EARLY BELFAST

George Benn (1801–82),
historian of Belfast

EARLY BELFAST

*The origins and growth
of an Ulster town to 1750*

RAYMOND GILLESPIE

THE BELFAST NATURAL HISTORY
AND PHILOSOPHICAL SOCIETY
IN ASSOCIATION WITH
ULSTER HISTORICAL FOUNDATION

THE BELFAST NATURAL HISTORY AND PHILOSOPHICAL SOCIETY, founded in 1821, encourages understanding of the human and natural environment of Ireland, both past and present. It has a particular focus on Belfast and its hinterland. It promotes original scholarship, and new ideas and interpretations, which are of an academic standard and yet are accessible to a wider audience.

First published 2007
by the Belfast Natural History and Philosophical Society,
c/o the Linen Hall Library,
17 Donegall Square North, Belfast BT1 5GD
in association with Ulster Historical Foundation
Unit 7, Cotton Court, Waring St., Belfast BT1 2ED

Distributed by Ulster Historical Foundation

Printed by Biddles, Kings Lynn, Norfolk
Design by Dunbar Design

To Bill Crawford

Pro tanto quid retribuamus

CONTENTS

PREFACE   xi

INTRODUCTION   xiii

1   A local landscape   1

2   The medieval inheritance   24

3   Chichester's town, 1603–60   53

4   Thomas Phillips's town, 1660–95   88

5   John Maclanachan's town, 1695–1750   128

    Epilogue: the transformation of Belfast   167

INDEX   175

LIST OF ILLUSTRATIONS

George Benn, historian of Belfast   frontispiece

Streets of central Belfast in 1901   xviii

The Antrim escarpment with Cave Hill and Belfast, from Knockbreda *c.* 1830   3

The site of Belfast   4

Raths and circular earthworks in the Belfast area   9

The medieval routeways at Belfast   13

Belfast from Belfast Lough, 1823   17

Distribution of mottes in the Belfast area   31

Parish church, High Street, 1715   39

Parish church, High Street, 1685   57

Bridge Street from the encumbered-estates maps of 1850   63

The Bridge Street marketplace, 1685   64

The castle and its gardens, 1685   70

Belfast *c.* 1660, showing the approximate line of the rampart   76

The Strand Gate, 1685   78

Down Survey of 1657 for the barony of Belfast   89

Thomas Phillips's perspective view of Belfast, 1685, redrawn from the original   90

Waring Street, 1685   94

Front and rear views of Tristram Beresford's seventeenth-century
house at Coleraine   96

The late seventeenth-century quay at the east end of High Street, 1685   98

The market house, Cornmarket, 1685   99

View of Belfast *c.* 1730, from a token issued by W. Johnston   100

The arms of the Chads family from the bridge that they constructed
across the River Farset   103

Extramural housing outside the Mill Gate, 1685   104

Extramural housing outside the North Gate, 1685   105

Housing filling between the rampart and the town inside the Mill Gate   106

The Long Bridge, from a sketch by Mary Delany, 1755   118

John Maclanachan's map of Belfast, 1715   130

Map of Belfast, 1757   131

First and second Presbyterian churches, 1715   134

First and second Presbyterian churches, 1757   134

The site of the castle in 1757   136

Waring Street, 1715   137

Early eighteenth-century drawing of a house to be built for a
Captain Chichester in Waring Street   138

The pottery and associated buildings, 1757   139

The military barracks in Barrack Street as it was shown in 1715 and 1757   144

The earliest phase of the development of the Belfast 'entries' in 1715   146

Isaac Macartney's development at Hanover Square as it was
shown in 1715 and 1757   150

St Anne's Church, 1823   170

The white linen hall of 1785   172

NOTES

The following abbreviations have been used in the notes:

Belfast atlas	Raymond Gillespie and S.A. Royle, *Irish historic towns atlas no. 12: Belfast, part 1 to 1840* (Dublin, 2003).
Cal. Carew MSS	*Calendar of the Carew manuscripts, 1515–74* etc. (6 vols, London, 1867–73).
Cal. S.P. dom.	*Calendar of state papers, domestic, 1547–80* etc. (London, 1856–).
Cal. S.P. Ire.	*Calendar of state papers relating to Ireland, 1509–73* etc. (24 vols, London, 1860–1910).
Excavations	*Excavations 1969–: summary accounts of archaeological excavations in Ireland* (Dublin and Bray, 1969–76, 1985–).
P.R.O.N.I.	Public Record Office of Northern Ireland
Reg. P.C. Scot.	*Registers of the Privy Council of Scotland, 1545–1569* etc. (38 vols, Edinburgh,1877–1970).
T.C.D.	Trinity College Dublin
T.N.A.	The National Archives: Public Record Office, London
U.J.A.	*Ulster Journal of Archaeology*

Dates have been given in old style except that the year has been taken as beginning on 1 January rather than 25 March, as was customary before 1752. Metric measures have been used except where imperial ones have been given in contemporary documents (as with measurements of burgage plots or shipping tonnage) and these have not been converted.

PREFACE

BOOKS EACH HAVE A UNIQUE HISTORY. Authors can, in the main, pinpoint how and when they chose to write about their own subject and set out an intellectual autobiography explaining how a work came to be written. This book is unusual in that I cannot do this. Since I was born and grew up in Belfast it would be impossible to isolate a period when I was not aware of the city's topography. However, for someone growing up in Belfast, finding a guide that would explain that topography, and particularly the early topography of the city, was difficult. There were several popular works on the history of Belfast, notably Cathal O'Byrne's eccentric and romanticised *As I roved out* (Belfast, 1946) but, with the exception of *Belfast: origins and growth of an industrial city*, edited by J.C. Beckett and R.E. Glascock (London, 1967), there was almost nothing available that explained the physical evolution of the city. George Benn's intimidating but magisterial *History of the town of Belfast from the earliest times to the close of the eighteenth century* (London and Belfast, 1877) was firmly locked away in the Central Library, as were most of the works in Noragh Stevenson's *Belfast before 1820: a bibliography* (Belfast, 1967).

Since then much has changed. There is now much more accessible writing on the history of Belfast than before, especially the popular work of Jonathan Bardon, and, crucially, a great deal more research on the history of other Irish towns. This writing is usually characterised by two features. Firstly, it is primarily focused on the nineteenth century, when Belfast was at the height of its economic and cultural power, and has relatively little to say about the earlier town. Secondly, it has approached the problem of Belfast's evolution through archival research, driven by questions formulated to deal with the political, economic and social evolution of Belfast. This book asks rather different questions and uses other types of evidence. In my lifetime the topography of parts of Belfast has been transformed as a result of urban redevelopment and terrorist activity. In that process there has grown an awareness of the importance of the physical fabric of the town as evidence for its past. In particular the Irish historic towns atlas project, including Raymond Gillespie and Stephen Royle's *Irish historic towns atlas no. 12: Belfast, part 1 to 1840* (Dublin, 2003), C.E.B. Brett, Raymond Gillespie and W.A. Maguire's *Georgian Belfast* (Dublin, 2004) and Raymond Gillespie and Stephen Royle's *Belfast c. 1600–1900: the making of the modern city* (Dublin, 2007) have been important in assembling basic topographical data on the early history of Belfast. This book should be seen as an outgrowth of this ongoing work. It is designed to make some of that material, particularly that relating to the early history of the town, more accessible and to place it in a wider context. If it makes those who live in Belfast and the surrounding area more aware of the make-up of their own place, and particularly the traces of the early town in the modern city, then it will have achieved some part of its aim of explaining how Belfast's past relates to the modern city. If it encourages others to continue that exploration it will have done even more than was intended.

None of this would have possible without the help of many people. Bill Crawford's enthusiasm for and exposition of the local past remains a powerful motivation, the importance of which is difficult to overstate. The Belfast Natural History and Philosophical Society, in the person of Angélique Day, have been by turns patient, sympathetic and constructive publishers. Those involved in the Irish historic towns atlas project in the Royal Irish Academy both forced me to systematise my knowledge of Belfast and encouraged and facilitated this outgrowth from it. I am indebted to them for permission to reproduce two maps that originally appeared in the atlas – on pages 13 and 76 of this volume. Other institutions have also granted permission for the reproduction of illustrations and these are credited in the relevant captions. Finally, Bernadette Cunningham has, as always, contributed more than she realises.

INTRODUCTION

> As for the early history of Belfast ... what can it be? Why firstly it
> is a tale of ignorant money grabbers trying to live: secondly, the
> tale embraces the building of places for education and
> superstition: thirdly, the tale informs us that some soldier of
> fortune thought the place worth robbing: then a library, a poor
> house and so on until water closets have been introduced and the
> town becomes a city: and then the respectable portion of its
> inhabitants become curious to learn its history.
>
> Thomas L'Estrange to George Benn, 29 September 1873[1]

Writing in 1823 Belfast's greatest historian, George Benn, declared:

> Belfast, though at present so conspicuous for commercial and
> political importance, is generally supposed to be of very modern
> origin. This is in great measure correct for there is not
> undoubtedly a town in this kingdom which has advanced to
> eminence with equal rapidity, or which has been so little
> distinguished in the ancient history of Ireland and so much in the
> modern. The notices which are to be found in the works of the
> early writers on Irish affairs relative to Belfast are brief and scanty,
> while the state and occurrences of places, now completely
> inconsiderable, are often accurately and precisely detailed.[2]

In this Benn was reflecting the views of a previous generation.
Henry Joy, the Belfast publisher and old radical, observed in 1817,
'Belfast is a town of modern creation and contains not a single
object deserving the notice of the antiquary,' although he conceded
that its history was 'highly interesting and important' as a
vindication of the contemporary political principle of liberty.[3] Over
time Benn's views hardened and he began his 1877 history of the
town with the unqualified declaration that 'Belfast as a town has no

ancient history'.[4] Indeed his contemporary and Celtic scholar William Hennessy congratulated Benn on the publication of his history, noting 'I think you have managed to do an almost impossible thing, namely to create a history for an unhistoric town'.[5] From Benn's point of view these statements are entirely understandable. When he was born in January 1801 Belfast had all the appearance of a recently built town. The activities of the landlords of the town, the earls of Donegall, in the 1750s and 1760s, had resulted in an almost complete reconstruction of the urban fabric. As Benn himself noted in 1823, 'there are no good houses in Belfast of more than sixty years standing and except, perhaps, two, no public buildings which have not been erected within the memory of persons living'.[6] In the late eighteenth century the older housing in the town had been swept away under conditions imposed in building leases. New streets, such as Donegall Street, had been laid out and modern public buildings, such as the poorhouse in Clifton Street, had been erected. The results impressed visitors; one American traveller in the 1770s went as far as to note that Belfast was 'a large, populous and beautiful town'.[7] As a result of all these initiatives Belfast lacked the antiquities of Carrickfergus to the north-east, with its medieval castle and parish church of St Nicholas. Nor could it boast a dissolved medieval religious house, as at Bangor, Newtownards or Downpatrick. Moreover, in comparison to the wealth of documentary evidence then being published by Benn's Dublin contemporary, J.T. Gilbert, Belfast had little to offer.

For all this pessimism, however, Benn recognised that Belfast did have an early history. In his work he printed some of the evidence on which that history might be based: references to Belfast in medieval government and ecclesiastical records, comments in the Irish annals, the fragmentary early entries in the corporation records and, perhaps most importantly, the maps of the town before 1750. Not much that is new has come to light since Benn wrote. A few extra documentary references have been unearthed and recent archaeological investigations have shed additional light on the area around the medieval settlement and its seventeenth-century successor, although archaeology has the potential to add very considerably to our knowledge in the future. Some evidence that

Benn was aware of but had little skill in interpreting, such as place-names, is now much better understood. Perhaps most important for evaluating the evidence for the early history of Belfast is that our sense of the context of its development has improved dramatically. Much more is now known about the history of medieval and seventeenth-century Ulster than was known in Benn's day. The story of the evolution of Ulster settlement has emerged from utter darkness into a thin mist.

However, we still need to recognise that the evidence is sparse. A succession of accidents has deprived historians of much of the raw material with which they could rebuild past worlds. The fact that the Belfast area lay within the liberty of the medieval earldom of Ulster means that it never featured prominently in the records of central government, a difficulty compounded by the fact that the records of that earldom, kept at Trim in the later medieval period, were said in 1495 to have been 'taken and embezzled by divers persons'.[8] Later disasters, such the destruction of the Public Record Office in Dublin in 1922, were of less significance, since Benn and his antiquarian confrères had already worked their way through that material and preserved much of local interest in their notes and published work. Most of what has survived, such as the Irish annals or the corporation records, is laconic in the extreme and its interpretation is fraught with difficulty. All that is no excuse for not trying, but it does shape the way we try to write the early history of Belfast. This book approaches the problem realising that the evidence, as we have it, will never allow us to write a narrative history of the early settlement, since there are too many gaps. Rather than such a history, then, this is an attempt to set out and look again at the surviving evidence. Absent, fragmentary and ambiguous evidence means that much of what happened in Belfast's past has to be inferred rather than demonstrated. Hence, interpreting what the evidence might say is as important as the evidence itself. There are many possible interpretations and many perspectives that can be brought to the evidence that survives. The one that I have adopted is primarily topographical, realising that how people shape the landscape around them can tell us a good deal about their lives and aspirations. The findings may at times seem fragmented and the answers uncertain, or at least as much the result of guesswork as empirical research. It is simply one attempt to shape the unwieldy body of evidence, interpretation and imagination into some sort of plausible sense, or perhaps even a kind of story.

NOTES

1 P.R.O.N.I., D3113/7/67
2 George Benn, *A history of the town of Belfast* (Belfast, 1823), pp 3–4.
3 Henry Joy, *Historical collections relative to the town of Belfast* (Belfast, 1817), p. iv.
4 George Benn, *A history of the town of Belfast from the earliest times to the close of the eighteenth century* (London and Belfast, 1877), p. 1.
5 P.R.O.N.I., D3113/7/52.
6 Benn, *History* (1823), pp 86–7.
7 Kenneth Morgan (ed.), *An American Quaker in the British Isles* (Oxford, 1992), p. 172.
8 10 Henry VII, c. 15 [Ire].

1

A LOCAL LANDSCAPE

Belfast as a town has had a great capacity to reinvent itself for each generation that has lived in it.[1] For some in the late twentieth century it was synonymous with rioting and civil unrest. For an older generation it was an industrial capital on a scale unmatched anywhere in Ireland; in 1901 it was briefly the largest urban centre on the island of Ireland in population terms, displacing even Dublin. Its name conjured up images of linen manufacture, heavy engineering, rope making and, above all, shipbuilding. For better or worse Belfast was best known to many as the birthplace of the ill-fated *Titanic*. Yet this industrial giant was itself a recent creation. Harland and Wolff's shipyard on Queen's Island, for instance, only came into being in 1861. In the middle of the nineteenth century the core of Belfast manufacturing, which employed half of the city's workers (as opposed to a third in Dublin or Cork), lay not in the heavy industry and shipbuilding of the east side of the city but in the textile mills of its northern part, around Smithfield and York Street. This was a classic industrial landscape, with large steam-powered factories and unsanitary housing, built in streets that were laid out in a grid-iron plan along Carrick Hill, North Queen Street and York Street. The middle class of this period escaped to the new suburbs along the Antrim Road and the Malone Road.[2]

For another generation, 50 years earlier still, this industrial landscape would have appeared strange. In the 1790s it was water power from the rivers flowing from the Antrim Plateau into the River Lagan, rather than steam engines, that provided the energy to manufacture yarn and cloth. Unlike the industrial workers of the middle of the nineteenth century, the majority of whom were involved in linen weaving, those in Belfast around 1800 were engaged in the

Opposite: Streets of central Belfast in 1901, from the Ordnance Survey of that year.

1

cotton trade. In 1800 the number of cotton looms in the town out-numbered linen looms by five to one.[3] Indeed, in 1800 much cotton weaving was not even done in factories but in the houses of weavers, concentrated in the north-west of the town around Smithfield, Peter's Hill and Carrick Hill.

Fifty years further back in time, in the middle of the eighteenth century, none of this activity would have existed. At that stage Belfast was not an industrial centre but a commercial one. Trading in its various forms dominated the world of Belfast. The town was a local market for those from the surrounding countryside who wanted to sell cattle, grain and linen yarn but it was also an international *entrepôt*. Belfast merchants such as Waddell Cunningham or Thomas Gregg had international connections that made it necessary for them to maintain a branch of their business in North America and to diversify their operations into commercially related activities such as banking and discounting bills of exchange.[4] The town had an international reputation to match this activity. In continental Europe in 1800 Belfast was said not only to be 'well known as a place of considerable trade' but in the 'first rank' of the commercial towns of Europe.[5]

An inhabitant of Belfast of about 1750 would have had more chance of recognising the town of a century earlier than they would have had of finding their way around the town that had developed by 1850. The layout of seventeenth-century Belfast resembled that of 1750 much more than that of 1850. The seventeenth-century market house and parish church were still intact (though both would be demolished by 1800). There were new features in the townscape, such as the linen hall, while older markers, such as the castle, had disappeared. While the seventeenth-century town might have lacked the sophistication of mid-eighteenth-century Belfast, it was still a town driven by trade, both with North America and continental Europe.

For all these changes, what remained constant over time was the landscape within which the human activity around Belfast took place. Travellers commented on that landscape's strong contrasts. The town itself was low lying, which some felt did not set it off to its best advantage. At the beginning of the nineteenth century Philip

Dixon Hardy observed that 'from the low situation in which the town [Belfast] itself is built, its appearance from a distance, is not only unimpressive, but mean and it is not till the stranger almost enters it that he is convinced of its extent, commercial importance and wealth'.[6] That sense of flatness is enhanced by the mountains overshadowing the town both to the north-west and south-east. According to George Benn, writing in 1823, these 'bestow uncommon grandeur and beauty on the general appearance of this town'.[7] To the north the Antrim basalt escarpment, overlying deposits of white chalk, dominates the town, rising to 390 metres at Black Mountain, 478 metres at Divis Mountain and 368 metres at Cave Hill, where the escarpment and the Iron-Age hillfort, McArt's Fort, combine to produce a dramatic silhouette. This was land that in the period after the Anglo-Norman colonisation was settled late, if at

The Antrim escarpment with Cave Hill and Belfast, seen from Knockbreda on the Castlereagh Hills c. 1830. Knockbreda parish church is on the left.

all. According to the hearth money rolls of the 1660s the population around Belfast was densest behind the town in the Lagan valley and along the roadway at Legoneil between Squire's Hill and Divis Mountain. The lower slopes of the Antrim Hills were thinly settled and the upper reaches had no houses at all.[8] Such was the thinness of people in the upper reaches of the hills that in the nineteenth century a tradition survived in Belfast that in 1692 'the last wolf in Ireland [was] killed with Irish wolf dogs on the hill of Aughnabrack near Belfast' and that Aughnabrack was subsequently renamed Wolf Hill.[9] In the 1800s these slopes became important escapes from the industrial town. Benn noted that the people of Belfast ventured out to the lower slopes of Cave Hill and McArt's Fort for 'convivial sports'. Later in the century Thomas Gaffikin reported the same exodus to this rural area on Sundays.[10] The rugged nature of the Cave Hill, with the enigmatic caves carved into its side, gave it a romantic quality that generated myths and legends about the place, many involving buried treasure. As early as 1556 Lord Deputy

The site of Belfast.

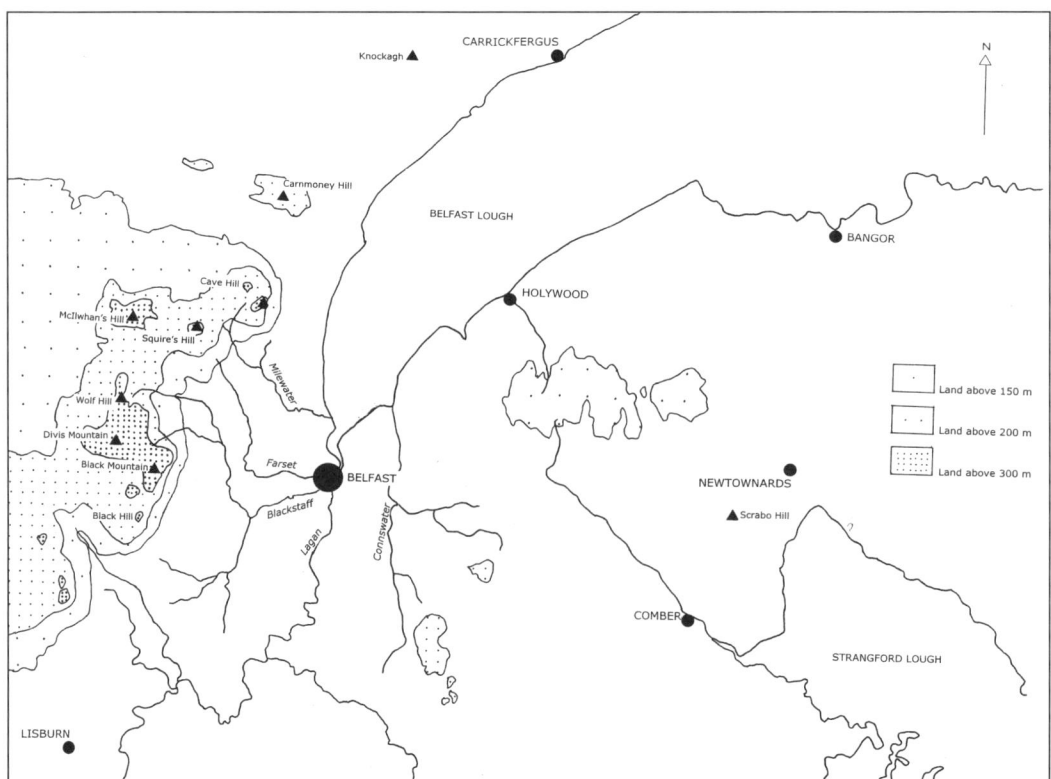

Sussex was told that in Ben Vadagan (an older name for Cave Hill) there 'is a great cave where is the treasure of the country of Clandeboy'.[11] To the south-east, on its County Down side, the town was overshadowed by the lower Castlereagh Hills and Holywood Hills. These gentler, fine-grained lower Palaeozoic sub-greywackes and slaty mudstones rise to 180 metres and 200 metres north of Dundonald and at outliers around Braniel. In most places this range of hills rarely rises above 150 metres but nevertheless forms an effective edge to Belfast, restricting the eastward development of the road network and forcing traffic along the coast. This line of hills is broken by the Dundonald Gap, which provides access to Newtownards and Strangford Lough.

Both of these areas of high land attracted human interest early. On the northern side of the River Lagan, which flowed in the broad valley between the high land, the flint deposits underlying the basalts on the Antrim Plateau proved to be a magnet for Neolithic people seeking raw material for the manufacture of tools and weapons. On Black Mountain and Squire's Hill above the town, for instance, there are Neolithic flint-working sites.[12] There is also evidence of other activities. At Ballyutoag there is a horned cairn and at Legoniel a possible chambered cairn.[13] At Ballyvaston, to the north, Neolithic pottery and hearths have been found, together with a large quantity of flint debris and some Bronze-Age pottery. There is a Bronze-Age barrow and a rath nearby. A Bronze-Age dress fastener has also been found on Cave Hill in the same area.[14] A probable Bronze-Age burial can be associated with Black Mountain and there may be another Bronze-Age cremation on Cave Hill at Ballyvaghagan.[15] More convincing evidence for Bronze-Age settlement in the area around Belfast is provided by excavation of an enclosed hut platform with a round house and worked flint of late Bronze-Age date at McIlwhan's Hill in the townland of Ballyutoag, just to the west of Cave Hill.[16]

Between the Antrim escarpment and the Castlereagh Hills lay the broad valley, floored with Triassic sandstone, along which the River Lagan meandered. Prior to the last glaciation, the Lagan in the Belfast area adopted a slightly different course from its present one, then flowing through what is now called the Bog Meadows.[17] In fact, the last glaciation altered the shape of the valley itself. Much of the area was covered with boulder clay as ice moved across east Ulster. As that ice retreated eastward and blocked the Lagan Valley a lake formed, in which a layer of clay and considerable quantities of sands and gravels were deposited. These 'Malone sands' were to have a considerable impact on the human landscape of the area around Belfast. Their importance lay in the fact that wherever they were deposited they formed ridges or nearly flat areas of higher land on which roads or settlements could be built. The settlements to the south of central Belfast, around the Malone Road and Stranmillis, are founded on Malone sands. The platform of the Malone sands rises from the raised beach on Malone Road at Methodist College, forming a platform that falls off to the River Lagan on one side and the River Blackstaff on the other. The three main roads in this area, the Malone Road, the Lisburn Road and the Stranmillis Road, all utilise the higher land formed by the Malone sands. This area, described as the 'plains of Malone' as early as 1611, contains some of the earliest indications of human activity around Belfast.[18] It seems clear that an early undulating routeway followed a line roughly similar to that now taken by the Malone Road. The prehistoric finds along this route extend over a long period. Neolithic flint flakes have been found there in some numbers as well as some Neolithic pottery.[19] At Danesford, a number of very large polished porcellanite axes have been found in a context that suggests a ritual deposit.[20] There is at least one Bronze-Age burial associated with the Malone Road.[21] There were also several rural settlements established on the platform of Malone sands along which the routeway passed. One such site on the route of the present Malone Road was discovered and partially excavated in the 1930s, producing flint flakes and souterrain ware.[22]

After the deposit of the Malone Sands ice readvanced into the Lagan Valley, producing a layer of boulder clay above the sands in some places, before finally retreating eastward. What followed was a period in which the sea level, and hence the shoreline, fluctuated considerably. Land rose and fell as the weight of the ice was removed and the volume of water rose as the ice melted. Peat beds formed, which were inundated again. This inundation resulted in the deposition of estuarine clay or 'sleech', as it is termed in the Belfast area. This blue-grey clay underlies much of central Belfast in varying thicknesses and, while it is easy to work, it provides unstable foundations for substantial buildings. At Cornmarket the sleech is some 17 metres deep, thinning to the south and east of the City Hall to about 1 metre, although it thickens rapidly to 9 metres at Donegall Square North and 6.4 metres at Oxford Street. A second thick deposit of up to 9 metres of sleech occurs along the Bog Meadows and the line of the River Blackstaff.[23]

The final shoreline adjustment raised this estuarine clay above sea level and created the series of raised beaches visible at the Shore Road and in breaks in gradient at the northern end of the Malone Road above Shaftsbury Square and on the Ormeau Road south of Ormeau Bridge. Along this fluctuating coastline there are some signs of human activity but these are rather transient. At Ormeau Bridge finds of Mesolithic flints suggest hunter-gatherer activity and four other such sites occur along the north Down coast close to Belfast.[24]

As the post-glacial landscape stabilised, two things of importance for the evolution of Belfast occurred. First, the landscape was colonised by vegetation. On the hills hazel bushes were cleared by Neolithic and Bronze-Age settlers to produce a grassy, weedy vegetation suitable for habitation, which was subsequently covered by peat. In the valley bottom the growth of trees was much more luxuriant. The initial peat layer formed after the glacial retreat contains hazel, birch, pine, oak and elm. The wooded nature of the later landscape is clear from some of the older townland names, now vanished but preserved in the seventeenth-century inquisitions and land grants: Ballynyculnytry (the townland of the holly-abounding area) around the Grosvenor Road area; Ballysillan (townland of the willows); Ballycullo (possibly the townland of the yews); Ballywonard (townland of the high thicket) and Ballyfaighnamony (townland of the wood of the bogs).[25] There is even more direct evidence for the importance of woodland in this area before the seventeenth century. According to a note on a map of Belfast Lough of 1570, 'Along this river [the Lagan] by the space of 26 miles groweth much woods as well as oakes for timber as other wood which may be brought in the bay of Carrickfergus with boat or by dragge'.[26] Traces of this dense woodland cover could be seen into the eighteenth century around Cromac Wood, in the Cromac Street area, through which passes had to be cut. The straight line of Donegall Pass is one reminder of these routeways.[27]

By the late sixteenth century there was a willingness to exploit whatever timber remained in the Belfast area. Timber was used for building works, and the construction of Belfast Castle, and probably the parish church, in the second decade of the seventeenth century were carried out using timber from the Lagan Valley.[28] As early as 1568 the possibility of shipbuilding at Belfast was envisaged. Nothing came of it at that time, but it was remarked again in 1583 that Belfast was a place fit for shipbuilding.[29] In 1610 these sentiments were echoed and it was noted that the woodland around the town was not good enough for pipestaves but was good enough for building and shipping.[30] By the 1630s at least one ship had been built there and was used in an attempt to transport to North America those who would not conform to the established church.[31] Shipbuilding was not the only industry to feed off the timber in the area around Belfast. Timber, in the form of charcoal, was important as a raw material in iron working. As early as 1612 an ironworks was established at Stranmillis by the Edinburgh entrepreneur Nathaniel Udward who utilised the local woodland, and later drew on timber from north Down, to feed his operation. By 1616 he had sold this to Sir Fulke Conway, an associate of Sir Arthur Chichester who held land around Lisburn, and by 1636 it passed into the hands of the Belfast merchant Robert Barr, who had recently arrived there from Derry.[32] By the 1630s a charcoal-burning ironworks had been established at Old Forge and New Forge with another at Ardoyne by 1640. The forge at New Forge was clearly a substantial structure. In the early 1640s Robert Lawson, the son-in-law of its owner, described the losses at the works as a result of the rebellion as £2,000 worth of sow iron, much iron ore, 1,000 tons of squared timber, 1,000 loads of charcoal as well as land and houses.[33] Timber was also required as part of the tanning process since bark, not used in charcoal making, produced tannin for the processing of skins, which were available from the butchers in the town. There were a

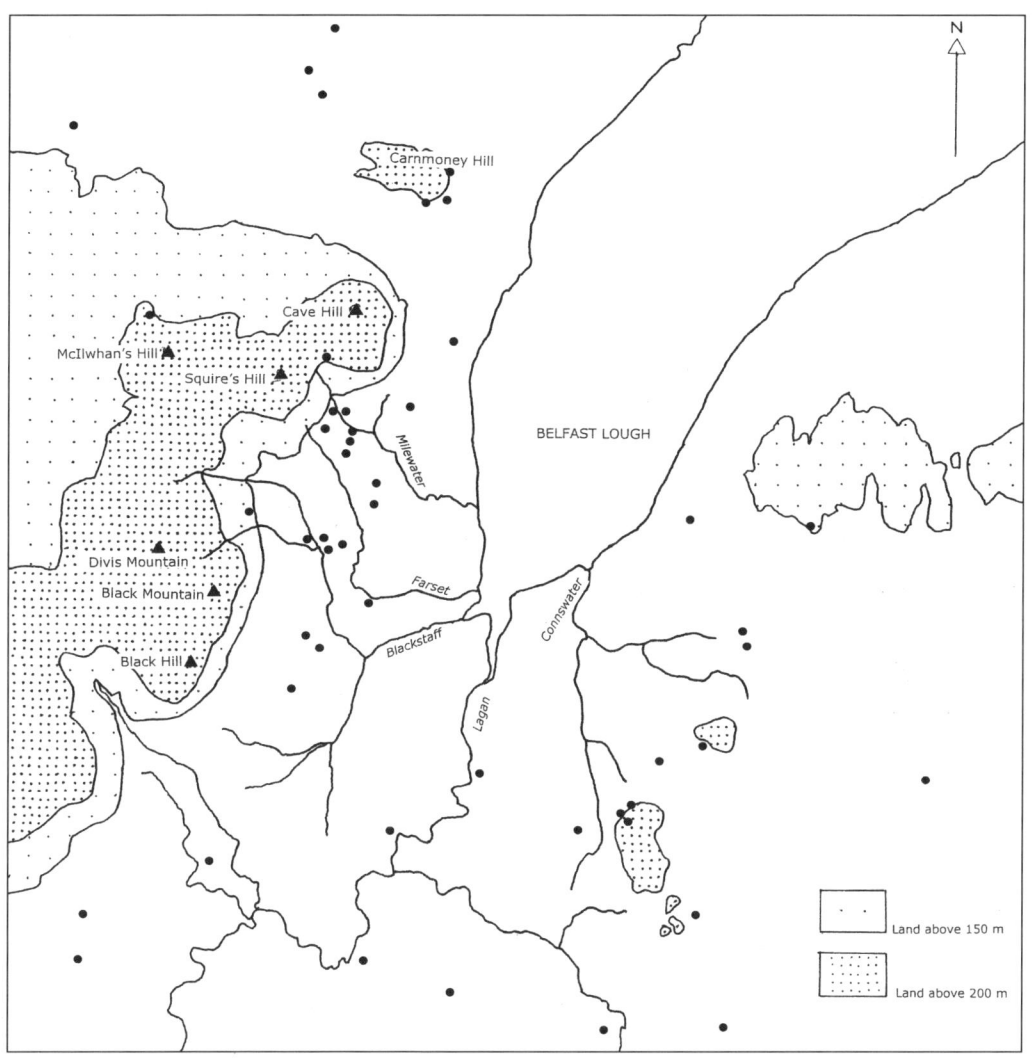

Raths and circular earthworks in the Belfast area.

number of tan pits located within Belfast in the middle of the seventeenth century, at Waring Street and in other places, and a large number of tanners and other leatherworkers were admitted to the freedom of the town in the early seventeenth century.[34]

A combination of a valley bottom that was waterlogged in places and heavily wooded in others meant that the earliest permanent settlement in the areas around what became Belfast was on the undulating lower slopes of the surrounding high land. Raths, or ringforts, may well provide some of the earliest evidence for permanent settlement on a significant scale in the Belfast area, although excavations have not yielded much evidence for dating. Not all the surviving raths were occupied simultaneously and some may even be Anglo-Norman.[35] As they are shown on the Ordnance Survey map of the 1830s these features hug the high ground above the Lagan Valley, above the 50-metre contour but below the 100-metre one. The pattern is repeated on the County Down side of the valley and the investigation of place-names containing the elements 'lis', 'rath' or 'dun' confirms the more general pattern.[36] It is worth noting that the place-names containing personal names in Belfast area also follow this distribution. This distribution is not confined to raths. Other known monuments of the same date around Belfast, such as souterrains or crannogs, avoid the valley bottom also, clinging to the lower slopes of the Antrim Plateau.[37] The most dramatic exception to this is, of course, McArt's Fort, a large Iron Age fort located on Cave Hill at a height of 360 metres, which dominates Belfast Lough. It utilised the sheer drop of the mountains on three sides, while a dry ditch secured the fourth. It is possible that it formed a tribal centre at this period, perhaps paralleling the hill fort at Scrabo on the other side of Belfast Lough. Some of the rath structures on the higher land above 100 metres may not have been permanent settlements but temporary villages for summer cattle herding. The bone evidence from excavations of a rath at Shaneen Park, on the edge of the main belt of rath distribution, certainly suggests that cattle dominated the livestock economy on this sort of site, with evidence of only a few pigs and almost no sheep.[38] Excavations at Ballyutoag, above the Cave Hill, have identified other rath-like structures. A number of house sites, perhaps as many as 23, were associated with large curvilinear fields. These dated to the 700s, with some reoccupation in the tenth century, but it was clear that the houses had been rebuilt on a number of occasions. This is perhaps best understood as part of a transhumance village for summer occupation.[39]

The second important landscape feature in shaping the Belfast area consists of the rivers flowing from the high land of the Antrim escarpment and Castlereagh Hills into the River Lagan. On the southern side of the valley, Purdy's Burn discharged into the Lagan and the Connswater flowed into Belfast Lough. Some of these rivers powered the many mills depicted on the maps of the County Down side of the River Lagan, drawn by Thomas Raven in 1625.[40] The limited height of the Castlereagh Hills meant that these rivers did not have the power of those falling from the Antrim Hills into the Lagan. In the late eighteenth century the rivers on the Antrim side of the Lagan – the Mile Water, the Farset, the Colin and the Blackstaff with its tributaries including the Clowney and the Forth rivers – provided the power for the early industrialisation of the Belfast area by powering factories and supplying water for bleach greens. Earlier in the seventeenth century such rivers had powered corn and fulling mills in and around the town.[41] Two of these rivers are of particular importance for the evolution of Belfast. The first is the Farset, which rises above Legoniel, flows past the medieval parish church at Shankill, through Millfield and under High Street (giving that street its curving appearance) to enter the Lagan to the east of the Albert Clock and High Street. The second river of importance is the Blackstaff (or Owenvarra). The Blackstaff's course has been altered at least twice in its history but its original line began at Divis and, gathering size from a number of tributaries, meandered through the Bog Meadows until it reached what is now Sandy Row, then curved behind what is now the City Hall to enter the sea in a large marshy area with extensive mudflats, covering the site of the present Victoria Square. This river was tidal at least as far as Sandy Row.

Where these two rivers entered the larger River Lagan they created an ismuth of land and at this a sandbar formed, providing the foundation for a ford that was constructed on the site and giving Belfast its modern name: *Béal Feirste* – the approach to the sand-bank ford.[42] This was not, of course, the only ford across the Lagan. In the seventeenth century there was a ford at the highest point at which the Lagan was tidal, at Stranmillis.[43] Again, it seems that there was a ford at Shaw's Bridge, which was replaced by a bridge in the 1650s. This crossing point may have been associated with the near-by late-Neolithic henge monument, the Giant's Ring at Ballynahatty. This complex had a series of associated monuments and hence was clearly a centre of regional importance that required access, probably including a river crossing.[44] However, the significance of the ford at Belfast is that it was the lowest point at which the Lagan could be forded and hence provided the most convenient route northwards to Carrickfergus and eastwards into north Down. Thus, in the 1570s the earl of Essex found the ford at Belfast an easy way across the River Lagan at low tide.[45] At times the passage was easy, as one Irish poem of the early seventeenth century put it the Lagan was the 'silent stream' of Belfast.[46] However, sometimes using the ford was neither a simple nor a risk-free way of crossing the Lagan. In 1573, for instance, the earl of Essex discovered that at Belfast the water 'being high and swollen with rain and a northerly wind they could not pass at the ford'.[47] Later he would encounter similar difficulties with an impassable River Lagan, swollen by rain.[48] In 1575 Lord Deputy Sidney encountered similar problems at Belfast, where 'by reason of the tide's extraordinary return our horses swam, and the footmen in the passage waded very deep'.[49] Again, the rivers flowing from the mountains around Belfast could become dangerously swollen with rain (the Colin River for instance can rise 1m above its normal level in flood conditions) and this combined with high tides often led to local flooding. The ford was important but it also presented challenges to those wishing to use it.

Identifying precisely where the ford at Belfast was poses a number of problems. Indeed, more than one ford may have been constructed on the site over the long period of time during which it was in use. Its origins are lost in antiquity but it may be worth noting that three Iron Age swords have been found in the Lagan at Belfast, suggesting that some sort of crossing point was in use very early on indeed.[50] A ford had been constructed by 668, when the *Annals of Ulster* note a battle there between the Ulaid and the Cruithin, two of the main population groups in early east Ulster.[51] Such contests at the site may have been commoner than this single annalistic entry suggests. A ninth-century poem by Mael Mura of Othain celebrating the deeds of the semi-mythical hero Tuathal Techtmar, preserved in the later Leabhar Gabhála, lists one hundred battles that he is supposed to have fought, twenty-five in each province. Among the Ulster battles is 'Cath Fersde' or the battle of the sand-bank ford, which probably refers to the same place as the annal entry of 668.[52] Given the highly structured nature of the entries in the poem and its mythological context there is no reason to presume that this refers to an actual pre-Christian battle but the inclusion of the site in the list is probably a reflection of the fact that this was a place where battles did take place. In the nineteenth century antiquarians proposed a number of sites for the ford. Some commentators placed it north of where the Farset entered the Lagan and argued that Waring Street was the continuation of it.[53] Another theory favoured the other side of the Farset, near the Long Bridge, which was eventually built to replace the ford and which was, in turn, replaced by the present Queen's Bridge.[54] Yet a third possibility – that the ford was even further upstream – was canvassed by some.[55] While it is not possible to reconcile all these pieces of evidence, enough survives to allow a tentative position to be established. There is some evidence in the form of records of timber and stone dredging in the late eighteenth and mid-nineteenth century from the area opposite Chichester Quay and the end of High Street that may suggest that some sort of structure existed under the Lagan at this point.[56] However, this cannot be seen as conclusive because

The medieval routeways at Belfast.

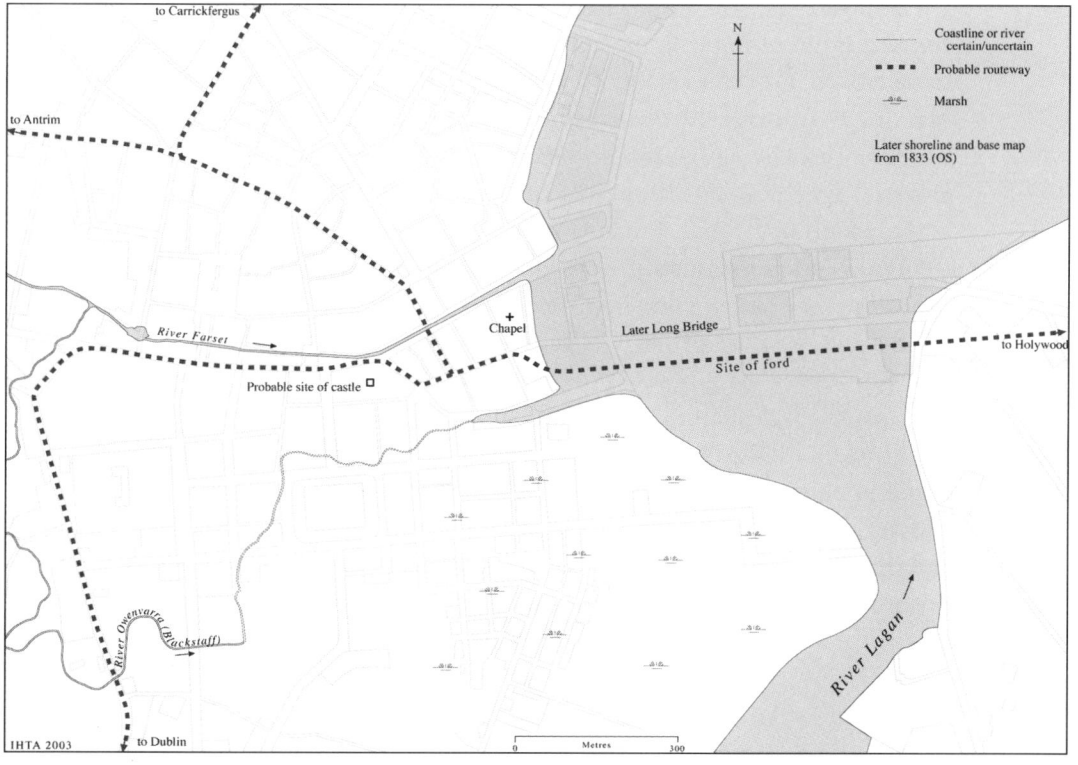

in the 1840s, during the building of the Queen's Bridge, stonework rather like a causeway was found under the river on the site, which may also suggest the presence of a ford.[57] It seems that the ford was not fixed at one point in the landscape for its entire life: it may have migrated over time. There is some evidence to indicate that the site near the Queen's Bridge, beside where the Blackstaff entered the river, may have been the main fording point. A map of 1696 marks a feature at this site called the Long Cross, which appears to be a causeway across the Lagan, and this may represent the ford.[58] Secondly, the position of the medieval 'chapel of the ford' can be identified with the present site of St George's Church on High Street. Based on a depiction of this church on Thomas Phillips's map of Belfast in 1685, the entrance was not from High Street but from the Ann Street side. This suggests that those crossing the ford would have done so to the west of where the Farset enters the Lagan rather than to the east. All this would seem to indicate that the question of the principal site of the ford, which gave rise to legal proceedings in the nineteenth century, was somewhere in the area of what is now the Queen's Bridge and probably on the site of the Long Bridge that replaced the ford in the 1680s.

The position of the ford is important, since it controlled the main crossing point of the river and hence helped to shape the local communications network in the Middle Ages and later. The approach from Ballymacarret on the south side of the Lagan was by a road indicated on the early-seventeenth-century Raven maps of north Down.[59] By the 1620s this part of north Down had become known as the 'plains of Belfast', presumably as a result of the importance of the ford to the surrounding area.[60] On the town side of the ford the routeways were more complex. The line of Ann Street probably represents the main routeway leading away from the ford. Travellers going towards Carrickfergus probably crossed the Farset somewhere near where Bridge Street is now and a bridge certainly existed here on Thomas Phillips's map of 1685. After crossing the Farset they made for high ground along what is now the line of North Street to Carrick Hill and so followed the high ground of the raised beach, crossing the Mile Water and on to Carrickfergus. Alternatively, some seventeenth-century travellers rode at low tide along the Strand beside the Lagan on the north side of the Farset before joining the coast road at Whitehouse.[61] If travellers' destinations lay inland they probably followed the line of what is now the Shankill Road, where the medieval parish church of Shankill was located, and crossed the Antrim Plateau at Legoneil on the col between Squire's Hill and Divis Mountain. Those travelling south probably followed the Farset up what is now Castle Street to meet the continuation of the Carrickfergus Road along Durham Street to cross the Blackstaff at Boyne Bridge, which was certainly in existence by the 1640s and known as the 'great bridge at Belfast'. From this point they could follow the sandy ridge between the sleech of the Bog Meadows and the flood plain of the Blackstaff. This became the winding line of Sandy Row, whose curving way contrasts with the later straight, planned lines of the Dublin Road and Great Victoria Street, laid out in the nineteenth century. From this the routeway rose onto the platform of the Malone sands following the line probably now taken by the Malone Road. Thus the ford provided a focal point for communications between Antrim and Down. It was, as the traveller Fr Edmund MacCana put it in his 1643 description of the area, 'in the navel, as it were, and the central point of the two regions'.[62]

The ford at Belfast had one other important attribute: it was eminently defensible. The spur of land between the Blackstaff and the Farset was a neat and naturally easily defended position from which to guard the ford. The seventeenth-century townland name for this peninsula, where the medieval castle of Belfast would later be built, was Ballycullcallaghy or Ballycoolcallagh – townland of Calgagh's corner or recess – a name giving the impression of an area neatly tucked away as a self-contained unit.[63] However, this does not mean that the site was without problems for any settlement that might be created there. The low-lying landscape meant that it was subject to periodic flooding. The original wide flood plain of the Blackstaff, in the Victoria Square and Ann Street areas, was often flooded in winter. As late as the flooding of 1902 the Blackstaff could still flood to the full limits of its alluvium, notwithstanding significant engineering works in the nineteenth century to limit such occurrences.[64] The flooding was particularly acute at times of exceptionally high tides. Thomas Gaffikin recalled that in the 1830s the area around

Ann Street and its area would flood 'to a depth of several feet' at spring tides while the Belfast Improvement Act of 1800 observed of the old churchyard on High Street: 'the water from the sea occasionally overflows the said yard and the burying of the dead bodies therein by the reason and means aforesaid [has] become a public nuisance'.[65] Belfast suffered from such flooding in 1775, 1796, 1819, 1838,1869, 1895 and 1906. Much earlier, the 1696 map had marked areas along High Street that were subject to flooding.[66] The area liable to flooding provided a limit to the southern expansion of the town, which was not breached until the nineteenth century when the Blackstaff was finally culverted. As a result the southern side of Belfast was late in developing. Measures were taken by a number of groups to try to deal with this problem. The landlord of the town included in one lease of 1656 the condition that the lessee on High Street was to 'wall or pale in so much of the river or stream running through the said town [the Farset] and pave so [much of] the same as front the said tenements', the walling of the river being partly an anti-flood measure.[67] In 1664 the corporation ordered that the banks along the Farset were to be built up with stone, presumably in an attempt to prevent such flooding.[68] As a result of this sort of activity High Street was raised by at least a metre and excavations in the 1850s revealed a path below the present one that was probably the original pavement.[69]

Despite this surfeit of water, Belfast would also have problems with its water supply. The Lagan was tidal up to Stranmillis, where the place name *an Sruthán Milis* – the sweet stream – indicates the change from salt water to fresh.[70] The Blackstaff was tidal up to the Boyne Bridge on Sandy Row, indicated by the fact that the bridge was formerly known as the Saltwater Bridge. The Farset was also tidal into Castle Street as well as being heavily polluted since it was used as a dumping ground for butchers' waste. All this meant that supplies of fresh water in Belfast were very limited and the town had to be supplied from wells that drew on the water-bearing sandstone under some of the town or from the surrounding countryside. However, water in any quantity is heavy and difficult to transport and supplying this commodity was a logistical problem that was not overcome for some time.

Belfast from Belfast Lough, from Benn, *History* (1823).

In topographical terms Belfast needs to be seen not only in terms of the hills that overshadowed it and the mud on which it rested but also in relation to the sea beside which it is perched. James Adair Pilson, writing in the 1840s, contrasted the 'lowness and flatness' of Belfast that 'renders the exterior aspect of the town tame and uncompromising' with the view 'seen up the Lough at night [when] it looks like a focus and divergence of light amid a world of darkness'.[71] The relationship between Belfast and the lough on which it is situated has been vital for its history. As Fr MacCana pointed out in 1643, Belfast was 'accessible to the inhabitants of either districts (Antrim and Down) as well as of Scotland': on this its future prosperity was to rest.[72] The deep indentation of Belfast Lough gave the early harbour protection. It was, as Walter Harris described it in the 1740s, 'as safe and spacious a bay as any in Ireland'.[73] During the Williamite campaign of the 1690s, for instance, Belfast Lough provided a safe harbour from which the Williamite force could occupy Carrickfergus and Bangor. By 1691 the lough was so full of ships laden with provisions and ammunition to supply the Williamite force that 'it seem'd to be like a wood there between six and seven hundred sail of ships'.[74] This safe haven was not an unmixed blessing, since the lough also provided a convenient place from which privateers could operate in the late seventeenth and early eighteenth centuries. These illicit enterprises, many of which were French, had an impact on the trade of the town as pirates ambushed ships carrying high value cargoes such as tobacco setting sail from or sailing into Belfast or Carrickfergus.[75] Indeed one early eighteenth-century Belfast merchant urged ships carrying goods consigned to him to put into Larne until they had ascertained that Belfast Lough was free from privateers.[76]

Belfast Lough is long and narrow, becoming shallower as it approaches Belfast itself. As one commentator in the 1880s observed, 'Belfast is neither an inland town nor one situated on the open seaboard.'[77] Navigating the lough was not an easy task, and in the late seventeenth century finding the shipping channel through the mud deposits could be difficult.[78] There were several sandbars that needed to be navigated before ships could approach Belfast.[79] At Belfast itself the water was shallow, around three metres at high tide but less than half a metre at low tide. In the early nineteenth century some ships needed the assistance of several tides before they could land at the quay but over time land reclamation pushed quays out into deeper water.[80] This was not as much of a problem as it might seem. First, while ships engaged in long-distance transatlantic trade may have been large vessels, most of the ships trading with England or Scotland, which accounted for most of the town's business, were smaller craft. The *Mary Fortune*, which traded between Belfast and Bristol in the 1680s was 30 tons, the *Charlemont* and the *Peter of Bilbao* on the same route were 30 and 40 tons respectively. Other ships, trading with Chester, were described as ketches or small sailing ships.[81] Secondly, opposite Holywood there was a deeper area known as the Pool of Garmoyle that was used by ships discharging in Belfast and Bangor in the early seventeenth century. Here, up to 20 ships could anchor at low water and their goods were taken to Belfast by smaller boats. This sheltered aspect of the port accounts for the rather primitive infrastructure that existed there in the seventeenth and eighteenth centuries. At Derry the fast-flowing and deep water of the River Foyle made it necessary for the quays to jut out into the river to protect shipping. At Carrickfergus ships had to be protected from the sea by a quay and a harbour. None of this was necessary in the placid waters around Belfast.

Navigating one's way along Belfast Lough into the town was not always a simple task since the channel could become blocked with weeds. It was the responsibility of the water bailiff in Belfast in the late seventeenth century to ensure that the channel was kept clear and marked with 'perches'.[82] The local importance of Belfast Lough was at least as great as its role in international trade. Moving goods by sea was easier and a good deal more cost effective than carting them across land. In the 1590s the garrison at Belfast was maintained with men and supplies shipped from Carrickfergus.[83] It is clear from the reports of the surveyor of the customs that in the early seventeenth century there was a significant coastal trade in goods within Belfast Lough.[84] That coastal trade continued into the early nineteenth century.[85] Belfast was therefore linked by its lough into a regional world of north Down and south Antrim and as it developed it drew not only goods but people from these areas.

While the physical landscape did not entirely determine how the town of Belfast would develop over subsequent centuries it did provide a series of possibilities that could be exploited. The ford in particular had the potential to attract as settlers those who wished to control access between the coastal parts of Antrim and Down. The appeal of settling in such a strategic site had to be balanced against difficulties such as the flooding and heavy wood cover encountered there; and the communications advantages presented by Belfast Lough had to be offset against the problems of piracy and navigation through such a shallow channel of water. Such challenges helped to shape the character of the people who lived in and around Belfast and influenced how they in turn shaped their local world, giving the region its own indescribable personality.

NOTES

1   For the fluidity of Belfast's identity see Nicholas Allen and Aaron Kelly (eds), *The cities of Belfast* (Dublin, 2003), pp 7–18.

2   Trevor Carleton, 'Malone, Belfast: the early history of a suburb' in *U.J.A.*, 3rd ser., xli (1978), pp 94–101.

3   John Dubourdieu, *A statistical survey of the county of Antrim* (Dublin, 1812), p. 509.

4   Thomas Truxes (ed.), *The letterbook of Gregg and Cunningham, 1756–1757* (Oxford, 2001).

5   Dubourdieu, *Statistical survey*, p. 505.

6   P.D. Hardy, *Twenty-one views in Belfast and its neighbourhood*, ed. C.E.B. Brett (Belfast, 2005), p. 9.

7   Benn, *History* (1823), p. 3.

8   Trevor Carleton, *Heads and hearths: the hearthmoney rolls and poll tax returns for Co. Antrim, 1660-69* (Belfast, 1991), p. 48.

9   J. Compton, *A compendious system of chronology* (Belfast, 1823), p. 135.

10 Benn, *History* (1823), pp 209–10; Thomas Gaffikin, *Belfast fifty years ago* (Belfast, 1894), pp 9–10, 13.

11 *Cal. Carew MSS 1515–74*, p. 254. For the caves and the stories attached to them see Philip Reynolds and Samuel Turner, 'The caves in Ben Madighan' in *U.J.A.*, 2nd ser., viii (1902), pp 73–82; R.M. Young, *Historical notices of old Belfast* (Belfast, 1896), p. 266 and Samuel Ferguson, *The Hibernian night's entertainments* (New York, 1852), pp 308–431. The most dramatic story of treasure is that of a diamond that it was claimed had been found on the Cave Hill and sent to Madame Tussaud's in London in 1887. It was said to measure 11 inches and weighed one pound. Its whereabouts are now unknown.

12 E.M. Jope (ed.), *An archaeological survey of County Down* (Belfast, 1966), p. 11; 'Notes on excavations' in *Proceedings of the Prehistoric Society*, iv (1938), p. 322.

13 I.J. Herring, 'The forecourt Hanging Thorn cairn, McIlwhan's Hill, Ballyutoag, Legoniel' in *Proceedings of the Belfast Natural History and Philosophical Society* (1936–7), pp 43–9.

14 *Excavations 1986*, p. 9; *Excavations 1994*, p. 2; *Excavations 2002*, p. 3.

15 Samuel Lewis, *Topographical dictionary of Ireland* (3 vols, London, 1849), i, p. 193; J.W. Pilson, *History and view of the rise and progress of Belfast* (Belfast, 1846), p. 11; *Excavations 1994*, p. 2.

16 Philip McDonald, Naomi Carver and Mike Yates, 'Excavations at McIlwan's Hill, Ballyutoag, Co. Antrim' in *U.J.A.*, 3rd ser., lxiv (2005), pp 43–61.

17 P.I. Manning, J.H. Robbie and H.E. Wilson, *Geology of Belfast and the Lagan Valley* (Belfast, 1970), pp 123–4, Pl. 9.

18 The 1611 Plantation Commissioners referred to this area as the 'plains of Malone' (Benn, *History* (1877), p. 85).

19 S. Andrews and O. Davies, 'Prehistoric finds at Tyrone House, Malone Road, Belfast' in *U.J.A.*, 3rd ser., iii (1940), p. 154.

20 Andrews and Davies, 'Prehistoric finds', pp 152–4; E.E. Evans, 'An archaeological miscellany' in *U.J.A.*, 3rd ser., xxxviii (1975), p. 14; E.R.C. Armstrong, 'Associated finds of Irish Neolithic celts' in *Proceedings of the Royal Irish Academy*, xxxiv (C) (1917–19), p. 84; W. Gray, 'On some stone celts found near Belfast' in *Journal of the Royal Society of Antiquaries of Ireland*, xii (1873), p. 138.

21 'Proceedings' in *Journal of the Royal Society of Antiquaries of Ireland*, xii (1872–3), p. 138.

22 D.B. Quinn, 'An early Iron Age settlement at Malone, Belfast' in *Proceedings of the Belfast Natural History and Philosophical Society* (1930–1), pp 46–9.

23 Manning *et al.*, *Geology of Belfast*, pp 144–52, Pl. 10.

24 R. Day, 'Flint flakes at Ormeau Bridge' in *Journal of the Royal Society of Antiquaries of Ireland*, x (1868–9), pp 147–8; W.A. Adams, 'Prehistoric sites near the Ormeau Bridge, Belfast' in *U.J.A.*, 2nd ser., v (1898), pp 5–8; Jope, *Archaeological survey of County Down*, Fig 5b, p. 69.

25 Deirdre Flanagan, 'Belfast and the place names therein', trans. A.J. Hughes, in *Ulster Folklife*, xxxviii (1992), pp 87–94; Patrick McKay, 'Belfast place-names and the Irish language' in Fionntán de Brún (ed.), *Belfast and the Irish language* (Dublin, 2006), pp 18–29; Deirdre Morton, 'Former townland names in Tuath Cinament' in *Bulletin of the Ulster Place Name Society*, v, pt 2 (1957), pp 49.

26 T.N.A., MPF 1/77. For the authorship of the map see J.H. Andrews, 'Christopher Saxton and Belfast Lough' in *Irish Geography*, v, no. 2 (1966), pp 1–6.

27 Benn, *History* (1877), pp 552–3.

28 James Morrin, *Calendar of the patent ... rolls of Chancery in Ireland of the reign of Charles I* (Dublin, 1863), p. 65; *Inquisitionum in officio rotulorum cancellariae Hiberniae asservatarum reportorium* (2 vols, Dublin, 1826–9), ii (Down, Charles I), no. 105. When the seventeenth-century church was demolished in 1773 it was noted that oak, probably from the same source, had been used there also, P.R.O.N.I., T1893, 30 Dec 1773, George Portis to C.H. Talbot.

29 T.N.A., SP63/26/5; *Cal. Carew MSS 1575–88*, p. 370.

30 *Cal. S.P. Ire. 1608–10*, p. 89.

31 Thomas McCrie (ed.), *The life of Mr Robert Blair* (Edinburgh, 1848), p. 140.

32 K.W. Nicholls, 'Woodland cover in pre-modern Ireland' in P.J. Duffy, David Edwards and Elizabeth FitzPatrick (eds), *Gaelic Ireland 1250-1650: land, lordship and settlement* (Dublin, 2001), P. 201. On Barr see Raymond Gillespie, *Colonial Ulster: the settlement of east Ulster, 1600–41* (Cork, 1985), pp 178–9. For Barr at Stranmillis in 1636 see Manx Museum and Library, Douglas, Isle of Man, *Liber Cancellarii*, 1636, 58–9.

33 *A true relation of the several acts, passages and proceedings performed by Captain Robert Lawson* (London, 1643), pp 7–8.

34 Raymond Gillespie, *Colonial Ulster: the settlement of east Ulster, 1600–41* (Cork, 1985), pp 180–1; R.M. Young (ed.), *The town book of the corporation of Belfast, 1613–1816* (Belfast, 1892), pp 7, 55–6.

35 For example, *Excavations 1971*, p. 6; E.E. Evans, 'Two Belfast raths' in *U.J.A.*, 3rd ser., xv (1952), pp 84–6.

36 Jope, *Archaeological survey of County Down*, p. 110; Ivor Herring, 'Place-name maps of the Lagan Valley' in *Irish Naturalist's Journal*, viii (1943), pp 63–4.

37 J.P. Mallory and T.E. McNeill, *The archaeology of Ulster* (Belfast, 1991), p. 195; 'Investigation of a crannog in the townland of Ballygolan' in *Proceedings of the Belfast Natural History and Philosophical Society* (1918–19), pp 78–82.

38 E.E. Evans, 'Rath and souterrain at Shaneen Park, Belfast' in *U.J.A.* 3rd ser., xiii (1950), p. 12; Bruce Proudfoot, 'Further excavations at Shaneen Park, Belfast' in *U.J.A.* 3rd ser., xxi (1958), p. 36.

39 B.B. Williams, 'Excavations at Ballyutoag, Co. Antrim' in *U.J.A.* 3rd ser., xlvii (1984), pp 37–49.

40   The originals are held in the North Down Heritage Centre, Bangor, County Down, but there are copies at P.R.O.N.I., T811.

41   Young, *Historical notices*, p. 128.

42   The evidence for this and other interpretations of the evidence is reviewed in Flanagan, 'Belfast and the place names therein', pp 80–6; McKay, 'Belfast place-names', p. 16.

43   E. Hogan (ed.), *The history of the warr of Ireland from 1641 to 1653* (Dublin, 1873), p. 100. For a suggestion that this is where Edward Bruce crossed the Lagan in the insurrection of 1315 see Leo McKeown, 'Historical itineraries in Antrim and Down' in *Down and Connor Historical Society Journal*, viii (1937), pp 33–4.

44   Barrie Hartwell, 'Late Neolithic ceremonies' in *Archaeology Ireland*, viii, no. 4 (winter 1994), pp 10–13; idem, 'A Neolithic ceremonial timber complex at Ballynahatty, Co. Down' in *Antiquity*, lxxvi (2002), pp 526–32.

45   T.N.A., SP63/48/52.

46   Osborn Bergin (ed.), 'Irish grammatical tracts' in *Ériu* ix (1921–3), supplement p. 108. The poem is dated from the fact that it does not appear in a 1552 manuscript of this text but is present in a mid-seventeenth century copy.

47   T.N.A., SP63/42/38.

48   T.N.A., SP63/46/10, 12.

49   Arthur Collins (ed.), *Letters and memorials of state ... by Sir Henry Sidney* (2 vols, London, 1746), i, p. 76.

50   Jope, *Archaeological survey of County Down*, pp 48, 67.

51   Seán Mac Airt and Gearóid Mac Niocaill (eds), *The annals of Ulster* (Dublin, 1983), p. 183.

52   The poem is unedited but it is reproduced in Kathleen Mulchrone (ed.), *The Book of Lecan* (Dublin, 1937), ff 8v–9.

53   Edmund Getty, 'The true position of the ford of Belfast' in *U.J.A.*, 1st ser., iii (1855), pp 300–15.

54   T.K. Lowry, 'The true position of the ford at Belfast' in *U.J.A.*, 1st ser., iv (1856), pp 253–60; Benn, *History* (1877), pp 751–3.

55   Lowry 'True position of the ford', p. 260.

56   Getty, 'True position of the ford', pp 309–11.

57   T.K. Lowry (ed.), *The Hamilton manuscripts* (Belfast, 1867), p. 54n.

58   *Belfast atlas*, map 6.

59   P.R.O.N.I., T811.

60   Lowry (ed.), *Hamilton manuscripts*, appendix, pp xxxiii–xxxiv.

61   George Hill, *The Macdonnells of Antrim* (Belfast, 1873); p. 385; *An exact account of his majesty's progress from his first landing in Ireland until his arrival at Hillsborough* (London, 1690).

62   William Reeves (ed.), 'Irish itinerary of Father Edmund MacCana' in *U.J.A.*, 1st ser., ii (1854), p. 57.

63   Morton, 'Former townland names', p. 47–8.

64   G.W. Lamplugh *et al.*, *The geology of the country around Belfast* (Dublin, 1904), p, 127. For a view of the Blackstaff flooding Great Victoria Street in 1902 see Lyn Gallagher, *The Grand Opera House, Belfast* (Belfast, 1995), p. 36 and in photographs in P.R.O.N.I., D 3038/1/7/11, D2547/10. A map of the areas liable to flooding from the Blackstaff appears in Andrew Malcom, *The sanitary state of Belfast with suggestions for its improvement* (Belfast, 1852).

65   Gaffikin, *Belfast fifty years ago*, p. 27; 40 Geo III, c. 37 [Ire], sect. 67.

66   *Belfast atlas*, map 6.

67 P.R.O.N.I., D509/13.
68 Young, *Town book*, p. 98.
69 John Grainger, 'Results of excavations in High Street, Belfast' in *U.J.A.*, 1st ser., ix (1861–2), p. 116.
70 McKay, 'Belfast place-names', p. 23.
71 Pilson, *History of the rise*, p. 9.
72 Reeves, 'Irish itinerary', p. 57.
73 Walter Harris, *The antient and present state of the county of Down* (Dublin, 1744), p. 127.
74 Samuel Mulleneux, *A journal of the three months royal campaign of his majesty in Ireland* (London, 1691).
75 For example, *The correspondence of Sir John Lowther of Whitehaven, 1693–1698*, ed. D.R. Hainsworth (London, 1983), p. 392; Benn, *History* (1877), pp 566–7; *Calendar of treasury books 1693–6,* pp 879, 899; *Cal. S. P. dom, 1700–2*, p. 46; P.R.O.N.I., D501/1, pp 118–9, 133, 151–2, 316 .
76 P.R.O.N.I., D501/1, p. 148
77 'Belfast drainage scheme' in *Irish Builder*, 1 Nov. 1885, p. 289.
78 For example, see Richard Dobbs's comments of 1683 in Hill, *Macdonnells of Antrim*, p. 387.
79 Harris, *Antient and present state*, pp 127–8.
80 Gaffikin, *Belfast fifty years ago*, p. 6.
81 T.N.A., E190/1138/1, ff 34, 72, 190; E190/1139/3, f. 61; E190/1140/3, f. 8; E190/1344/6, f. 4v.
82 Harris, *Antient and present state*, p. 127; Young, *Town book*, p. 121. For ships at Bangor using Garmoyle in the early seventeenth century, see British Library, Harley MS 2183, ff 175–5v.
83 *Cal. S.P. Ire., 1596–7*, p. 396.
84 For examples see British Library, Harley MS 2138, ff 174v, 177v.
85 Gaffikin, *Belfast fifty years ago*, p. 12.

2

THE MEDIEVAL INHERITANCE

On the face of it the site of Belfast does not seem to be a prime candidate for settlement. It was at the head of a poorly drained and heavily wooded river valley and its site was underlain mainly by unstable estuarine clays. However, its significance as a crossing point over the River Lagan was well known. As early as 668 the *Annals of Ulster* recorded its strategic significance, noting 'the battle of the Fersat between the Ulaid and the Cruithin'.[1] The ford was important to the population group known as Dál Fiatach (or the Ulaid), who were expanding northwards from south Down into Antrim. According to the Ulster annals two years earlier two kings of the Antrim grouping Dál Araide (or the Cruithin) had died in quick succession to be succeded by Cathassach mac Fiacha Luirgéne. It may be that this was seen by the Ulaid as an opportune moment to seize the strategic ford and, according to the annals, in the ensuing battle Cathassach himself was killed.[2] By the middle of the ninth century control of that ford meant that the Dál Fiatach were well established in the area around what would become Belfast. They left their traces in place-names such as Ben Madagain (Cave Hill) and McArt's Fort, both of which seem to derive from the personal name Matudán – probably Matudán son of Muiredach son of Eochaid, who died in 857 and who appears in a genealogy of Dál Fiatach. Again, the place-name Glengormley, a town to the north of Belfast, would seem to originate as a description of the family of Gormlaithe, descended from Muiredach son of Eochaid, and Dunmurray may have similar origins.[3] Those that they dispossessed may also have left traces of their presence in the place-names of Taughmonagh and Knockbreda.[4]

The existence of the ford on the River Lagan meant that the crossing was an important asset for whoever could control it.

Attempts at control probably began early. One interpretation of the name recorded in the seventeenth-century grants for the site of the later Belfast Castle gives its meaning as 'the townland of the rath of Calgach's corner'.[5] The individual called Calgach cannot be identified (although it is an unusual name in the annals and genealogies) so it is impossible to date what is probably the earliest layer of settlement. It is likely, however, that some sort of pre-Anglo-Norman structure was located on the site that became Belfast. Unpromising as the site might be for a medieval settlement, strategic considerations meant that defensive work and ultimately settlement would spring up against the odds.

I

Tantalising as all the early references to pre-Anglo-Norman activity at Belfast are, it is only from the early fourteenth century that it is possible to see the kind of settlement that grew up at the crossing of the Lagan in the High Middle Ages. Paradoxically, the best evidence we have of that settlement comes after its destruction. In 1333 William de Burgh, the 'brown' earl of Ulster, was killed somewhere near Belfast in an insurrection by John Logan and others. The exact location of the murder is unknown but it is tempting to fix it at the townland of Skegoniel (meaning 'the thorn bush of the earl'), located to the north-west of the present city.[6] The inquisition of the earl's lands taken after the murder mentions 'Le Ford', or Belfast:

> There is at Le Ford a manor in which there was a castle, now thrown down by John Logan's war, and worth nothing. There was a borough town there, now all burnt and destroyed by the said John, and worth nothing at present, but in the earl's time it was worth in prerequisites of the court and other profits £1.
>
> In demesne at the Ford 7 carucates [about 840 acres] formerly worth £2 each carucate, now nothing on account of the above war; 4 carucates at Castelconnaugh, formerly worth £1 10s. each, but now nothing; 2 carucates in Ymenaught formerly worth £1 a carucate, now nothing; £4 from 6 carucates which formerly Robert de Mandeville held freely in fee, but now nothing for the same reason.
>
> Formerly £1 6s. 8d. and 24 days work of reapers in August worth 1d. a day, from 8 carucates in Legolghtorp which David O

Colaran, an Irishman, held in fee, who now pays nothing for the same reason. There was a watermill, of which the profits of the toll were worth 6*s*. 8*d*. but now nothing because waste by burning of John Logan.

Extent of the castle and manor of Ford etc. £28. 15*s*. 4*d*. by old extent and now nothing by new.[7]

To this picture of Belfast we can add more information drawn from an ecclesiastical tax levied by Pope Nicholas IV in the 1290s. The assessments made for its collection in the dioceses of Down, Connor and Dromore for 1306–7 survive. According to these assessments, 'The White Church with the chapels of the Ford, of Henrystown and of Westone all these are worth 12 marks.'[8] The 'White Church', or '*Ecclesia Alba*', is readily identifiable as the parish church of Shankill and is referred to in the 1622 visitation records as 'the White church of the ford alias Belfast' ('*ecclesia de Albo vaddo alias Belfast*').[9] The chapels are less easily identifiable. 'Westone' is probably to be located in Ballyvaston, to the north of the city, where a castle and church are recorded in the seventeenth-century inquisitions. 'Henrystown' may be associated with Ballyhenry, although that is now just outside the boundary of the civil parish of Shankill. The 'chapel of the Ford' refers to a church established somewhere near the ford at Belfast. Thus, by the early fourteenth century the present site of Belfast had a church, a castle, a town of sorts and possibly a mill. Perhaps the best way to understand how this settlement had evolved is to consider each of these elements in turn.

The position of the church is relatively easy to determine. The 1622 visitation seems clear enough that the medieval church at the ford was what became the parish church of Belfast in the early seventeenth century, when the older building lay in ruins. This stood on the site now occupied by St George's Church in High Street and became redundant with the building of St Anne's as the new parish church in 1774–6 on the recently created and fashionable Donegall Street.[10] It is not known when the medieval chapel was built but it seems to have been part of an emerging parochial structure in the twelfth and early thirteenth centuries. While the church at the ford may have lain in the damp land beside the Farset and the Lagan, the main medieval parish centre is now represented by a graveyard on the Shankill Road that was the location of the parish church. This was well above the low-lying and damp lands around the Lagan, lying on the 30-metre contour, and is in a similar location to its contemporary, the church of Knock-Columcille (now Knock), on the County Down side of the Lagan Valley and like most other early south Antrim churches was situated beside a river, the Farset, on a slope. Moreover, the Shankill Road seems to have been the main routeway from the ford northward over the Antrim hills. Those crossing at Belfast probably followed the line of North Street to Peter's Hill and onward along the line of the Shankill Road. There is evidence of activity at the site of the church in the thirteenth century, with finds of coins of King John and Edward I in the graveyard.[11]

There are two important pieces of evidence about the emergence of medieval ecclesiastical organisation in the Belfast area. Unfortunately, both are late. The first comes from a terrier, or listing, of the ecclesiastical possessions of the diocese of Down, which was copied in the early seventeenth century but clearly compiled much earlier, since it appears that the religious houses had not been dissolved at the time when it was written. There is no internal evidence to provide a firm date for this document but a guess of about 1500 may not be too far out. The document records that by this date the dedication of the church of Shankill was to St Patrick. This need not imply any Patrician connection with the church, since in other parts of Ireland most of the Patrician dedications are no older than the Anglo-Norman reorganisation of the local dioceses, when new lords attempted to absorb a native cult.[12] The second piece of evidence comes from the extents taken at the dissolution of the Benedictine Cathedral Priory of St Patrick in Downpatrick in the early sixteenth century. This lists among the property of the cathedral priory the rectory or church of Shankill 'in the country of Brian Fertagh', which clearly relates to the parish of Shankill or Belfast.[13] This is confirmed in the 1622 visitation, which records the tithes of Shankill as being in the hands of the countess of Kildare, whose family had acquired the impropriations of the Downpatrick priory in the sixteenth century.[14] It is difficult to know when the rectory of Shankill came into the possession of the priory. A confirmation of the cathedral's property in 1183 does not contain any mention of the parish and hence it is probably later than that date.[15] However, if we assume it was likely to have been given to the founder of the priory as one of its endowments then the grant must have been made by John de Courcy, who founded the priory and endowed it with property elsewhere in County Down. This would mean that the endowment was made after 1183 but before de Courcy's expulsion from Ulster in 1204–5. At this point the church of Shankill may have taken the dedication to St Patrick – that of its mother church at Downpatrick.

What may have been at work here was a particularly complex game of ecclesiastical chess. At the synod of Rathbreasail in 1111 it seems that only one diocese was created for east Ulster, the diocese of Connor, which encompassed the present dioceses of Down, Connor and Dromore. In 1136 or 1137 the reforming archbishop of Armagh, Malachy, retired from that see and began a campaign for reform in east Ulster by creating the bishopric of Down, which included the parish of Shankill. It seems that he based himself not at the later centre of the see, Downpatrick, but at the Augustinian house in Bangor, which he may well have seen as the diocese's cathedral. Some credence is given to this view by the fact that as late as 1224 the canons of Bangor maintained that Bangor was the cathedral of the diocese and that they had the right to elect the bishop.[16] When John de Courcy established his Anglo-Norman cathedral at Downpatrick in the late 1170s, after Malachy's death, this was a direct challenge to Bangor. Endowing Downpatrick with Shankill, which (as we shall see) had been a high-status parish close to Bangor (and possibly under its control since the proxies from one of the chapels of Shankill were payable to Bangor), sent a clear message about the nature of the new order and about who was now in control. Something of these developments may be suggested by the architectural evidence of this early church. This is meagre since the church was already in ruins by 1604 and by 1823 it had been demolished.[17] Modern attempts at excavation at the site have not found any remains but in 1823 George Benn noted 'an enormous foundation stone was discovered last year in making a grave. It was of so great a size that it required to be blasted with gunpowder.'[18]

Masonry of this size is often associated with some of the earliest surviving Irish stone churches and in another context it has been suggested that churches described as 'white' in the middle ages (as Shankill was) were built of stone.[19] Such stone churches in this area seem to be associated with Malachy's twelfth-century reforms since according to St Bernard's contemporary life of Malachy it was the bishop who introduced stone-built churches. This, it was claimed, cause some distress to the local population who had not seen a stone church before Malachy's building activities.[20] Thus both limited archaeological evidence and documentary sources point to a twelfth-century rebuilding of the church at Shankill in stone, suggesting an important site, tied with ecclesiastical politics of some complexity.

However, these complex twelfth-century political games do not explain the origins of the church at Belfast. It is clear that the parish of Shankill had a history that stretched back before the thirteenth century. In one account, by the Kilkenny chronicler James Grace, of the murder of the brown earl of Ulster in 1333 the murder was said to have taken place 'between the castle of Sancles and Gregfergus' ('*inter castrum de Sancles et Gregfergus*').[21] The latter is clearly the castle of Carrickfergus but the former place name is more confusing. One possibility is that it represents an attempt to render Shankill, the castle of Shankill being that at the ford at Belfast. If that is so then the parish name of *Sean Chill* (old church) was already well established in the early fourteenth century and the church was already an old one. There is a piece of evidence for earlier ecclesiastical activity on this site in the form of three fragments of an episcopal crozier, now in the National Museum of Ireland, all of which came from this site. One piece represents the ferrule, another the drop of the crozier with its reliquary box and the third part the crozier's foot. On the basis of the decoration these have been dated to the late eighth or ninth centuries.[22] This probably indicates an episcopal presence at the site. Such episcopal churches, associated with monastic centres, were more common in early-medieval Ireland than was previously thought and each major family may well have had an episcopal church. It is likely that Shankill was the episcopal church for the local power group. If Shankill had such status, that would help to explain the curious trajectory of the diocese of Down's boundary. When that diocese was created in the early twelfth century out of the larger diocese of Connor, the diocesan boundary was drawn along the minor River Glas an Bradden and the Ballymartin River to include Shankill and a number of south Antrim parishes (Umgall, Mallusk and Carngraney) rather than following the obvious topographical division of the River Lagan. Since the diocese was demarcated in Down's favour the boundary may have been placed northwards to include the high-status site of Shankill. This desire to include Shankill in the diocese of Down may have been the result of Bishop Malachy wishing to link it with his cathedral at Bangor, as discussed above.

If Shankill was indeed an episcopal church, although there are no identifiable entries in the annals that demonstrate that it was, then this would certainly increase the status of the site. Such sites often had additional activities associated with them, such as markets or fairs, and in that context it is worth noting the find of hack silver, comprising two arm rings and an ingot, at nearby Cave Hill.[23] Such hoards not containing coins are usually dated between *c.* 850 and *c.* 950, which is not far away from the probable date of the crozier fragments.[24] This hoard, later concealed at Cave Hill, could well be an indication of commercial activity near the Shankill site.

As the parochial structure within which Belfast evolved took shape around the church a similar secular process was under way around the castle. It is difficult to date the foundation of the castle that appears in the 1333 account quoted above. In the 1860s T.K. Lowry, editor of the seventeenth-century Hamilton manuscripts, noted that he had seen in the now-destroyed pipe roll of 1262 an entry that:

> Richard of Exeter accounts for £254. 7*s.* 6*d.* for many debts etc.; £30 granted by the king's son, Edward, to him for the custody of the castle of Carrickfergus, £20 for the custody of the castle of Antrim, £[blank] for the Castle Del Rath; £10 which Edward, the king's son, granted to him for the custody of the castle of the ford and £10 for the custody of Greencastle.[25]

If Lowry read the entry correctly this is the first reference to a 'castle of the ford' at Belfast. The appearance of such a reference is a reflection of the status of the earldom of Ulster at the time. In 1242–3 Hugh de Lacy, earl of Ulster, died without an heir and the earldom reverted to the crown. Ten years later the earldom was granted to Queen Eleanor as part of her dowry and the following year it became the property of the future Edward I, son of Henry III, who was then lord of Ireland.[26] However, the debts incurred clearly predate the entry in the pipe rolls of 1262 and they had been outstanding for some time, possibly as far back as the acquisition of the Ulster lordship by Lord Edward in the 1250s. It is thus possible that the castle of Belfast was in existence at this date. It is also clear that when the debts were incurred the castle at the ford had only recently been constructed. The pipe roll of 1211–12, when the earldom was also in royal hands, makes no mention of any castle at the ford, despite recording work at a wide range of Ulster castles.[27]

Distribution of mottes in the Belfast area.

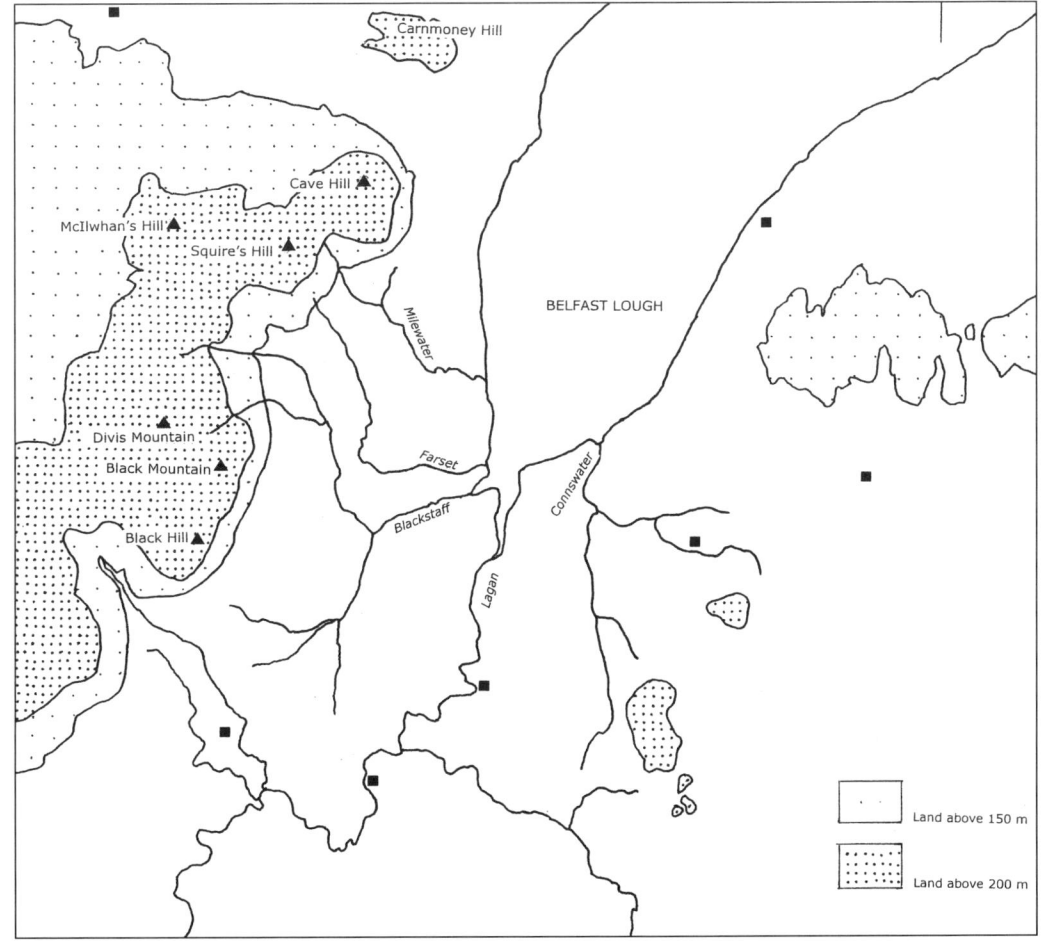

If this speculation is correct the castle at Belfast may be a creation of the 1250s. Such a date would fit with what is known about the evolution of communications in this area in the late twelfth and early thirteenth centuries. Early Anglo-Norman crossing points on the River Lagan are easily identified because they were fortified with motte structures. Here a clear pattern of mottes across north Down may suggest a routeway that did not pass through the ford at Belfast. The route from Dundonald to Knock was clearly an important one but it seems to have veered off towards the motte at Belvoir Park and Edenderry, which probably marked crossing points on the river, before moving into the western part of Antrim. Indeed, when John was at Carrickfergus as lord of Ireland in 1212 he sailed from there to Holywood rather than ride along the coast through the ford at Belfast. This arc of mottes indicates not only the main Anglo-Norman communications route but also a chain of defences creating a secure enclave in the upper Lagan Valley. Within this easily defended enclave the creation of settlements was clearly a strong possibility and Belfast was a prime location for a castle or town.

According to the evidence, as the thirteenth century advanced interest in the ford and its hinterland from those at Carrickfergus increased. Settlement probably moved southward from Carrickfergus towards the ford, rather than from any other Anglo-Norman centre, such as Newtownards on the County Down side of the River Lagan. The place-names in Shankill that can be shown to have Anglo-Norman associations are all located in the north-eastern part of the parish, in the area closest to Carrickfergus, along the shore of Belfast Lough.[28] Moreover, all these place-names occur in the northern part of the division of the parish of Shankill known in later inquisitions as 'Tuatha Cinament'. The origin of the term 'cinament' is the subject of some debate but a Norman-French derivation seems possible – which again points to Anglo-Norman influence, probably from Carrickfergus, in this area.[29]

All this suggests Anglo-Norman penetration southwards from Carrickfergus towards the ford at Belfast, possibly in the first half of the thirteenth century. This is also suggested by the pattern of medieval coin hoards in the area, most of which occur north-east of Belfast, towards Carrickfergus. It seems highly likely, therefore, that the castle at Belfast was established by Anglo-Norman settlement from Carrickfergus, pressing southwards along the coast of Belfast Lough in the early thirteenth century.

There is no hard evidence for the precise location or appearance of the castle. The most probable site is that occupied by the later medieval tower house and the plantation castle of the seventeenth century, around the modern-day Castle Lane and Castle Place. This would be a logical and strategic site on which to position a castle. From that point it was possible to dominate both the peninsula of land formed by the Rivers Farset and Blackstaff on the north and south and the Lagan to the east. However it may be possible to infer something of its appearance by considering some of the contemporary Ulster castles. From 1242–3, when de Lacy died, until its regrant to Walter de Burgh in 1264 the lordship was in the hands of the king or his son. Over this period there was a sustained campaign by the crown to reassert its authority over Brian O'Neill, of the Tyrone lordship, who was also trying to expand his authority. This resulted in a period of castle building. The greater castles of the lord, Carrickfergus, Greencastle and Dundrum, were all repaired and some of the castles of the lord's vassals, such as Clogh, were extended. More significantly, new castles were built. Drumtarsy, near Coleraine, was constructed in 1248, Magh Cobha (Seafin in County Down) in 1252, Caol Uisce (Narrow Water, apparently in Fermanagh) in the same year and also probably Doonbought in County Antrim.[30] Others, such as Connor, Cross and Court McMartin, all in County Antrim, may be of a similar date since they are similar in form to the dated examples. These castles have similarities with that at Belfast in terms of their siting. Most are sited beside rivers and on high land. Belfast Castle was certainly built at the bend in the river and it was located on land that was higher than that around it, and it is possible that it was raised on an artificial platform. To the east was the Lagan and south and west the flood plain of the Blackstaff occupied deep sleech around Donegall Square. In the case of Seafin and Doonbought the castles were built on top of existing raths and this also seems to be case of Belfast since the place-names suggest a habitation site. Finally all these castles of the 1250s were on the margins of the lordship. Belfast too lay outside

the main area of the lordship before the 1250s with most settlement
to the north and west of the mottes surrounding it. All this suggests
that Belfast was similar to these castles of the 1250s. If that is so then
it began life as a polygonal enclosure, probably enclosed by a rude-
ly built stone wall, which was probably no more than 30m across,
with a surrounding ditch and a keep within the wall, as at Seafin.[31]
The main aim of this rather crude fortification was to act as a garrison to protect the ford. However over the next fifty years a manor,
which provided the legal and administrative framework within
which local life operated, was erected here. It is not known when
the manor referred to in 1333 was created. There is certainly a reference to the 'manor of the ford' ('*manor de Vado*') in 1293 in a fine
recorded in a later abstract of a set of de Mandeville charters.[32] It
may be that the castle was enlarged to meet its new role as manor-
ial centre but its position is a reminder of its original role. While the
manor may have been a resource territory, the positioning of the
castle on the manor's edge was essentially strategic, to protect a
communications node, rather than to fulfil an economic or administrative role.

Following the establishment of church and castle, the next logical
development was the creation of a town. The 1333 inquisition
describes the settlement as a borough, suggesting that it had a legal
form and some kind of charter. However, the inquisition says nothing about the town's economic functions. There is, for example, no
documentary evidence of a market but one almost certainly existed. If the evidence of the 1333 inquisition is to be trusted at least
some rents were to be paid in cash, which presumes some form of
local market to turn agricultural produce into money. In terms of
valuations of boroughs in the Ulster lordship in 1333 Belfast came
near the bottom of the list, well below Carrickfergus, Holywood
and Greencastle. The pattern of distribution of ecclesiastical wealth
was little different. The borough and surrounding parish were poor
in relation to the area around them.[33] Thus, a settlement at Belfast
might best be seen not as a fully functioning town but as a rather
smaller 'rural borough'.

There is little evidence for the town's physical appearance or precise location. However, excavations in 2003 have produced evidence

for a set of property boundaries fronting onto Cornmarket and lying under those of the seventeenth century. Some thirteenth- or fourteenth-century imported pottery was also found in a gully on the High Street side of the site.[34] This may well be the site of the medieval settlement and it would support the possibility (mentioned in the previous chapter) that the medieval routeway from the ford followed the line of the present Ann Street. Later building work on Ann Street has probably destroyed much of the archaeological evidence for this early settlement.[35]

Close to this castle, church and town were a number of smaller dispersed dwellings. In 1928 excavations at Ekenhead Presbyterian Church on North Circular Road revealed one such settlement, which can be dated by the presence of a coin hoard to c. 1315–18.[36] This was a rectangular earthwork of a moated site type about 9 metres across, probably with some form of stone structure in the middle. Again, excavations at what seemed to be a rath at Poleglass produced not only quantities of coarse pottery but also a silver penny of 1280–1.[37] At Ballysillan and Shaneen Park the excavation of earlier raths may also provide some pottery evidence of temporary reoccupation during the Anglo-Norman settlement.[38]

II   the burning of 1333

What happened to the settlement of Belfast after the burning of 1333 is very unclear. There is no direct evidence of what might have occurred there for more than a century afterwards. When the place appears in the sources again it is in the late-fifteenth-century *Annals of Ulster*. Under the year 1476 the annalist noted:

1476
1486
castle

> A great hosting by Ua Neill (namely Henry) against [Conn], son of Aedh Ua Neill the Tawney and he went against the castle of Bel-Feirsdi and the castle was taken and broken by him and he went to his house with triumph of victory.

The early-seventeenth-century *Annals of the Four Masters* reported the same events in much the same words.[39] The second reference from the Ulster annalist appears ten years later, in 1486, when he described the following:

> The castle of Bel fersdi was taken by Feidhlimidh, grandson of

[Aedh] Ua Neill the Tawney and by the son of Savage, namely and by the sons of Brian the Foreign, son of Brian the Freckled, from the warders of Brian, son of Aedh the Tawney, son of Brian the Freckled, in summer.[40]

The third reference, equally enigmatic, appears in the *Annals of Ulster* for 1489:

Ua Domnaill, namely Aedh, son of Niall the Rough, went into Trian Conghail at the end of harvest this year. And great raids were made by him on Mac Uibilin in the Route and the son of Ua Domnaill, namely Conn, was wounded there and the castle of Bel-Fersdi was taken by Ua Domnaill on that incursion and he went safe to his house.[41]

These entries, slight as they may appear, are important in establishing a number of facts about Belfast in the late fifteenth century. Firstly, there was a castle; secondly, that castle was under the control of the O'Neills of Clandeboy by 1476; and thirdly, it was of enough significance to tempt O'Donnell to raid it – despite the fact that the main aim of his raiding was located in north Antrim, in the Route. These pieces of information may help us to understand how the settlement at Belfast had evolved.

How long the castle at Belfast had been under the control of the Clandeboy O'Neills is not clear but it may have been a recent acquisition. However given that this was a substantial stone castle, as discussed below, O'Neill power must have been well enough established in the area to extract the resources from the local population to build such a structure. It is possible to push the date back a little before 1476. In 1468 two factions of the O'Neills clashed on the Cave Hill in what was clearly by then the core of O'Neill territory.[42] Even earlier in 1442 there was a dispute between two parties over the right to the rectory of Breadac, or Knockbreda, which was referred to the archbishop of Armagh for a resolution. The resulting judgment was to be enforced by Odo Flavus O Neyll, or Aodh Buidhe O'Neill of Clandeboy if necessary, providing clear evidence that this branch of the family represented the secular lords of the Belfast area at this point.[43] The Clandeboy O'Neills, an offshoot of the main branch of the Tyrone O'Neills, took advantage of a much-weakened Anglo-Norman colony to spread their influence in the late fourteenth century. However, this was a slow process and the lordship certainly did not collapse after the burning of Belfast and the murder of the brown earl of Ulster in 1333. As late as 1374 an Anglo-Irish lord was still controlling the area of the parish of Camlin to the west of Belfast.[44] Moreover, the commercial influence of the centre of the lordship, Carrickfergus, seems to have continued. Three Irish groats of Edward VI and Henry VII were found near Belfast in the nineteenth century and a hoard at Knockagh, to the north of Belfast, of about 1395 had a significant number of Scottish coins, all of which suggest trading contacts with a wider world, probably through Carrickfergus.[45] However, given that the Belfast area was late colonised, probably only in the 1250s, it was probably also one of the early areas to be surrendered.

It may be that the period between the death of the brown earl of Ulster and the consolidation of power by the Clandeboy O'Neills in the region in the early sixteenth century saw considerable activity in the Belfast area. For instance, the ford was a complex man-made structure, if the evidence of dredging in the Lagan discussed in the previous chapter is to be believed. Such a structure had to be maintained: this required a locally organised group of people and possibly even a settlement. In return, presumably, levies for use of the ford were imposed by the O'Neills. Whether other services, such a quay, were provided by O'Neill in return for payment is not known but possible. Other evidence also indicates a well-organised landscape in the Belfast area in the later Middle Ages. Land grants and inquisitions from the early seventeenth century record an already existing complex organisation of land units. The simplest unit was clearly the townland, a unit that had been evolving throughout the Anglo-Norman period. Ballyvicustullie (now Greencastle), for instance, preserves the Anglo-Norman surname de Angulo in its Hibernicised form of Costello: therefore, that townland must have been named after the Anglo-Norman settlement. However the early-seventeenth-century inquisitions also recorded more complex units described as 'tuatha' or 'cinaments'. To the north of the castle lay Tuath Cinament. To the west was the Tuath of Le Fall and Malone and to the south was the Cinament of

Derryvolgie. The origin of the word 'cinament', as discussed above, appears to be Anglo-Norman and it is possible that 'Le Fall' may also have an Anglo-Norman origin.[46] For such reasons these units must date from the thirteenth or fourteenth centuries. They are clearly later than the townland network since their boundaries, as recorded in seventeenth-century inquisitions, bisect some townlands. They also appear to be later than the parish of Shankill since, again, they are not coterminous with the parish boundaries.[47] As such they may preserve features of later-medieval landscape organisation. It is difficult to understand the functions of these boundaries. One possibility is that they represented taxation units and another explanation is that they are settlement units. The latter appears the more likely since the 1604 land grant to Sir Arthur Chichester of the castle and its lands specifies that the lands were described as the tuatha of Malone, Fall and Cinament.[48] The term 'tuath' in sixteenth century land grants appears to refer to lands associated with one extended family but a personal name is normally part of the place-name. In this case it appears that the O'Neills took over the earlier description and boundaries of the land around Belfast and parcelled it out among a number of the families of their followers. If this is so it does suggest enough continuity of individuals between the Anglo-Norman settlement and the O'Neill colonisation for boundaries to be remembered in an age when they were not mapped. What also seems likely is that these three land units comprised the demesne lands of the late-medieval castle, which are referred to in later grants as the lands of the castle of Belfast, held by the Clandeboy O'Neills, and were very roughly coterminous with the civil parish of Shankill, within which the castle lay. If so they were probably occupied by the principal families of the immediate O'Neill household.

It is also clear that there was large-scale ecclesiastical reorganisation in the same period. The taxation of 1306–7 had recorded the parish of Shankill as having three dependent chapels. The terrier of c. 1500, however, notes that Shankill had six dependent chapels: Cromac, Kilpatrick, Ballyvaston, Killemna, Cloghcastally and Tullyrusk. The church at the ford is not mentioned and is probably to be identified with Cromac, since this would be the place closest to the site of the chapel. Ballyvaston appears in the 1306–7 taxation but the other chapels were later creations.

These arose in two ways. Firstly, the chapel of Tullyrusk equates with the parish of Karryn (or Knockcairn), recorded as a separate parish in 1306–7. By *c.* 1500 it seems that Shankill had absorbed this parish and reduced the former parish church to the status of a chapel. Of the remaining three chapels at least two must be new creations and one may conceal the older chapel of Henrystown, although it is equally possible that it was replaced by 'Cloghcastally' (probably Greencastle), which is near Ballyhenry, provisionally identified as the site of this chapel. 'Kilpatrick', identified in later inquisitions as being in Malone near Stranmillis, is probably now represented by Friar's Bush graveyard and 'Killemna' may be associated with the townland of Kilmakee in Dunmurray.[49] The meaning of these developments is very unclear but the annexation of Karryn to Shankill may be the result of the growing power of the Clandeboy O'Neills, anxious to increase the status of the parish associated with their castle. There is one other indication that this is so. Richard Pococke, visiting Belfast in 1752, noted that 'the church

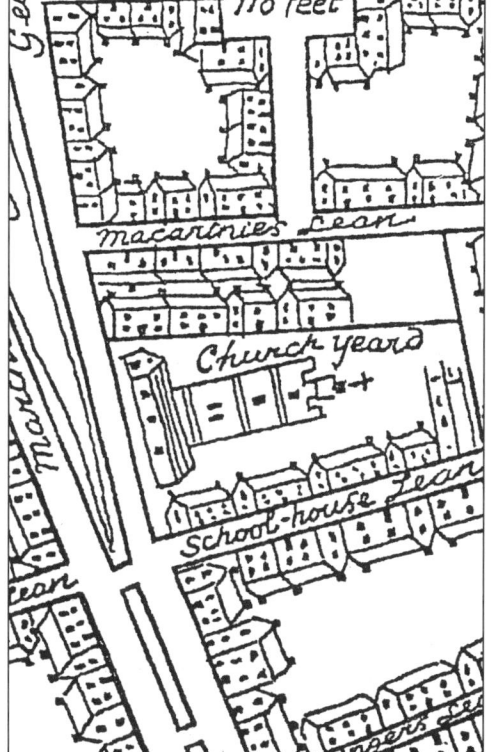

seems to be an old tower or castle, to which they have built so as to make it a Greek cross, and is very mean fabric for such a considerable place'.[50] The unusual nature of the tower is confirmed from the rather crude sketch included in John Maclanachan's map of 1715, in which the tower seems out of proportion to the rest of the building. It is possible that the tower of the seventeenth-century church was a survivor of an older late-medieval building. If so, the church at the ford

Parish church, High Street from John Maclanachan's map of 1715. Note the disproportionate size and irregular nature of the tower, possibly representing the fabric of an older medieval building.

39

may have been rebuilt in the late fifteenth or early sixteenth century by the O'Neills as an indicator of their status. A hint that the O'Neills acted in this way is provided in the 1640s by Fr MacCana, who noted the church dedicated to St Columba at Knock, 'which Niall O'Neill, chief of Trian Congall, endowed with valuable lands and many privileges'.[51] This is almost certainly Niall Mór O'Neill, who was lord of the area from 1482 to 1512 and who reconstructed the Franciscan friary at Carrickfergus in 1497. A date such as this would fit the sort of ecclesiastical reorganisation taking place around the O'Neill castle at Belfast. Secondly, the creation of new chapels may indicate the expansion or redistribution of population in the area around Belfast. While the chapels mentioned in the 1306–7 taxation were all in the northern part of the parish, two of the new creations were in the southern part, which might indicate a growing population there. There is one other hint that this may be the case. Excavations in raths that lay on the slopes of the hills to the north of Belfast in the 50-100m range suggest that many of these were reoccupied in the thirteenth century but there is no evidence for later occupation in the fifteenth century. This may suggest that settlement was moving into the lower land and onto sites that have not yet been located.

The annalistic entries do not reveal much about the siting, form or fabric of the castle at Belfast. It does, however, seem reasonable to conclude that the castle stood on the site of the early-seventeenth-century fortification around Castle Place. In the 1590s Sir John Chichester described how at Belfast 'boats may be landed within a butt shot of the said castle', suggesting it was some way from the mouth of the River Farset.[52] In 1611 the Plantation Commissioners described how the builders of the new castle 'had taken down the ruins of the decayed castle there almost to the vault of the cellars' and built a brick house joined to the new structure.[53] The mention of a vault suggests that this was a stone castle, although it is important to remember that annalistic entries of the later sixteenth century do suggest that the fifteenth-century structure was rebuilt a number of times, and it is just possible, though unlikely, that the castle observed by the commissioners was a later creation. Certainly in 1553 the castle at Belfast was described as 'old', whereas the other

O'Neill castle at Castlereagh was not.[54] The Plantation Commissioners' reference to cellars seems unlikely, given that the castle would have been located on the Belfast mud or sleech and that any cellar would be likely to flood. What the commissioners may have seen was not a vaulted cellar underground but the vaulted ground floor of a tower house of a type that was becoming increasingly common in the late fifteenth century. There are no contemporary descriptions of this sort of building at Belfast but in 1738 there was a tradition that the castle at Belfast had been 'an old square castle with a court or bawne', which would conform to the description of a tower house.[55] Part of this castle may well have survived until relatively late, having been incorporated into the seventeenth-century brick-built castle at Belfast that was destroyed by fire in the early eighteenth century. In 1823 George Benn reported of this later castle, 'it is only a few years since the remaining walls were removed, when they were found to be eight feet in thickness'.[56] A wall that thick would make no sense in a brick-built structure of the seventeenth century but could describe the lower part of the walls of a tower house or the bawn surrounding it. Unfortunately Benn was not precise about the location of these walls and the 1757 plan of the town offers too many possibilities to guess where it may have been. Another part of the bawn wall may also have survived under the market house at the corner of Cornmarket and High Street. When that structure was dismantled in 1813 Benn recorded the 'removal of great stones of which the building was composed'. From other sources it is known that the market house was made of 'small red bricks' with sandstone dressings.[57] However, excavations at Cornmarket in 2003 revealed two large stone walls about one metre in width: these are probably part of the castle structure, other parts having been demolished in 1817.[58]

It is possible to argue for this sort of structure at Belfast on one other basis. The Clandeboy O'Neills had at least two other castles in the immediate area, one at Castlereagh and another near Antrim at Edenduffcarrick. The Castlereagh site was clearly a stone tower house and surrounding square bawn of stone with a ditch outside and flanking angle towers on at least two of the corners. The results of excavation, however, did not suggest a very robust structure.[59]

The similarities of that structure to what is known about Belfast are striking and it seems likely that Belfast was similar to that at Castlereagh, although probably older.

In the early part of the sixteenth century this emerging centre at Belfast attracted increasing attention from the annalists. Under the year 1503 the *Annals of the Four Masters* noted:

> A hosting by the same earl [of Kildare], attended by the English and Irish of Leinster to Magh-line [and] to Carrickfergus; and he demolished the castle of Belfast and made the son of Sandal constable of Carrickfergus.[60]

In 1512 Kildare was back:

> An army led by Garrett, earl of Kildare, lord justice of Ireland, into Trian-Chongail; and he took the castle of Belfast, demolished the castle of Makeon of the Glynnes, plundered the Glynnes and a great portion of the country, and led the son of Niall, son of Con [O'Neill] away into captivity.[61]

The rationale for hostage-taking, according to the *Annals of Ulster*, was that the hostages would be 'in pledge [of compliance] with his [Kildare's] own award'.[62] In 1523 Kildare made another foray into east Ulster. He attacked and 'broke' Aodh O'Neill's castle of Belfast in revenge for O'Neill's rescue of the crew of a Scottish boat that had run aground while the earl was chasing it.[63] Kildare was not the only person interested in Belfast. For 1537 a number of annalists recorded that the son of Conn O'Neill was taken prisoner at the castle of Belfast, presumably rebuilt, while his father was on campaign in east Ulster.[64] Compared to the 50-year period between 1450 and 1500 Belfast was attracting increasing attention. The context of all this lay in the complexities of factional politics at national level. In the late fifteenth century Henry O'Neill, lord of the Tyrone O'Neills, had consolidated his position as the effective ruler of Ulster by the paradoxical move of submitting himself as a vassal of Edward IV, who was also earl of Ulster by right of inheritance.[65] By this means O'Neill acquired royal support in imposing his authority on the other Ulster lords, including the Clandeboy O'Neills. By the 1450s he had done this thoroughly, although relations were to prove difficult. The attack on Belfast Castle in 1476 is one indication of that. Royal support for the overlordship of the Tyrone O'Neills over those of Clandeboy continued into the sixteenth century. It was given a more personal edge by the marriage of the sister and daughter of the lord deputy, the earl of Kildare, to senior members of the Tyrone O'Neill family. Thus the 1503 and 1513 incursions against Belfast Castle were less about imposing the will of the Dublin administration on the O'Neills of Clandeboy than about supporting Kildare's family contacts and the vassals of the crown, the O'Neills of Tyrone, against local dissent in Antrim.

III

After 1550 Belfast began to attract further attention from the Irish annalists. For 1552 the *Annals of the Four Masters* noted:

> A hosting was made by the lord justice into Ulster against the son of Niall og (i.e Hugh O'Neill [of Clandeboy]) and the Scots. A party of English and Mac tSabhaoisigh preceded them with a force in quest of preys, but the son of Niall og met these at Belfast and he rushed on and defeated them and slew Mac tSabhaoisigh together with forty or sixty others. The other troops went across [the River Lagan] and proceeded to erect a castle at Belfast but they gained no victory and obtained no spoils or hostages.[66]

Hugh subsequently submitted to the Dublin administration and was regranted Belfast Castle.[67] The entry in the annals is rather unclear. The reference to 'erecting' a castle at Belfast implies that the site did not already have a functioning fortification, possibly because it was still in ruins from the campaigns of the 1530s. In 1553 Lord Chancellor Cusack described Belfast as 'an old castle standing upon a ford out from Ard to Clandeboy which, being well repaired, being now broken, would be a good defence betwixt the woods and Carrickfergus'.[68] These observations suggest that the site of Belfast had begun to take on a strategic significance it had not had in the previous 20 years. The context was the internal disputes that had erupted within the O'Neill family. For 1555 the annalists recorded the death of Niall Óg O'Neill, lord of Clandeboy, killed by Scots 'with the shot of a ball'. The lordship was then partitioned between two contenders.[69] The division between upper and lower Clandeboy meant that Belfast was the main way of crossing from one to the other. This internal disruption, of itself, was not crucial to the future of east Ulster but internal feuding allowed Scots mercenaries from the Isles to exploit the situation and destabilise the political arrangements in east Ulster. There may even have been a Scottish settlement close to Belfast. According to a survey of royal possessions in Ulster of 1540:

> There are two lordships or manors pertaining to Knockfergus. On the one side is the manor of Molynne, which is four miles long from the castle to the water or river of Scarrenenegragh, and on the other side the lordshipp of Ardd, in length four miles from the castle [of Carrickfergus] to the Blackstaffe called in Irish Mayddedowneard where the Scots now inhabit twelve towns by force of arms[.][70]

It is difficult not to identify the Blackstaff with the river near the site of the castle of Belfast as opposed to the River Blackstaff that formed the boundary of the barony of Ards, since the latter was a much greater distance from Carrickfergus than the four miles specified. It may then be possible to conclude that there was a Scottish settlement in the Belfast area.

The problem of the Scots in east Ulster in the late sixteenth century was a growing one with which the Dublin administration would have to contend. Politically the Scots were a volatile grouping who would ally themselves with whatever party suited them best. In 1553 there was an alliance between the O'Neills and the Scots, while under the year 1555 the annalists noted the appointment of a new lord deputy, Thomas Radcliffe, earl of Sussex, who 'at the ins[iste]nce of O'Neill' organised a campaign 'to expel the sons of MacDonnell and the Scots who were making conquests in the Route and Clannaboy'.[71] Sussex on his expedition visited Belfast and noted that the castle was in ruins but if repaired would be an important defensive site, and other soldiers campaigning against the Scots agreed.[72] Such comments reflect changed priorities, since in 1542 the lord deputy had been happy to grant Clandeboy to the O'Neills, reserving only Carrickfergus, Larne and Coleraine to the crown. He disregarded Belfast entirely.[73]

In the 1560s new urgency was given to the problem of instability in Clandeboy, with the growing power of Shane O'Neill in west

Ulster and the outbreak of war in 1566, as well as the continuing problem of Scottish incursions into Antrim and Down.[74] Shane O'Neill, keen to establish his power east of the River Bann, claimed overlordship of the O'Neills of Clandeboy and ownership of the castle of Belfast.[75] As a result of these developments Belfast again appeared in the writings of those in the Dublin administration concerned with establishing strategic defences in east Ulster.[76] By 1567 the castle had been repaired and a small troop of 15 horsemen was garrisoned there. There may also have been an even more substantial settlement. In early 1568 Captain Nicholas Malby, governor of Carrickfergus, claimed that Belfast had cost him dearly to build but that he had farms there and hoped to develop it further.[77] However, none of this halted the feuding between the two branches of the Clandeboy O'Neills, which drew the Dublin army into the territory. In 1568 Lord Deputy Sidney attempted to regularise the situation by drawing up an agreement between the two claimants to the lordship of Clandeboy. This provided that the castle would be maintained as a garrison to separate the two parties and that they would build a bridge over the ford at Belfast as well as cutting roads through the woods. They were also to compensate Malby for the improvements he had carried out there.[78] Brian MacPhelim O'Neill recovered the castle of Belfast.

Such piecemeal solutions had limited value in maintaining stability and new options were resorted to. The parliamentary act of attainder of Shane O'Neill in 1569, after his failed rebellion, claimed all of Ulster for the crown. Queen Elizabeth then proceeded to grant some of the land to settlers who would secure it. In 1570 north Antrim was granted to Sir Thomas Gerard and his company, despite a request by Brian MacPhelim O'Neill for such a grant, and in 1571 Sir Thomas Smith received a grant of Clandeboy. Neither of these schemes prospered and in July 1573 the queen granted the greater part of County Antrim to the earl of Essex. Essex arrived at Carrickfergus in August and immediately met resistance. He recognised the strategic importance of Belfast and suggested a garrison of 300 footmen and 100 horse be based there.[79] As he observed,

> [Belfast] is a place meet for a corporate town, armed with commodities as a principal haven, wood and good ground, standing

upon a border and a place of great importance for service. I think it convenient that a fortification be made there at the spring, the fortification for the circuit and a store house for victuals to be at her majesty's charge and other buildings at mine and such as shall inhabit it'.

A bridge across the Lagan was also thought to be a necessity.[80] Early in the following year he resolved to fortify Friarstown, near Belfast, with a garrison of 400 foot and 50 horse.[81] Friarstown is relatively easy to identify. It occurs as 'Freerestone' on a map of *c.* 1570.[82] It is marked as part of a cluster of buildings on higher land to the south of the castle of Belfast. In an inquisition of 1618 it is recorded as 'Ballenebraher al[ias] Frierstown'. It seems that the latter was a fairly free English translation of the former and it need not imply a religious house but rather the 'town of the brothers' (which could mean friars). Given the possibility, discussed above, that the church at the ford may have been rebuilt in the late fifteenth century by the same man as built the Franciscan house at Carrickfergus, it is possible that a Franciscan house was planned for this site but never developed, leaving the place name as its only trace. By the eighteenth century it had become known as Friar's Bush, a graveyard on the Stranmillis Road. The large mound in the centre of the present graveyard may represent the remains of some of the buildings marked on the map of *c.* 1570, which were erected by Essex because he intended to build a stone house on the site.

By May 1574 Essex reported to the Privy Council that he had begun to entrench a large town at Belfast, although this was probably nearer the castle than the original proposed site of Friarstown.[83] Soldiers were to be used for the construction and Brian MacPhelim O'Neill also promised labour.[84] By July it was planned that a brewhouse, storehouse and mill were to be finished before the end of the year, despite an outbreak of disease among the garrison in May and the ambush and execution of Brian MacPhelim O'Neill in November. The cost was estimated at £2,000 but it was hoped that letting houses would bring in £100 a year.[85] Plans became more elaborate as time progressed. In October a walled town was envisaged, with a storehouse, bakehouse, brewhouse and mill so that the town would not have to be supplied from Carrickfergus. By

November the dimensions of the walls (given as 4 feet thick and 16 feet high with a circuit of 3,200 feet) and timber storehouse (100 feet by 24 feet) had been decided on; the rampart was said to be 'viewed and plotted out' but there was a shortage of craftsmen for the actual construction.[86] This evidence allows us to understand the scale of the operation that was planned at Belfast. The proposed rental of £100 needs to be seen against the rental of £274 realised from Newry in 1575.[87] Again, a walled circuit of about 975 metres matches Carrickfergus's 1,000 metres, Newry's 1,300 metres or Downpatrick's 1,200 metres.[88] This suggests that Essex had in mind a substantial town, similar to other major east Ulster towns in the mid-sixteenth century, rather than simply a garrison settlement. However, all was not well. By June 1575 little seems to have been done, although Essex wrote defiantly to the queen, 'I resolve to build in one place, namely Belfast and that at little charge. A small town will keep the passage, relieve Knockfergus with wood, and horsemen being laid there shall command the plains of Clandeboy.' Such a garrison could, he hoped, be funded from the rents of the Irish, who would be left on their lands in Clandeboy.[89] By then the project was dead. In May 1575 the queen had withdrawn her support for his colonisation scheme and no further progress was made. However, as Lord Deputy Sidney emphasised, Belfast needed to be kept in crown hands for security reasons and a garrison was maintained there in 1585.[90]

The long-term impact of all this activity is not clear. Belfast certainly had established itself as a castle but it is possible that there was more to it than that. There have been many finds of late Elizabethan coins in the Belfast area. In 1824 George Benn in his history of Belfast observed that 'coins of Henry VIII, Elizabeth, James and Charles I are very numerous' but he did not provide examples of such finds, save to say that they occurred in 'lots'.[91] Further silver coins, probably Elizabethan, were found near St Anne's Church in the 1840s by the Belfast antiquarian Edmund Getty.[92] In the 1850s, during roadworks in the area between Skipper Lane and Store Street, 'a good many silver coins were found, chiefly of Elizabeth, which found their way to the silversmith. There were likewise a number of base metal.'[93] Such coins certainly continued in use long after they were issued and some of these finds may represent deposits of the seventeenth century. However, it is probable that some do relate to sixteenth-century trading activity around the castle at Belfast. Such castle sites were generally trading centres and it is no coincidence that in the nineteenth century Elizabethan coins were also found at the site of the O'Neill castle at Clandeboy.[94] Given the position of the castle on the ford at Belfast some sort of trading function, however infrequent, is highly probable. This can hardly have been much more than a beach market of only local significance, trading on the edge of the subsistence-commercial economy, rather than a regular market with associated craft workers such as developed in the early seventeenth century.

Whether any sort of temporary settlement grew up around the castle of Belfast is not known. The only indications that this might be so are on a map of north-eastern Ireland *c.* 1580, which shows a large schematic castle at Belfast with a number of adjoining cabins. Another map of 1601, attributed to Ralph Lane, also shows several cabins on the site. It is also possible to infer the existence of a number of houses on the site from the comment in 1574 during Essex's occupation that there were men 'lodged in the town'.[95] By the late sixteenth century the origins of the later town as a centre of commerce can be at least vaguely discerned.

IV

The idea of establishing a settlement on the site of the lowest fordable crossing point of the River Lagan had a long, if somewhat discontinuous, history. When a viable town did emerge there in the early seventeenth century it did not appear from nowhere. The human landscape around the town had been moulded by several groups of people who had been responsible for establishing the key sites of church and castle around which settlement clustered. They had also been responsible for creating the territorial framework of townlands, parishes and tuatha that the seventeenth-century settlers found convenient for managing their activities. While the later inhabitants of Belfast might not always have been aware of their medieval inheritance it was certainly a reality in their lives. The castle provided visual evidence of the continuity of settlement on the site and also of its defensive importance. Medieval Belfast was not a construction of the mind but an important context for the development of the modern town.

NOTES

1 Mac Airt and Mac Niocaill, *Annals of Ulster*, p. 139.
2 MacAirt and Mac Niocaill, *Annals of Ulster*, pp 136–9. The succession is recorded in a king list edited in Kuno Meyer (ed.), 'The Laud synchronisms' in *Zeitschrift für celtische Philologie* ix (1913), p. 480.
3 McKay, 'Belfast place-names', pp 15–16, 22, 27–8.
4 Ibid., pp 23, 30.
5 Morton, 'Former townland names', pp 47–8.
6 Deirdre Flanagan, 'Corrigenda and addenda' in *Bulletin of the Ulster Place-Name Society*, 2nd ser., ii (1979), pp 53–4.
7 G.H. Orpen (ed.), 'The earldom of Ulster, ii: inquisitions touching Carrickfergus and Antrim' in *Journal of the Royal Society of Antiquaries of Ireland*, xliii (1913), p. 139.
8 William Reeves (ed.), *Ecclesiastical antiquities of Down, Connor and Dromore* (Dublin, 1847), pp 6–7.
9 T.C.D., MS 550, p. 248.
10 William Cassidy and H.C. Lawlor, 'The chapel of the Ford, Belfast' in *U.J.A.*, 3rd ser, viii (1945), pp 50–1.
11 W.A. Seaby, 'Medieval coin hoards in north-east Ulster' in *Numismatic Chronicle*, 6th ser., xv (1955), p. 166; L.N.W. Flanagan, 'Ulster Museum: archaeological acquisitions of Irish origins' in *U.J.A.*, 3rd ser., xxiii (1960), p. 54.
12 For example, see John Brady, 'Anglo-Norman organisation of the diocese of Meath' in *Irish Ecclesiastical Record*, lxvii (1946), p. 234.
13 P.R.O.N.I., DIO 1/24/26/5.
14 T.C.D., MS 550, pp 242, 248.
15 Gearóid Mac Niocaill, 'Cartae Dunenses, xii–xiii céad' in *Seanchas Ard Mhacha*, v (1969–70), pp 419–20.
16 For this see H.J. Lawlor, 'The genesis of the diocese of Connor, including Down and Dromore' in *Proceedings of the Belfast Natural History and Philosophical Society* (1930–1), pp 64–6.
17 *Irish patent rolls of James I: facsimile of the Irish Record Commissioners' calendar* (Dublin, 1966), p. 49, Benn, *History* (1823), p. 249.
18 Benn, *History* (1823), p. 249n.
19 John Blair, *The church in Anglo-Saxon society* (Oxford, 2005), p. 372.
20 H.J. Lawlor (ed.), *St Bernard's life of St Malachy of Armagh* (London, 1920), pp 109–10.
21 James Grace, *Annales Hiberniae*, ed. Richard Butler (Dublin, 1847), p. 126.
22 Susan Youngs (ed.), *'The work of angels': masterpieces of Celtic metalwork, 6th to 9th centuries* (London, 1989), pp 168–9.
23 C.S. Briggs, 'A lost hoard of Viking-age silver from the Cavehill, Belfast' in *U.J.A.*, 3rd ser., xlvi (1983), pp 152–3.

24 John Sheehan, 'Early Viking age silver hoards from Ireland and their Scandinavian elements' in H.B. Clarke, M. Ní Mhaonaigh and R. Ó Floinn (eds), *Ireland and Scandinavia in the early Viking age* (Dublin, 1998), p. 169.

25 Lowry, *Hamilton manuscripts*, p. 51n.

26 *Calendar of documents relating to Ireland* (ii, 1252–84), no. 255.

27 Oliver Davies and D.B. Quinn (eds), 'The Irish pipe roll of 14 John' in *Ulster Journal of Archaeology*, 3rd ser., iv (1941), supplement, pp 53–65.

28 The names are Balllyvaston, Greencastle, Low Wood (probably Listollard, which has not survived but refers to a motte), Bally Cros an tSeanascail (which is recorded only in seventeenth-century sources but lies between Legoniel and Ballyaghagan) and Skegoneil. See Morton, 'Former townland names', pp 46–53; McKay, 'Belfast place-names', pp 25, 26, 27.

29 Deirdre Morton, 'Tuath divisions in the baronies of Belfast and Masserene' in *Bulletin of the Ulster Place Name Society*, iv, pt 2 (1956), pp 38–9; Prof. Reid, 'A note on "Cinament"' in *Bulletin of the Ulster Place Name Society*, v, pt 1 (1957), p. 12; K.W. Nicholls, 'Mandeville deeds' in *Analecta Hibernica*, no. 32 (1985), pp 3–4.

30 T.E McNeill, *Anglo-Norman Ulster* (Edinburgh, 1980), pp 29, 65–8; G.H. Orpen, *Ireland under the Normans* (4 vols, Oxford, 1911–20), iii, pp 267–8, 279; E.M. Jope (ed.), *An archaeological survey of County Down* (Belfast, 1966), pp 219–20.

31 For plans of these castles see T.E.McNeill, *Castles in Ireland: feudal power in a Gaelic world* (London, 1997), p. 156.

32 British Library, Add. MS 6041, no. 33.

33 McNeill, *Anglo-Norman Ulster*, pp 35, 91.

34 'Belfast excavations' in *Archaeology Ireland*, xvii, no. 4 (2003), p. 4 and in greater detail in *Excavations 2003*, p. 3.

35 For example, *Excavations 2002*, p. 3.

36 E.M. Jope and W.A. Seaby, 'A square earthwork in north Belfast: the site of the Ekenhead early 14th century coin-hoard' in *U.J.A.*, 3rd ser., xxii (1959), pp 112–15.

37 *Excavations 1971*, p. 6.

38 Evans, 'Two Belfast raths', pp 84–5; E.E. Evans, 'Rath and souterrain at Shaneen Park, Belfast' in *U.J.A.* 3rd ser., xiii (1950), pp 32–4; Bruce Proudfoot, 'Further excavations at Shaneen Park, Belfast' in *U.J.A.* 3rd ser., xxi (1958), pp 20, 23..

39 W.M. Hennessy and B. MacCarthy (eds), *Annála Uladh: Annals of Ulster* (4 vols, Dublin, 1887–1901), iii, pp 258–9; John O'Donovan (ed.), *Annála Ríoghachta Éireann: Annals of the Kingdom of Ireland by the Four Masters* (Dublin, 1851), iv, pp 1100–01.

40 Hennessy and MacCarthy, *Annals of Ulster*, iii, pp 306–7.

41 Ibid., iii, pp 340–1.

42 Ibid., iii, pp 220–1; A.M. Freeman (ed.), *Annála Connacht: Annals of Connacht* (Dublin, 1944), pp 544–5.

43 Reeves, *Ecclesiastical antiquities*, p. 15, note u.

44 Katharine Simms, 'Gaelic lordship in Ulster in the later middle ages' (Ph.D. thesis, Trinity College Dublin, 1976), pp 219–20.

45 Seaby, 'Medieval coin hoards', pp 162, 166.

46 Morton, 'Tuatha divisions', p. 7–8.

47 J.B. Arthurs, 'Stranmillis, Derryvolgie and the Cinament' in *Bulletin of the Ulster Place Name Society*, iii (1955), pp 10–12, 35–42; Morton, 'Tuatha divisions'.

48 J.C. Erck, *A repertory of the inrolments in the patent rolls of chancery in Ireland: James I* (Dublin, 1846), p. 23.

49 Older studies, such as Benn, *History* (1823), p. 252 were inclined to associate this chapel with burial sites but this appears unlikely since burials and baptisms were the prerogatives of a parish church rather than a local chapel.

50 John McVeagh (ed.), *Richard Pococke's Irish tours* (Dublin, 1995), p. 38.

51 Reeves, 'Irish itinerary' in *U.J.A.*, 1st ser., ii (1854), p. 56.

52 *Cal. S.P. Ire. 1596–7*, p. 396.

53 Benn, *History* (1877), p. 86.

54 *Cal. Carew MSS 1515–74*, p. 243.

55 T.G.F. Paterson, 'Belfast in 1738' in *U.J.A.*, 3rd ser., ii (1939), p. 110.

56 Benn, *History* (1823), p. 73.

57 George Benn, *A history of the town of Belfast from 1799 till 1810* (London, 1880), p. 118; C.E.B. Brett, *Court houses and market houses of the province of Ulster* (Belfast, 1973), p. 44.

58 'Belfast excavations', p. 4 and in more detail in *Excavations 2003*, p. 3.

59 T.E. McNeill, 'The castle of Castlereagh, Co. Down' in *U.J.A.*, 3rd ser., l (1987), pp 123–7.

60 O'Donovan, *Annals of the Four Masters*, v, pp 1270–1.

61 Ibid., v, pp 1318–9. The account is given in the same terms in William Hennessy (ed.), *The annals of Loch Cé* (2 vols, London. 1871), ii, pp 213–5.

62 Hennessy and MacCarthy, *Annals of Ulster*, iii, pp 498–9.

63 *Stat .Papers, Henry VIII*, ii, p. 99.

64 Freeman, *Annála Connacht*, pp 700–1; Hennessy, *Annals of Loch Cé*, ii, pp 304–6; O'Donovan, *Annals of the Four Masters*, v, pp 1,440–1.

65 Katharine Simms, '"The king's friend": O'Neill, the crown and the earl of Ulster' in James Lydon (ed.), *England and Ireland in the later Middle Ages* (Dublin, 1981), pp 214–36.

66 O'Donovan, *Annals of the Four Masters*, v, pp 1524–5.

67 *Cal. Carew MSS 1515–74*, pp 233–4.

68 *Cal. Carew MSS 1515–74*, p. 243.

69 O'Donovan, *Annals of the Four Masters*, v, pp 1538–9.

70 D.B. Quinn, 'Anglo-Irish Ulster in the early sixteenth century' in *Proceedings of the Belfast Natural History and Philosophical Society*, 1933–4, p. 77.

71 *Cal. Carew MSS 1515–74*, pp 242–3; O'Donovan, *Annals of the Four Masters*, v, pp 1538–9.

72 *Cal. Carew MSS 1515–74*, p. 243; T.N.A., SP61/3/65i.

73 T.N.A., SP60/10/86.

74 T.N.A., SP63/19/36.

75 *Cal. Carew MSS 1515–74*, p. 306.

76 For example: T.N.A., SP63/17/20; SP63/22/49; SP63/22/51, 67, 69; SP63/23/32i, 39; SP63/24/38ii

77 T.N.A., SP63/23/39.

78 T.N.A., SP63/26/5.

79 T.N.A., SP63/40/65; SP63/42/55, 58.

80 *Cal. Carew MSS 1515–74*, p. 448.

81 T.N.A., SP63/44/22.

82 T.N.A., MPF1/77.

83 T.N.A., SP63/46/12.

84 *Cal. Carew MSS 1515–74*, p. 475; T.N.A., SP63/46/12.

85 T.N.A., SP63/46/13; SP63/48/36; British Library, Cotton MS Titus BXIII, ff 453v.

86 T.N.A., SP63/48/9, 46i; British Library, Cotton MS Titus BXIII, ff 453v, 455, 456.

87 Harold O'Sullivan, 'A 1575 rent roll with contemporaneous maps of the Bagenall estate in the Carlingford Lough district' in *County Louth Archaeological and Historical Journal*, xxi, no. 1 (1985), p. 36.

88 Avril Thomas, *The walled towns of Ireland* (2 vols, Dublin, 1992), ii, pp 40, 70, 180.

89 T.N.A., SP63/52/5.

90 T.N.A., SP63/52/60; SP63/121/7.

91 Benn, *History* (1823), p. 255.

92 Royal Irish Academy, MS 12 L 8/91.

93 Grainger, 'Results of excavations', p. 115.

94 James Carruthers, 'On hoards of coins found in Ireland' in *U.J.A.*, 1st ser., i (1853), p. 166.

95 T.N.A., SP63/48/52.

3
CHICHESTER'S TOWN
1603–60

The late-medieval settlement at Belfast was a rather restricted affair, based on a castle that defended a ford, a small chapel and possibly a cluster of houses. For the most part it was controlled by the most powerful local family, the O'Neills of Clandeboy. In the late sixteenth century that family was far from being a cohesive unit. In the 1550s the lordship had been divided in two, a division confirmed by Sir John Perrot, the Irish lord deputy in 1583.[1] However, neither party was happy with the arrangement and Belfast Castle, lying on the boundary between the two parts of the lordship, was coveted by both families. Sir Nicholas Bagenall, marshal of the army, noted in 1586 that the division of Clandeboy was one 'whereby great dissension doth depend between them [the two branches of the O'Neills] and great slaughter on both parts often committed'.[2] In normal circumstances such internal rivalry might have been managed but the outbreak of war in Ulster in 1594 made this a difficult and dangerous process. In 1596 one of the Clandeboy O'Neills, Niall Mac Aodh of lower Clandeboy, petitioned the lord deputy for the castle of Belfast after the death his brother Aodh in 1595. However, it was his cousin, Sean Mac Briain, who had succeeded to the lordship, and seized the castle in 1597, massacring the small garrison. The castle was retaken the following day.[3] The episode convinced the Dublin administration that allowing local lords to control the castle at Belfast was too dangerous a strategy to be pursued in the volatile years of the 1590s. The castle, said to be fit for a ward of 20 or 30 men and clearly much smaller than Essex's plans of the 1570s, was granted to the muster-master general, Sir Ralph Lane. By 1599 the possibility of building a town at Belfast, perhaps like the settlement planned by Essex in the 1570s, was again being canvassed but it came to nothing.[4]

As the Nine Years War drew to a close in the early part of 1603 Belfast Castle was said to be ruinous and in July of that year the governor of Carrickfergus, Arthur Chichester, offered to rebuild it in return for a grant of the castle and the surrounding property.[5] In August 1603 he obtained a king's letter for the governorship of Carrickfergus and the castle of Belfast, together with its lands – which, it was claimed, he already occupied. A patent was issued in November 1603 but subsequently surrendered, as a new grant was made in November 1604.[6] Together the royal grant of 1604 and the subsequent town charter of 1613 were vital in providing the legal framework for the transformation of a late-sixteenth-century beach-head market into a fully fledged trading town. They created property rights, which allowed the building of a formal quay structure, market rights, enabling the exchange of goods with legal protection, and the position of urban freeman, which permitted the development of local craftwork. Through the grant of 1604 and the charter of 1613 Sir Arthur Chichester, whose family later became earls of Donegall, became landlord and developer of what would become Belfast.

I

With the legal formalities complete, the castle of Belfast was now firmly in Chichester's grasp. He began developing his newly acquired property so that it would generate an income. There is little doubt that this was Chichester's primary intention for the site. The original king's letter for the grant of the property explained that its aim was 'that his [Chichester's] tenants in the lands may be the better encouraged to plant and manure the same when they may have from him some certain estate therein'.[7] The site was clearly unsuitable for agriculture but its position on the River Lagan at the junction of a number of important routeways made it a good location for a market with an associated port. This is what Chichester intended to develop. As early as 1607 Belfast had been identified as a site for a corporate town, together with Coleraine and Bangor, although relatively little development can have taken place on the site.[8] Most of what we know of the early development of Belfast comes from a report made in 1611 by commissioners appointed to survey progress on the newly established Ulster plantation. In addition to reviewing developments in the planted counties the commissioners also reported on the 'voluntary works' undertaken by settlers outside the plantation scheme, including Chichester's Belfast. Based on this report and a few other sources, it is possible to reconstruct something of the topography of the early-seventeenth-century town. We can identify four topographical elements to the settlement. The first is the fate of the castle, the second the church, the third the streets of the new town laid out by Chichester and finally the settlement's marketplace.

The first of these elements, the castle, was described by the 1611 commissioners when they reported that at Belfast:

> we found many masons, bricklayers and other labourers at work who had taken down the ruins of the decayed castle there almost to the vault of the cellars, and likewise laid the foundation of a brick house 50 foot long which is to be adjoined to the said castle by a staircase of brick which is to be 14 foot square.
>
> The house is to be made 20 foot wide, and two stories and a half high. The castle is to be built two stories above the cellars, all the rooms thereof to be vaulted and the platforms to be made thereupon. The staircase is to be made 10 foot higher than the castle, about which castle and house there is a strong bawne almost finished which is flankered with four half bulwarks. The foundation of the wall and bulwarks to the height of the water table is made with stone, the rest being in all 12 foot high above the ground, is made with brick. The bawn is to be compassed with a large and deep ditch or moat which will always stand full of water. The castle will defend the passage of the ford at Belfast between the Upper and Lower Clandeboye and likewise the bridge over the Owenvarra between Malone and Belfast. This work is in so good forwardness that it is like to be finished by the middle of the next summer.[9]

What the Plantation Commissioners described is a structure quite different from that shown on later maps of Belfast but much more akin to the sort of buildings that were put up in other places as part of the Ulster plantation scheme. The reuse of an older castle, as at Dungiven, was not unusual, particularly given its strategic position. Of the 43 castles recorded by the Plantation Surveyors in the early

1620s seven had reused older buildings. Moreover, the dimensions of the castle were not unusual in a plantation context. Roughan Castle in Tyrone was described in 1622 as being 30 feet square with two and a half storeys while Lord Lambert's estate in Cavan had a stone and lime house 60 feet long, 21 feet broad and two storeys high. Among English settlers in Fermanagh one house at Drumken was 68 feet long, 25 feet broad and three stories high. Like Chichester's Belfast building it had a large square staircase on the back of the house. This was also typical of vernacular buildings in south-west England, from where Chichester came. Overall, most English plantation houses were fewer than three storeys tall and had rectangular ground plans. Few were more than 20 feet wide but they were between 40 and 60 feet in length.[10] At 50 feet by 20 feet with two and a half storeys, the house that the Plantation Commissioners described as being built at Belfast was typical of many being constructed across Ulster at this stage. What is unusual about this structure is the use of brick, which was uncommon in Ulster at this stage. While brick was reported as a building material further along the Lagan valley in was rare elsewhere. The availability of brick clay is certainly one explanation for this but cost may have been the crucial factor since no good building stone was available locally.

In contrast to the detailed report on the castle the commissioners said nothing about the second element in the new town plan, the church at the ford. Here ecclesiastical records can help to fill out the picture. The ecclesiastical visitation of 1622 reported tersely, 'Ecclesia de Albo vaddo alias Belfast built from the ground and repaired.'[11] There is no evidence that the older parish church at Shankill was ever repaired and this reference must be taken to refer to the old chapel of the ford at Belfast. Chichester doubtless felt that this was a more convenient location for the inhabitants of his new town to worship than the more remote site at Shankill, although no formal transfer of the site of the parish church was made until 1774, when an order in council relocated the parish church to the town of Belfast.[12]

It appears that Chichester's rebuilding took place fairly speedily. By 1615 the town corporation ordered that fines be levied on those

Parish church, High Street, redrawn from Thomas Phillips's perspective view of Belfast, 1685. The entrance is from the Ann Street side rather than the High Street side, suggesting that this was the medieval routeway from the ford. The building behind the church is the earl of Donegall's school, established in the 1660s.

who did not attend church 'within the said corporation' – which implies that the chapel of the ford was already functioning as a parish church. The order was repeated in 1617.[13] How much rebuilding was carried out at this stage is not clear but the comment of the visitation implies that it was extensive. Benn, writing in 1823, noted that those who remembered the church described it as 'without any external ornament, and principally built of brick', as the rest of the town was, and shingled.[14] Some of the fabric may have survived from the older chapel, given the unusual size of the tower. The Phillips maps of the 1680s contain both a perspective drawing of the church and a ground plan, which enable a reconstruction of this early seventeenth-century church. What is striking about this church is its scale. According to Phillips's survey the church measured 150 feet along its east–west axis and 100 feet from north to south. The nave was aisled with six bays and there were two transepts. The cathedral of St Columb in Derry, built in the late 1620s at a cost of £4,000, was 140 feet on its long axis before its enlargement in the 1880s. It too was aisled with six bays. However, it lacked transepts and hence was a much narrower rectangular structure. The 'planter's Gothic' of Derry Cathedral is replicated at Belfast in the large window in the north transept depicted in Phillips's sketch of the church.[15] Such architectural embellishment was rare in Ulster plantation churches. Only on the Grocers' estate at Muff in County Londonderry was a parish church built with such a window and this was paid for by the London landlord rather

than the local parish.[16] What this suggests is that while Chichester's
funds for rebuilding the church may have been limited he was prepared to include one grand gesture to highlight the importance of
the building as the Grocers did at Muff. In terms of scale Belfast was
closer to St Nicholas's Church in Carrickfergus, which was also
rebuilt by Chichester in 1614. At 160 feet this is slightly longer than
Belfast but the width of the transepts is the same, at 100 feet. Given
that St Nicholas's was the parish church of Chichester's main settlement and contained his mortuary chapel, building a church on the
same scale in Belfast expressed considerable ambition for the growth
of the early settlement.

The church and the castle on the south side of the River Farset
represented continuity with the medieval settlement on the site. On
the north side of the river new developments were taking place that
were to change that settlement's shape radically. In 1611 the commissioners reported:

> The town of Belfast is plotted out in good form, wherein are
> many families of English, Scotch and some Manksmen already
> inhabiting, of which some are artificers who have built good tim-
> ber houses with chimneys after the fashion of the English pale, and
> one inn with very good lodging which is a great comfort to the
> travellers in those parts.
>
> Near which town the said Sir Arthur Chichester hath ready
> made above twelve hundred thousand of good bricks, whereof
> after finishing of the said castle, house and bawn, there will be a
> good proportion left for the buildings of the other tenements
> within the said town.[17]

The comment by the Plantation Commissioners leaves no doubt
that Belfast was a planned town – one that was 'plotted out'. What
is more difficult to discover is what form its plan took. A clue may
be provided by an inquisition of 1621, which recited an earlier land
grant of January 1616 from Chichester to John Vesey of a property
in the broad street (*platea*) of the town of Belfast.[18] It is clear that the
street called Broad Street since 1619 was, in fact, the modern Waring
Street. Why the street should have attracted this name is not clear,
since archaeological investigation suggests that the modern street
line follows the line of the seventeenth-century one and it is not

particularly broad (certainly no more so than North Street, also built up in the seventeenth century) but it probably reflects the narrowness of some pre-existing trackways.[19] If the width of the street is not difficult to fix, neither is its length. The eastern end must have been much the same as that shown on Thomas Phillips's 1685 map of the town, which ends at the strand alongside the River Lagan. The western end poses more of a problem. A grant of a fee farm from Chichester to George Theaker (probably the father of Chichester's agent and sovereign in the 1640s) in August 1619 stipulates that land lay on the west side of Broad Street. A later grant noted that Broad Street lay between North Street and the Presbyterian meeting house.[20] This suggests that Broad Street in 1619 extended across Bridge Street and into what is now Rosemary Street, a name that only seems to have come into use at the end of the seventeenth century. If the measurements in the deed are correct, Theaker's freehold would have ended at the point where Rosemary Street now curves at the top of Lombard Street. This is the point where the street stops on the 1685 map of the town also. If this reconstruction is correct that would give a town which was about 335 metres long along its main axis. Derry, by comparison, was almost 488 metres long within the walls along its main axis and Carrickfergus, Chichester's other town, was about the same length as Belfast. While Belfast may not have been conceived as a settlement on the scale of these other two, lacking their housing density, it was by no means an inconsequential place.

The plan of the early seventeenth-century town was therefore one of a single wide street built on a green-field site opposite the older medieval settlement. The migration of the focus of the settlement stems from the irregular flooding in the area between the Farset and Blackstaff, inundating the area between the church and the castle, where the medieval village had lain. By the standards of the planned towns of Derry or Coleraine the new Belfast was an unambitious scheme, having more in common with Lurgan or Newtownards, linear towns that grew up along existing roadways, than more exotic town layouts. However, the scheme's simplicity reflects the Chichester family's lack of funds rather than their lack of ambition. Part of the laying-out process would have included the creation of tenements or burgage plots of land set out at right angles to the street. It is possible to reconstruct some of these tenements from nineteenth-century estate maps and later deeds. In a survey of Belfast in 1850 the plots along both sides of Waring Street have street frontages of between 37 and 43 feet, although some of the plots had been amalgamated or subdivided. These seem to represent seventeenth-century divisions. According to one early eighteenth-century lease a burgage share in Belfast was 42 feet.[21] Another lease of property on High Street of 1656 stated that a half burgage was 21 feet in front, implying a full burgage plot was 42 feet.[22] The shape and distribution of the plots reflect something of the early geography of the planned town. On the face of it they seem large, certainly in comparison to the older medieval town of Carrickfergus. However, when Archbishop Hampton leased an area of Armagh to two developers in 1615 he stipulated that the tenements to be created were to measure 50 feet in front and extend back 150 feet. On these sites houses 40 feet long, 16 feet broad and 15 feet high were to be built. Each tenement had 36 statute acres attaching to it in the previously common land around Armagh.[23] Again in Derry, on the basis of an eighteenth-century survey that preserved earlier arrangements, the most typically sized plots measured from 25–30 feet to 33–40 feet.[24] One final example, that of Lurgan in County Armagh, suggests that the houses built in the town were on average 30 feet wide, which may suggest plots of roughly the same dimensions as those in Belfast.[25]

There is very little evidence to suggest what the houses constructed on these plots looked like. The Chichester family had little money to develop their town and they probably resorted to a technique frequently used in Belfast during the late seventeenth and early eighteenth centuries – the building lease. This required tenants to build a house on their property in addition to paying the rent and entry fine. The cost of the building was offset by a lower rent or extended lease term. The lease usually contained few requirements about the sort of houses to be built and thus there were problems in controlling the appearance of the town. This problem was compounded by the shortage of local stone for building and the low-lying nature of the site, which meant that cellars for storage, common in most towns, were not practicable. The Plantation Commissioners' comment that some of the inhabitants had built good timber houses like those in the Pale may mean that timber-framed buildings were erected in the town. This form of construction was quick and cheap, using local materials although in the case of the Londonderry settlement frames were shipped in from elsewhere. The frame was filled in with the brick that the Plantation Commissioners reported was made in large quantities near the settlement. Similar timber-framed buildings survived in Chichester's other town, Carrickfergus, into the nineteenth century.[26] No brickfields of seventeenth-century date have been identified but a roof-tile kiln may have existed in the open area of what is now Cornmarket.[27] Given the prominence of timber in building, the danger of fire was clearly a problem. This was not unique to Belfast. Newry had burned down in 1600 and Bangor had almost been destroyed by fire in 1625.[28] This danger lay behind the banning of wooden chimneys and new malt kilns in Belfast by the corporation in 1638.[29]

Initially, outside the main thoroughfare of Waring Street, there was relatively little development of streets and house plots, although series of older routeways meant that the site was not an entirely green-field one. At right angles to Waring Street lay the old medieval routeway towards Carrickfergus, now followed by North Street. Judging from the fact that the North Street plot patterns on nineteenth-century maps are much more irregular than those along Waring Street and High Street, there was some unplanned building along this road. There were also some houses around the church, which were demolished in 1651 for the widening of a road.[30] Further west, up Ann Street, some archaeological evidence from a property boundary provides a dendrochronological date of 1610–28 for timber recovered.[31] The cartographic evidence and that of the plot patterns would not support the laying out of plots in that area as early as this and it seems highly probable that this timber was reused. One indication of the limited nature of the early seventeenth-century development is that, on the basis of the evidence of later leases, only holdings running north and south to the River Farset from Waring Street attracted shares in the burgage lands. These are probably, then, the areas covered by the earliest leases. However, not all development was confined to Waring Street: it extended into Waring Street's immediate vicinity. Probably nearly contemporary with the laying out of Waring Street is Skipper Street, although there are no documentary references to it until 1670. Skipper Street, which may mark the eastern end of Waring Street in the early seventeenth century, was most likely created to provide access for merchants from Waring Street to the town quay, which lay at the east end of what is now High Street, opposite the parish church. The town quay was, presumably, a rather simple affair. There was no customs house before the 1660s and even later maps do not show any evidence of cranes or berths for ships.

Fairly quickly, a pathway developed from the town quay along the north bank of the River Farset, linking it to the marketplace at Bridge Street. This was probably an early development and may have been planned. A deed of 1617 refers to a grant of property in the high street ('*alto vico*') of the town of Belfast and by the 1650s, at least, the name had become established for the street. The dimensions of the plot were described as a frontage of 84 feet extending 126 feet behind, which is a double burgage share (as described above), which suggests that this was laid out in the same way as the plots on Waring Street.[32] This development had the effect of opening up the rear of the tenements that ran from Waring Street to the river. This was the origin of the northern side of High Street and presumably it continued down into Castle Place, providing access to the marketplace from that side also. Thus early streets such as High Street and Skipper Street can be seen as the sinews of the nascent town, connecting the quay, marketplace and main street, the town's main features. Belfast stands in contrast to Derry or Coleraine, where streets formed a geometric pattern within the walls rather than linking together economic and social centres in the town. Here the lack of walls around early Belfast proved to be an asset since the port did not require an expensive system of water gates to enter the town, leaving the quay free to develop according to the needs of trade.

The final element in the layout of the early settlement was a marketplace. This had been an important element in the conception of the place because from its inception Chichester had intended Belfast to be a marketing centre. The earliest grant of a market at Belfast, creating a legal framework for market courts and trading rights, was in 1605. This grant was made not to Chichester but to the north Down landowner Sir James Hamilton. Why Hamilton should have received such a grant is not clear. One possible explanation is that it was purely speculative, but another possibility is that the grant reflects older marketing connections. Hamilton also received grants of markets at Castlereagh, Holywood and Bangor (all on his estates) in that year: these may have been confirmation of older, sixteenth-century markets at these locations. If, as suggested in the previous chapter, Belfast was also the site one of these informal markets, including it in a grant to Hamilton would appear logical since it would have belonged to the network these markets formed. The grant did not last long. By 1608 it had been surrendered and a new one made to Chichester's nephew, Arthur Basset.

Bridge Street and its associated property boundaries, from the encumbered-estates maps of 1850. Note how the east–west properties become smaller as High Street is approached, suggesting a triangular market place filled in with later property units.

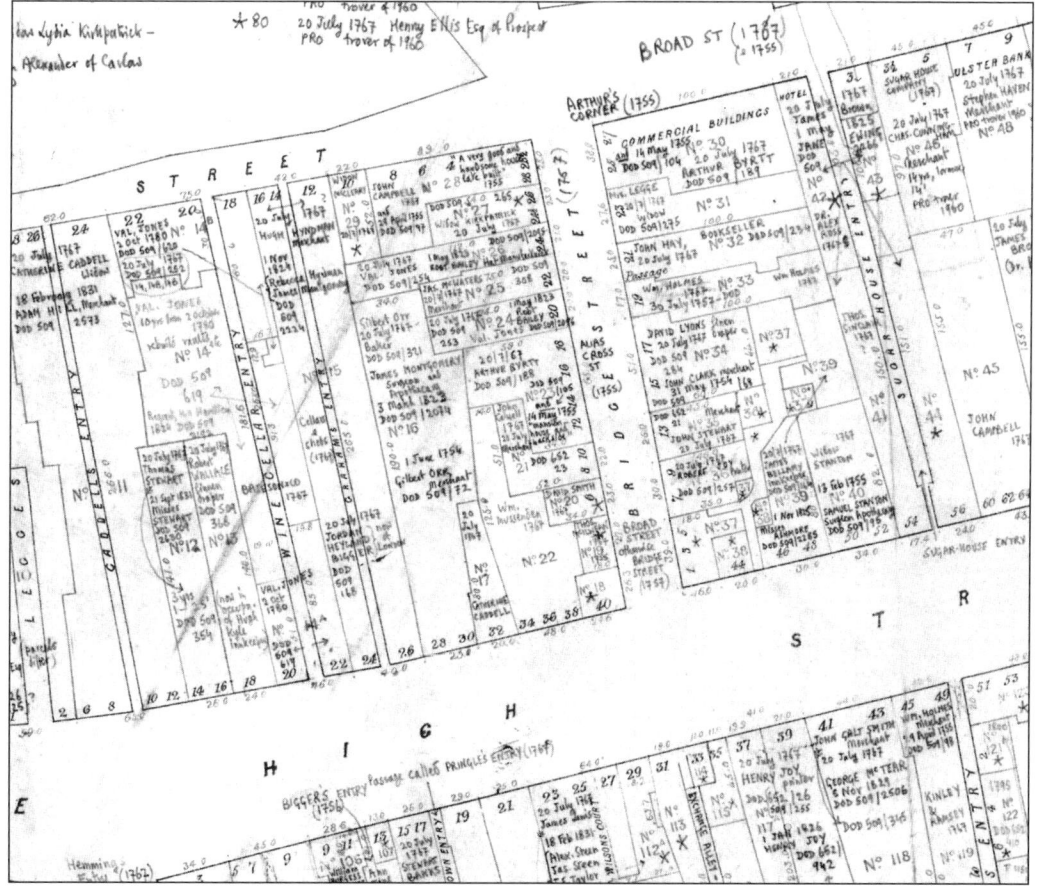

The Bridge Street market-place as it appears on Thomas Phillips's perspective view of Belfast, 1685. The large warehouse-like buildings on the top right were probably built in the old marketplace after it fell out of use. The early seventeenth-century town hall probably stood some-where near the position of this warehouse.

By the 1620s the rights to hold markets and fairs had been transferred into Chichester's own hands.

The organisation of the market is difficult to recon-struct. There was clearly a well-defined marketplace in the town – the corporation decreed in 1639 that 'the market be kept round together and not scattering up and down but all together in the market place'.[33] It is not possible to be absolutely certain of the position of the marketplace, but the most likely location is at what is now Bridge Street. Here the recently laid-out Waring Street met the older medieval routeway on the line of North Street, which crossed the Farset and joined with the medieval route now followed by Ann Street. This was a central point in the life of the town. The patterns of older plots on Bridge Street, clearly shown on nine-teenth-century maps of property ownership, suggest that this space was not originally linear but triangular, with the broad base of the triangle at the Waring Street side, allowing the marketplace to blend into the main street. The apex of the triangle focused on the stone bridge across the Farset, which formed a natural closure for that side of the market. When this marketplace fell into disuse, probably in the late seventeenth century, the sides were filled in with east–west plots that became longer towards North Street. Thus Bridge Street took on its modern appearance.[34] The process can be seen on Thomas Phillips's map of 1685, where the infill area is occupied not by houses but by a long chimneyless building – probably a recently constructed warehouse.

At least initially, the market was probably rather informally organised but by 1639 the corporation and the Chichesters agreed a 'settled course' for its organisation. Much of this comprised the sort of standard regulations associated with markets in many Irish towns, such as the weights and measures to be used, the provision that there was to be no forestalling of grain and that there was to be no trading before the ringing of the market bell at ten o'clock. However, some of the regulations do reflect local conditions. Livestock, for instance, was to be kept in pens while waiting to be sold, which suggests a large, well-organised, open market space. Standings for pedlars and butchers were also described. These were temporary constructions intended to accommodate a horse load of goods; the rent cost a penny. At the edge of the marketplace, along its walls, there seem to have been more permanent stalls, which suggests that the market was a frequent and regular affair.[35]

The 1639 arrangements for the market hint at the sort of goods that were sold there. They mention grain of various sorts (including wheat, rye and oats), cattle, sheep, pigs and horses as well as salt, hides and tallow. Undoubtedly grain from the surrounding countryside was necessary to feed the population of the expanding town. Meat, too, was a necessary food. Butchers were an important group within the town and there are a number of references in the corporation minutes to conflicts between the butchers of Belfast and the corporation. By 1640 the largest source of corporation revenue was from the customs charges for cattle passing through Belfast.[36] However, it is equally clear that a considerable portion of what was sold in the marketplace was for export. The correspondence of one Whitehaven merchant, Christopher Lowther, suggests that in the 1630s cloth and salt were the main imports into Belfast and the principal exports were beef and timber.[37]

By the 1640s almost a quarter of those who were admitted to the freedom of the town described themselves as merchants, the largest occupational designation. Such people did not necessarily live in the town but they certainly traded there, some of them infrequently. Robert Barr, for instance, began his trading life in Derry in 1635 but by 1638 was in Belfast, exporting iron from his own ironworks at New Forge. In 1639 he was in Scotland. George Martin was in Carrickfergus in 1633, but by 1637 he was in Lisburn and in 1639 he was in Belfast. John Corry spent only a brief period in Lisburn and Belfast before buying land in Fermanagh. Even John Vesey, one of the early sovereigns of Belfast, was described in a legal pleading of 1624 as being of both Belfast and Derry, suggesting he had interests in both places.[38] This mobility may help to explain why the Belfast merchants, unlike those of Carrickfergus, never established a merchants' guild, even though the original town charter had allowed for it. In addition, the charter of 1613 created a system whereby tradesmen could receive the freedom of the town and exercise their trade there, which provided protection for the emergence of craft skills. By the 1630s the freemen's rolls listed a range of such crafts operating in Belfast, including weavers, shoemakers, carpenters, wheelwrights, blacksmiths, joiners, glaziers and feltmakers. The most significant group comprised those from the clothing trades, much of whose output was for local consumption.

Thus, what emerged in early seventeenth-century Belfast was a planned town built along the central spine of what became Waring Street. This represented a new settlement, abandoning the older medieval structures for an almost green-field site to the north of a newly built town quay. This development reflected the town's changing function. Whereas the medieval settlement was focused on the ford and the strategic importance of the site, the new creation had different priorities. Unlike Carrickfergus, Chichester's other town, Belfast was unfortified and therefore was not designed to be defended in case of attack. The town clustered around the marketplace, suggesting that its main function was as a trading centre, not a strategic one.

II

By about 1630 Belfast could be said to have established itself as a real presence in the landscape. Physically it had emerged as a settlement with two foci: a medieval centre based on the church and castle and across the river a more modern trading centre. However, what was scarcely more than a small village also had a legal form that gave it an existence apart from its collection of buildings. In 1613 the town had been granted a charter that created an administrative structure within which it might function, as well being allowed to send two members to parliament. It retained this privilege until 1801 when its parliamentary representation was reduced to one. While the granting of the charter in 1613 provided a framework for the government of the town it was a very restricted basis for action by the fledgling corporation. All the land in the area was in the hands of the Chichester family, while the corporation held none. This was in contrast to Carrickfergus, where the corporation had over 16,500 acres in four major 'divisions', as well as the town parks, all of which was leased to the freemen and aldermen of the town and brought income to the corporation.[39] Derry and Coleraine also had 'liberties', which were leased to bring in income. However, Belfast Corporation had no income of its own (apart from the income of some of the market duties, most of which accrued to the Chichesters as holder of the patent for the market, and the revenue from the town's courts) to deal with emerging urban problems or day-to-day expenditures. Thus in 1633 the corporation declared that income from bequests and fines was to be used to defray the sovereign's hospitality bill.[40] Also, for instance, a fund to relieve the urban poor depended on bequests from individual townsmen, and the fund was administered by the corporation.[41]

If the Chichesters maintained a strict grip on the financing of the town, they exercised equally firm control over the make-up of Belfast Corporation. In line with other charters granted for Ulster towns in these years, the Belfast charter declared that the town was to be administered by a sovereign and twelve burgesses. The first holders of the posts were nominated by Chichester and specified in the charter.[42] The sovereign in successive years was to be elected from a list of three names presented by Chichester to the burgesses. The burgesses themselves were appointed for life or until they were judged to have forfeited their office by absence or misconduct, in which cases replacements were elected by the existing burgesses.[43] Freemen had little say in the running of the town and none in the election of its two members of parliament.

How this very early corporation conducted its business is poorly documented. In some respects it appears to have modelled itself on Chichester's other town, Carrickfergus. For example, one of the earliest customs in the town – that of giving the tongues of animals slaughtered by butchers to the sovereign – seems to be derived from the same practice at Carrickfergus.[44] This is hardly surprising given that both towns were under Chichester's control and that some of the early burgesses of Belfast (such as Waterhouse Crymble and Carew Harte) were also involved with Carrickfergus Corporation. This early Belfast Corporation does not appear to have kept minutes of its meetings and its only records are isolated resolutions copied into the later corporation minute book. Many of these early resolutions can be compared with entries from the older Carrickfergus records, which suggests that the corporation may simply have run Belfast on the basis of precedents elsewhere. However, from the middle of the 1630s the records were kept with greater care. From this point, indeed, there are increasing signs that the corporation was at least trying to become more effective. The challenges that they perceived they faced are suggested by the entries they chose to copy from their old records in the new corporation book in the late 1630s. The problem of social order was high on their agenda with the inclusion of older orders about attending church, selling ale, apprehending felons and keeping strangers in the town. Equally important was the challenge of enforcing the authority of the corporation. Orders dealing with dues to be paid by butchers, refusing the office of sovereign and the requirement to plead cases in the town court all reflect this concern. It may be that concern with the authority of the corporation led to an assessment made in 1639 for fitting out the town hall so that it could be used for the town courts.[45] The following year an assessment was made for 'arms', a town seal and a mace.[46] The term 'arms' presumably refers to a set of royal arms displayed, as was normal, in the town hall. These are the first hints that a town hall existed, although the charter had provided for one. It is not known when it was built or where it was located. However, in the regulations for the holding of markets it was stipulated that the measures for the sale of grain and liquids 'be made and kept in the town hall to regulate all other measures by'.[47] This implies that the earliest town hall was located in, or very close to, the marketplace. In the 1650s the Parliamentary Commissioners referred to the 'town hall and market house' as though they were in the same building.[48] This gave the marketplace an importance greater than simply that of a place for trading. It was an open space where public events associated with the workings of government happened, such as the reading of proclamations. Thus, in 1644, after Major General Munroe seized Belfast, the colours of the royalist force were torn to pieces in the marketplace as a public political statement.[49] On a more regular basis, if the corporation order of 1617 that the sovereign was to be accompanied from his house to church by the burgesses was enforced, that almost certainly entailed a procession through the marketplace.[50] Since most early sovereigns lived in Waring Street, reaching the church would have involved passing through the marketplace. In such public gatherings the abstract idea of a town corporation would have been made real to onlookers.

These signs of consolidation and expansion of the town in the 1630s are underpinned by some topographical changes. In 1635 Sir William Brereton, travelling from Carrickfergus, commented:

> At Belfast my Lord Chichester hath another dainty stately house (which is indeed the glory and beauty of the town also), where he is most resident, and is now building an outer brick wall before his gates. This [house] is not so large and vast as the other [at Carrickfergus], but more convenient and commodious; the very end of the lough toucheth upon his gardens and backside; here also are dainty orchards, gardens and walks planted.[51]

This description seems rather different to that of the castle given by the Plantation Commissioners in 1611, which recorded a small building 50 feet by 20 feet that had been erected before the house at Carrickfergus, which itself was probably built in 1618.[52] This is a great deal smaller that the castle at Carrickfergus. According to the ground plans drawn by Thomas Phillips in the 1680s, the Carrickfergus house comprised a central bow-window block with two long wings, making it 100 feet broad at the front and almost 100 feet deep, wings included.[53] Brereton's comment seems to suggest that the disparity between this and the house at Belfast was not that great. It seems likely that the Belfast building of 1611 had been

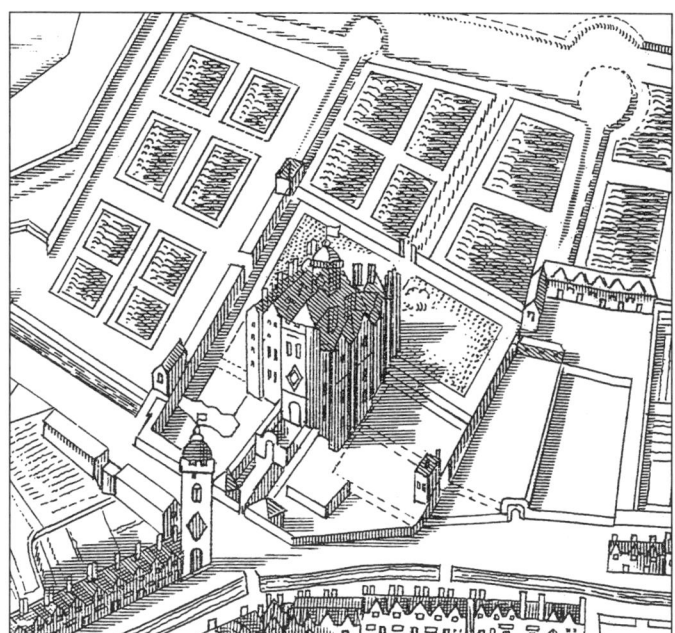

The castle and its gardens, redrawn from Thomas Phillips's perspective view of Belfast, 1685.

reconstructed to be closer to the castle as it is depicted on Phillips's 1685 map of the town of Belfast. This map shows the castle as a large Renaissance-style house with bow windows. It is an undefended building, most of the walling before the construction of the rampart in the 1640s being for ornamental purposes. If the castle described by Brereton is not that of 1611 then it is likely that it was rebuilt after the death of Arthur Chichester in 1625 and the succession of his brother, Edward, to the estate. It seems, though the evidence is slight, that about this time the Chichesters abandoned Carrickfergus and moved to Belfast. This may account for the rebuilding of the castle in the late 1620s in the latest fashion. Since it is unlikely that the castle at Belfast, described as having 40 hearths in 1660, was built in the 1640s or 1650s, a date in the late 1620s might fit such a reconstruction. It is equally possible that the building of the 1660s was the product of modifications over time and the castle seen by Brereton was some intermediate entity, the result of a partial rebuilding to which the wall around the gardens was a final touch. This finds some confirmation in the irregularity of the projection at the north-west corner, which is different from the other corners shown on Phillips's ground plan of 1685. This may suggest that an older structure was incorporated into more recent developments, possibly in stages over time. What is striking about this building is

70

how innovatory it was. Brick buildings on this scale were still a rarity in England and there were certainly none in Chichester's native Devon. The shaped gable shown in the gateway on Thomas Phillips's map of 1685 was an extremely modern feature since such shaped gables in brick only appear in England in the 1630s. The castle was certainly an impressive modern building at the cutting edge of fashion when it was built.

By 1640, the year in which Chichester received a regrant of his property under the Commission for Defective Titles, Belfast had grown to be a substantial settlement.[54] When the town was walled in 1642 the walls enclosed 30 hectares. By comparison the plantation settlements of Derry and Coleraine within the walls were 12 and 14 hectares respectively, while the older town of Carrickfergus covered 11 hectares, although it had recently been enlarged by Chichester.[55] Only the medieval town of Downpatrick at 40 hectares could rival Belfast as a substantial Ulster town.[56] But measurements of area are only one indication of a town's significance. Towns of equal size had greatly differing population densities and hence some attempt needs to be made to guess the population of Belfast. It is clear that the population was expanding rapidly in the years before 1640. The only definite evidence is from a cess list of 1640 made to raise money for a new town seal and mace and to pay the garrison. This contains 100 names that might be crudely equated with the number of households in town, although it is not clear how many of the urban households were exempt from the assessment. On this basis a crude guess is that Belfast's population lay between 400 and 500 people. If that is so, then notwithstanding its size its population was about one quarter that of Derry, which had 500 adult males (or upwards of 1,500 people) in 1630. Even Bangor had a population close to 1,000 in 1630.[57] However, it is clear that a significant population growth had taken place since 1611, when the town was laid out. This is indicated by the subdivsion of burgage plots to accommodate more people. By 1656 plots were being leased on High Street that were 21 feet wide, half the length of a standard plot, suggesting subdivision of property.[58] There is other evidence that suggests a rapidly growing town. In 1620, for instance, the corporation tried to outlaw the widespread practice of taking

71

subtenants, which suggests substantial migration into the town.[59] And in the early 1630s a very large number of those who left Chester for Ireland listed their destinations as 'Malone'. Many of these must have ended up in the town of Belfast.[60]

Belfast, then, was a large, sprawling town with a relatively low population density, a picture that accords with the idea that large plots were given to early settlers. Despite its sprawling character, Belfast had a clear urban appearance. Perhaps most important was the clear street line 'plotted out' and defined by the terraced housing on the building plots. Such an appearance differentiated it from some of the smaller north-Down towns depicted on the Raven maps of 1625, in which the detached buildings failed to form a coherent street line. Belfast had more in common with Holywood and Bangor, with their well-defined streets, than the scattered towns of Comber or Killyleagh. There are also signs that its economic structure was developing. In the early years of the town building activity was probably its main driving force, although the mention of an inn in the plantation commissioners' report highlights its role as a communications node, but by the 1630s the lists of freemen in the town book begin to record other trades, albeit those requiring limited capital such as butchering, tailoring and weaving. Certainly by the 1630s there are clear signs of the emergence of a well-defined merchant community, which represented the beginnings of the dominance of trade in the town's future. In all the town of Belfast was, as Fr MacCana noted in 1643, 'no mean one'.[61]

More than having become a substantial settlement, by 1640 Belfast had begun to achieve some status in the wider world. In 1636 the bishop of Down, Henry Leslie, chose to hold his ecclesiastical visitation at Belfast rather than the more traditional site of Downpatrick, where the cathedral was in ruins.[62] The centrality of Belfast was clearly a factor here but its size and local importance also influenced that decision. Indeed had the Restoration bishop of Down, Jeremy Taylor, not appointed Lisburn in 1662 as the meeting place of the chapters of Down and Connor to please the local landlord, Edward Conway (who was also his patron), Belfast might have acquired a cathedral sooner than it did.[63] Presbyterians, too, found Belfast a prominent enough place to meet in 1650.[64] In secular matters also Belfast was becoming more significant. According to the Presbyterian minister Patrick Adair it was 'the place where the country gentlemen and their officers then most haunted' in the 1640s – and the largest number of those admitted to the freedom of the town before 1644 described themselves as 'gentlemen'.[65] In social, administrative and economic terms Belfast had begun to rival its older neighbour, Carrickfergus.

III

What had characterised the history of Belfast before 1640 was fairly steady growth in the town and its trade. One indication of this is the valuation of the vicarage, which in 1622 was reckoned at £5 a year, a sum also recorded in a valuation of 1616. By the visitation of 1634 the valuation of the vicarage had risen to £50 and by 1640 it stood at £60 per annum.[66] Admittedly, some of this may have come from additional endowments provided by the Chichester family, since one of the family occupied the vicarage in 1634, but the bulk of the increase can be explained by the increased prosperity of the town and its surrounding area. A similar trend is shown by the growth of the Chichester family's rental income from the town and its surroundings. By the 1630s the town and manor of Belfast yielded the family £400 a year, more than Carrickfergus and most of their south Antrim manors.[67] Some context is provided for these estimates by the rental income from Derry, which was £665 in 1628, and Coleraine, which was £414 in the same year.[68] The population of Belfast had also grown in the early seventeenth century, largely through immigration. In a 1640 cess list of the town almost 44 per cent of the surnames were Scottish; 41 per cent were English and 7 per cent were Irish, the remainder being indeterminate. In the late 1630s circumstances conspired to change this situation. A series of bad harvests imposed strains on much of the population of east Ulster. That situation was made worse by political developments elsewhere. In Scotland, relations between the king and the Scottish Presbyterians had reached breaking point because of the introduction of a new prayer book. Inevitably the disturbances, which culminated in the two bishops' wars in 1638 and 1640, spread to the Scots in Ulster. To counter this development Lord Deputy Wentworth imposed an oath, known as the 'black oath', on the Scots in Ulster and added insult to injury by quartering an army intended for the Scottish wars on east Ulster. Belfast was not exempt and assessments for coal and candles for the army were imposed on the town in late 1640.[69] In addition to light and heat the soldiers quartered on the town needed to be fed. Poor harvests in 1640 and 1641 did not help that situation. The landlord, Sir Edward Chichester, observed in May 1641 that 'the inhabitants therein have spent their whole years [*sic*] provisions and have not the wherewith to furnish themselves with necessary victuals to maintain them and their families'.[70]

Politics mixed with this difficult economic situation and on the evening of 22 October 1641 a number of Ulster Catholics rose in an attempt to safeguard their rights, and those of the king, against what they perceived as a threat from a Puritan-inclined Dublin administration. News of this reached Belfast quickly. Two days later Sir Edward Chichester wrote to Viscount Montgomery telling him about the insurrectionists' bonfires, which could be seen from the town, and the seizure of a number of Ulster towns. Perceiving the undefended Belfast to be under threat, he fled to his more defensible town of Carrickfergus, where he had arrived by 17 November, leaving Belfast leaderless and undefended.[71] The immediate result in the town was panic. An account published in 1643 by a Captain Lawson described how he 'found most part of the inhabitants fled and flying and carrying away their goods to Carrickfergus'. At the Waring Street house of the sovereign, Henry le Squire, Lawson found 'seven or eight halberts, ready in the street to be shipped to Carrickfergus'.[72] Lawson mustered some 20 men from the town and, gathering others at the ironworks of New Forge, marched to Lisburn, where whatever British force could hastily be raised was congregating. Despite repeated attacks on Lisburn on 8, 22 and 28 November the insurgents failed to dislodge the settler force and, indeed, suffered considerable losses in the last attempt. For the moment Belfast was safe from attack.

The outbreak of war inevitably posed problems for the town. The securing of Lisburn against the Irish may have stopped a major onslaught on Belfast but there were some local disturbances. At Malone, about 5 kilometres from the present city centre, the house built by Moses Hill in 1611 was burnt by the insurrectionists and the nearby Stranmillis may well have suffered the same fate, as it is shown as ruined on the Down Survey map of 1657.[73] Likewise the ironworks at New Forge were destroyed in fighting in the early 1640s.[74] Despite this local activity Belfast was perceived, after the defeat at Lisburn, as a safe area and people began to flood into the town. Richard Head, then a child living near Carrickfergus, described in one of his later autobiographical works how when the rising broke out he and his family were guided to Belfast by an Irishman, where they 'were received with much pity of all and entertained and clothed and fed by some charitable minded persons'.[75] The numbers of people appearing on lists for assessments by the corporation grew, though the number admitted to the freedom of the town, practising trades there, collapsed. More importantly, the population became highly mobile. Of those assessed in 1642 only about half had been living in Belfast in 1640. Such a mobile population presented problems. One issue was clearly sanitation and attempts were made to improve hygiene by fining those who dumped manure and carrion in the streets and employing a man to bury carrion dumped in the town.[76] That did not solve the problem and during four months in 1643 disease swept through Belfast and some of the adjoining towns, temporarily reducing the population.[77] The influx of civilians was only part of the problem, since soldiers were billeted on the town as well. In December 1641 Belfast was said to have a garrison of 300–400, all of whom needed to be fed and housed.[78] By the middle of the 1640s the garrison stood at 400, which resulted in frequent assessments on the town for its support.[79] By 1647 the town was so full of soldiers that the corporation were forced to reserve seats in the church for themselves on Sundays.[80]

The most immediate problem was that of defence and in early 1642 the corporation decided to construct a rampart around the town. Gaps in the evidence for the early 1640s do not allow the documentation of this construction work in any detail. By June 1642 work had begun but the rampart was said to be unfinished and

1642–43 ramparts

there were complaints that assessments levied for the building of the rampart had not been paid.[81] In March 1643 a further cess was levied for the 'erecting of a bulworke at the Strand', which seems to be the large gate depicted on Phillips's map of 1685. The substantial sum of £30 was levied on the main inhabitants of Belfast for this building.[82] The rampart was clearly a substantial structure and its remains could still be identified into the early nineteenth century.[83] According to nineteenth-century tradition, combined with the cartographic evidence of Phillips's maps of 1685, the rampart ran from the junction of Castle Lane and William Street as far west as College Square and then to the junction of Royal Avenue and North Street, before proceeding east toward the river. The earliest map shows the rampart as incomplete, not extending much beyond a point on Donegall Street. However, some of Phillips's other maps continue the ditch, but not the rampart, until close to the position of the Strand Gate. There is some archaeological support for this in excavations at Gordon Street, close to the Strand Gate, which revealed a linear feature infilled with brown–grey clay that would

Belfast *c.* 1660, showing the approximate line of the rampart.

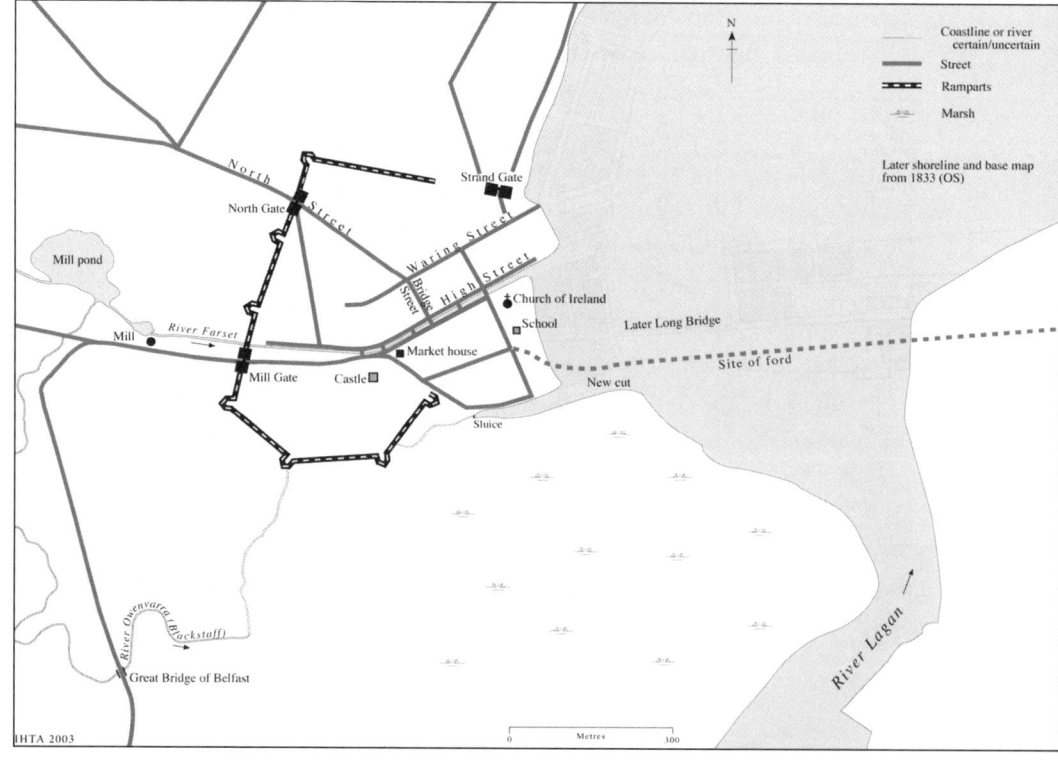

appear to be the remains of the ditch around the town. However, no indication of the presence of the rampart was found.[84] The incomplete circuit of the rampart, together with its hasty construction did not impress contemporaries. When in the 1650s the Cromwellian administration listed the walled towns of Ulster it did not include Belfast, presumably because its defences were so poor.[85]

Part of the rampart structure has been excavated on Donegall Street. On the outer side a ditch, later filled in, just over 3 metres wide and 1 metre deep (although in the nineteenth century Benn described it as 15 or 20 feet wide in places) was identified. On its inner edge were deliberately laid basalt boulders and stones, which were probably the foundation for an upcast earth bank.[86] This earth bank was interrupted by six bastions and three demi-bastions. These were arranged in such a way as to give some covering cannon fire to the entire circuit of the rampart, although this was concentrated on the western side. The close-range musket cover was poor, with only the north-west bastion properly covered. All this suggests that the rampart was a relatively weak defence and those who built it had a limited knowledge of how such structures worked.[87] It is worth noting the similarities of this rampart to defences erected in other Ulster towns at the same point. In particular it shows strong similarities to the earth wall built around Coleraine in 1610–13. In both cases the circuit was interrupted by six bastions and three demi-bastions, although the ditch around Belfast was not as deep as, and slightly narrower than, that at Coleraine.[88] It may be that the hastily erected ramparts at Belfast were modelled on those seen by their makers elsewhere (perhaps at Coleraine, for instance), rather than designed specifically for the site.

There were gates in this rampart at North Street, Mill Street and on the Strand. The Mill Gate, at the junction of Queen Street and Chapel Lane with Castle Street, was leased to a Robert Wilson in 1717 and referred to by Benn in 1823 when he mentioned 'part of the walls and arch of which remaining within the memory of many persons now living'.[89] The Strand Gate, erected later than the others and not connected to the main wall, was clearly a substantial structure, possibly of stone or brick, clearly identifiable in Thomas Phillips's 1685 map of the town. However, why such a substantial

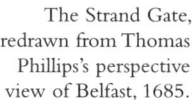

The Strand Gate,
redrawn from Thomas
Phillips's perspective
view of Belfast, 1685.

gate should have been made in this location is not clear. It does have a parallel at Coleraine – a Raven map of 1625 shows a similar structure on one of the main routeways into the town beside the river, although in Coleraine's case this may not have been constructed.[90] Since both structures were situated on main entrances to their respective towns it may have been thought that they would serve ceremonial as well as defensive purposes.[91] The other Belfast gates also seem to have been substantial structures in comparison to the earthen wall of the rampart. The assessment of 1645, for instance, made provision for bricks to construct a 'court of guard' (apparently in the town hall) and ironwork for the gates, as well as bridges at the gates, which were then under construction.[92] Again, Coleraine provides a parallel for this. Stone gates and smaller square stone towers were built into earthen ramparts there.

In the early 1640s Belfast remained under Chichester's command and his agent, Henry le Squire, was active in the settler army about the town.[93] However, Chichester's force was not the only one in the area. In June 1642 an army of Scottish soldiers landed at Carrickfergus under the immediate command of Robert Munroe. The force had been raised in Scotland by request of the king but paid for by the Westminster parliament and it lay outside the command of the settler forces in Ulster. The principal feature of this army was its militant Presbyterianism. The Scottish soldiers established the first presbytery at Carrickfergus in 1642. Inevitably there were tensions between the force of the Episcopalian Chichester at Belfast and Munroe's Presbyterian garrison at Carrickfergus. Locally, this was made worse by the fact that some of Munroe's force was actually garrisoned at Belfast and there had been problems between that force and the inhabitants of the town.[94] That tension worsened in 1643 when the Scots entered an agreement with the army's paymasters – the parliament in London that had been at war with the king since the previous August. The agreement, the 'Solemn League and Covenant', committed both sides to a Presbyterian religious settlement. It became one of the foundation stones of Ulster Presbyterianism but was not liked by the royalists, including Chichester. Tensions were exacerbated by the fact that the Dublin administration had entered a truce with the Ulster insurgents in September 1643 but the parliament in London had ordered Munroe's force to continue the war, fearing that a peace in Ireland would allow soldiers to be recruited to the royalist cause in England.

All this gave rise to mutual suspicion between Chichester's royalist force and Munroe's parliamentary one. In April 1644 the Dublin administration, under the control of the Irish lord lieutenant, the royalist marquis of Ormond, quickly sent money and supplies to Chichester at Belfast, fearing that Munroe was about to seize the town in the name of parliament.[95] On 13 May a number of the royalist officers of the settler army met in Belfast to discuss their position. Munroe feared that Chichester would hold the town against his authority and there was a rumour that the marquis of Ormond would send troops to support Chichester. Against this background Munroe moved, seizing Belfast without bloodshed on the morning of 14 May 1644. Many within the town clearly welcomed Munroe and the guards opened the gates at his approach.[96] Others were less sanguine. The sovereign, Thomas Theaker, was expelled from the town and fled to Dublin. The Solemn League and Covenant was taken by most of the inhabitants and they demanded changes in the government of the town so that the burgesses would be elected by popular vote, rather than selected by the Chichester family, and required to take the Covenant.[97] Signs of political unrest are discernable in the corporation records. According to the town book in the early part of the seventeenth century decisions about the running of the town were made by the sovereign and burgesses but in the middle of 1643 a new formula began to appear in accounts of corporation meetings. A cess of May 1643, for instance, was said to have been made by the 'burgesses and commonality'. By 1645 this formula was also being attached to more general decisions about the town and in 1646 'many of the commonality' were said to be part of the governing body of the town.[98] This radical political strain surfaced again in 1645 and 1646, when there were disputes about the nature of the sovereign's authority in the town. In 1645 the corporation had to declare that their lawful orders were to be obeyed and the following year burgesses were attacked on the street. Also in 1646, there appears to have been a dispute over the swearing in of the sovereign, which resulted in entries being removed from the corporation book.[99] All this seems to point to a significant radical attempt to move the locus of authority in the town away from the person of the landlord.

In August 1644 Munroe ordered the expulsion of Catholics from Belfast and demanded that Chichester's forces be disarmed. Chichester withdrew to London to complain to parliament about Munroe's actions. Political events there meant that relations between parliament and the Scots were becoming strained; parliament was clearly unhappy about the Scottish forces holding both Carrickfergus and Belfast. Yet the Scots were determined to do so since to hold the two ports was to control the supply of provisions for any army in the area. In December 1645 parliament insisted the town be surrendered to them but Munroe's army refused. A similar demand in late 1646 was also rebuffed. Munroe had clearly stamped his mark on Belfast. Indeed, there may even have been some settlement from Scotland. A pamphlet describing the fall of the town in 1649 noted that '800 Scots were afterwards turn'd out of the town, whither they had brought their wives and children to plant themselves there'.[100] Some supporting evidence for this is provided by the admissions to the freedom of the town, which rose from two in 1642 to 15 in 1644. By 1647, 30 freemen were admitted each year, suggesting a considerable influx of people for settlement rather than for safety. The numbers fell back to three in 1649, reflecting a more unstable political situation.

Matters took a more serious turn in 1648 when the Scots changed sides in the Second Civil War in England, now supporting the king. The parliamentarian commander in Ulster, General Monck, moved to seize Carrickfergus and Belfast, both of which fell without a fight. Belfast did not stay in Monck's hands for long. Reaction against parliament after the execution of the king in January 1649 led the royalist Hugh Montgomery, third Viscount Ards, to seize Belfast, which in turn provoked the intervention of the parliamentary commander Robert Venables, ordered north by Oliver Cromwell after landing at Dublin in August. The military action was short lived and its geography is unclear. According to a contemporary account cannon were involved but probably not needed – the attack came from the north of the town, where the rampart had been unfinished in 1642.[101] Belfast capitulated after a four-day siege. The Cromwellian victory was complete when the covenanter sovereign of Belfast, George Martin, fled to Scotland after his property had been plundered for his refusal to allow parliamentary troops to be quartered on it. Potentially even more devastating in the long run was a government plan to transport some of the main Belfast merchants to Tipperary to prevent them associating with their Scottish counterparts, who were still loyal to the exiled Charles II. Fortunately, this proved to be stillborn.[102]

IV

The impact on Belfast of the wars of the 1640s was limited. Perhaps the most serious damage to the physical fabric of the town came not from sieges or warfare but from the fortification of the former parish church by the Cromwellian army. Situated at the end of High Street, the church was well placed not only to control the ford over the Lagan but also to act as a lookout across Belfast Lough. In 1654 it was said to be in disrepair, since it had been used as a fort in the early 1650s, and consideration was given to rebuilding it. In fact, only repairs were carried out.[103] The nature of the fortification is unclear. There are mentions in the corporation records of demolishing houses near the 'Grand fort' in 1651, which may suggest that earthworks were erected round the church for artillery. Cannon were certainly removed from there to Carrickfergus when the building was restored for its original function in 1655.[104] It may also have served as a military hospital, since a surgeon was located at Belfast in 1655 but was no longer in the town by 1657.[105] It is clear from the fact that the church was said to be 'ruinated' in 1655 that more than the construction of earthworks was involved. It seems likely that the building was used as a barracks for soldiers. The church building may have been damaged but the institution was not. While the Church of Ireland was proscribed during the 1650s the Commonwealth preacher at Belfast, Essex Digby, was a former Church of Ireland minister at Geashill in County Offaly. It was probably no coincidence that he was also a nephew of Lady Donegall. The parochial structure also appeared little damaged since in 1654 Mathew Ferra, the parish clerk, was admitted free of the town.[106] Whatever about theological niceties the parish was too useful for local administration to be abolished easily.

War and its aftermath may have created problems for Belfast but it also presented opportunities. The new regime recognised the importance of Belfast over its older rival, Carrickfergus. The Parliamentary Commissioners based themselves there in 1650–1 and it became the centre of the revenue district thereafter. Elections were also held at Belfast rather than Carrickfergus in the 1650s.[107] Perhaps as a result of this Belfast was treated well by the Cromwellian regime. It was one of only a few boroughs, including Carrickfergus, Youghal and Dublin, that held on to their charters throughout the interregnum. One explanation may be the fact that charters had a restrictive nature, which meant that the Cromwellian military commander, Captain Francis Meek, could assume the powers formerly held by the Chichesters and effectively control the workings of the corporation by regulating the appointment of burgesses.[108] In fact, Meek was well practised at that task – he had been Chichester's constable of the castle in 1646, presumably later defecting to the parliamentary side. During the 1650s the town book no longer recorded the presence of the 'commonality' at meetings of the corporation, which suggests that the brief period of radicalism of the mid-1640s had been brought to an end by the new regime. In return the state took over the payment of the schoolmaster in Belfast, John Cornwall, who staffed the school established by the corporation in 1648, in an effort to direct young minds to godliness.[109]

It would be reckless to say that Belfast prospered in the 1650s since more general economic conditions did not permit that. A 1657 inquisition into the wealth of the parishes in Antrim noted that in 1640 the vicarial tithes of Belfast had been worth £60 but were at that time worth only £50.[110] However, there are signs that conditions did improve over the decade. The numbers admitted to freedom climbed gradually from five per year in the early 1650s to 31 in 1659, a figure that exceeded the level of pre-1641 admissions. The Cromwellian regime allowed many of these men to prosper. On the basis of the lay subsidy of 1663 one of the most prosperous men in Belfast was the tanner Thomas Waring. He had probably settled in Belfast about 1640 but had an unspectacular career until the early 1650s. Since he was English, was not a Presbyterian and was prepared to deal with the Cromwellian regime, he became sovereign of the town from 1652 to 1655 at a time when most other Irish towns were under military rule. Such an elevation propelled Waring into the upper echelons of Belfast society, a position from which he never lapsed.[111] In fact, the economic opportunities of the 1650s attracted into the town many who would become important later. George Macartney of Auchinleck in Scotland, for instance, came to the town in 1649 and was to become one of the most powerful economic and political forces in late seventeenth-century Belfast.[112]

V

By the end of the 1650s Belfast had begun to assume the form that it would take for the next century. It had begun in the seventeenth century as a green-field site, spurning the older medieval settlement, yet by 1640 the basic topography of the town had been laid out in a mixture of planned settlement at Waring Street and natural expansion along older routes such as North Street. The position of the town as a trading centre was already secure. Perhaps even more importantly, structures of government had been put in place by the charter of 1613 that allowed the town to function as an urban centre. However, the systems adopted were far from perfect. The power of the corporation was severely limited by its lack of funds and the control that the Chichester family exercised over appointments. Despite this they were solutions that functioned and were not challenged, except briefly in the 1640s. Belfast was, above all, a landlord town. It both reflected and contributed to the power and wealth of the Chichester family. It represented nothing less than the triumph of a new social and economic order.

NOTES

1   James Perrot, *The chronicle of Ireland, 1584–1608*, ed. Herbert Wood (Dublin, 1933), p. 36; *Irish fiants of the Tudor sovereigns* (4 vols, Dublin, 1994), iv Elizabeth, no. 4,960.

2   H.F. Hore (ed.), 'Marshall Bagenall's description of Ulster' in *U.J.A.*, 1st ser., ii (1854), p. 154.

3   *Cal. S.P. Ire. 1592–6*, p. 54; *Cal. S.P. Ire 1596–7*, pp 326–7, 396–7. The seizure of the castle is discussed in William Pinkerton, 'Overthrow of Sir John Chichester' in *U.J.A.*, 1st ser., v (1857), pp 188–209.

4   *Cal. Carew MSS 1588–1600*, p. 107; *Irish fiants*, iv Elizabeth, no. 6,235; Historical Manuscripts Commission, *Report on the Salisbury (Cecil) manuscripts at Hatfield House* (24 vols, London, 1883–1976), ix, p. 102.

5   Ibid., xv, pp 196–7.

6   Erck, *Repertory*, pp 23, 31, 100–10. For full text of the grant and a translation see P.R.O.N.I., D509/2, T956/4.

7   Ibid., p. 23.

8   *Cal. S.P. Ire. 1606–08*, p. 233.

9   Edited in Benn, *History* (1877), p. 86.

10 Philip Robinson, *The plantation of Ulster* (Dublin, 1984), pp 133–4.

11 T.C.D., MS 550, p. 248.

12 P.R.O.N.I., DIO 1/24/26/9.

13 Young, *Town book*, pp 3, 6.

14 Benn, *History* (1823), p. 73; Young, *Town book*, p. 42.

15 Alistair Rowan, *The buildings of Ireland: north-west Ulster* (Harmonsworth, 1979), pp 376–8.

16 D.A. Chart, *Londonderry and the London Companies, 1609-1629* (Belfast, 1928), plate 8, opposite p. 37.

17 Edited in Benn, *History* (1877), pp 86–7.

18 *Inquisitionum in officio*, ii, (Antrim, James I), no. 7.

19 *Excavations 1999*, p. 2; Ruairí Ó Baoill and Paul Logue, 'Excavations at Gordon Street and Waring Street, Belfast' in *U.J.A.*, 3rd ser., lxiv (2005), p. 116.

20 P.R.O.N.I., D271/1; D298/6.

21 Registry of Deeds, Dublin, 8/308/2810; C.E.B. Brett, Raymond Gillespie and W.A. Maguire, *Georgian Belfast: maps, buildings and trades* (Dublin, 2004), pp 16–17, 54–5.

22 P.R.O.N.I., D 509/13.
23 R.J. Hunter, 'Towns in the Ulster plantation' in *Studia Hibernica*, no. 11 (1971), pp 58–9.
24 Avril Thomas, *Irish historic towns atlas no. 15: Derry~Londonderry* (Dublin, 2005), p. 4.
25 Raymond Gillespie, *Settlement and survival on a Ulster estate: the Brownlow leasebook, 1667–1711* (Belfast, 1988), p. xl.
26 Angélique Day and Patrick McWilliams (eds), *Ordnance Survey memoirs of Ireland xxxvii: parishes of county Antrim, Carrickfergus* (Belfast, 1996), p. 29.
27 'Belfast excavations', p. 4.
28 *Cal. S.P. Ire. 1600*, p. 226; McCrie, *Robert Blair*, pp 59–60.
29 Young, *Town book*, pp 10, 11.
30 Ibid., p. 69.
31 'Belfast excavations', p. 4.
32 National Archives, Dublin, RC9/1, p. 30.
33 Young, *Town book*, p. 14.
34 Bridge Street is currently much wider than it was in the eighteenth and nineteenth century since the building line was moved back in reconstruction after bombing during the Second World War, 1939–45.
35 Young, *Town Book*, pp 13–15.
36 Ibid., pp 1–3, 4–5, 17.
37 D.R. Hainsworth (ed.), *The commercial papers of Christopher Lowther* (Gateshead, 1977), pp 1, 3, 10–12, 15, 29, 107, 110, 121, 123; Young, *Town book*, p. 11.
38 Gillespie, *Colonial Ulster*, p. 178; Young, *Historical notices*, pp 109–16; Manx Museum and Library, Douglas, Isle Of Man, *Liber Cancellarii 1624*, 15.
39 Philip Robinson, *Irish historic towns atlas no. 2: Carrickfergus* (Dublin, 1986), pp 3–4.
40 Young, *Town book*, pp 8–9.
41 For the early history of poor relief see R.M.W. Strain, *Belfast and its charitable society* (Oxford, 1961), pp 5–9.
42 The charter is printed in Young, *Town book*, pp 172–8.
43 Ibid., pp 15, 16, 24, 37–8, for examples.
44 Ibid., pp 1–2; Samuel Miskimmin, *The history and antiquities of Carrickfergus*, ed. E.J. McCrum (Belfast, 1909), p. 267.
45 Young, *Town book*, pp 11–12.
46 Ibid., p. 19. The uncollected sum was underwritten by Chichester's agent Henry le Squire, who was also sovereign (Benn, *History* (1877), p. 239).
47 Young, *Town book*, p. 13.
48 Benn, *History* (1877), p. 140.
49 T.C.D., MS 838, ff 6v, 15–15v.
50 Young, *Town book*, p. 6.
51 Edited in C. Litton Falkiner, *Illustrations of Irish history and topography mainly of the seventeenth century* (London, 1904), p. 370.
52 Miskimmin, *Carrickfergus*, pp 154–5.
53 Robinson, *Carrickfergus*, map 7.
54 For the regrant of 1640 see P.R.O.N.I., T956/25,26.
55 Figures from Thomas, *Walled towns* (2 vols, Dublin, 1992), pp 35, 39.
56 Jope, *Archaeological survey of County Down*, p. 273.
57 Gillespie, *Colonial Ulster*, p. 171.
58 P.R.O.N.I., D509/13.
59 Young, *Town book*, p. 7.

60 T.N.A., E157/17.
61 Reeves, 'Irish itinerary', p. 56.
62 Henry Leslie, *A treatise on the authority of the church, the sum whereof was delivered in a sermon preached at Belfast at the visitation of the diocese of Down and Connor the tenth day of August 1636* (Dublin, 1637).
63 W. Carmody, *Lisburn Cathedral and its past rectors* (Belfast, 1926), pp 93–6.
64 *A necessary examination of a dangerous design and practice ... by the presbytery at Belfast in the province of Ulster in Ireland* (London, 1649).
65 Patrick Adair, *A true narrative of the rise and progress of the Presbyterian church in Ireland*, ed. W.D. Killen (Belfast, 1866), p. 168; Gillespie, *Colonial Ulster*, p. 234.
66 T.C.D., MS 550, p. 248; MS 1067, p. 80; Bodleian Library, Oxford, Rawlinson MS A 491, f. 97.
67 Peter Roebuck, 'The making of an Ulster great estate: the Chichesters, barons of Belfast and viscounts of Carrickfergus, 1559–1648' in *Proceedings of the Royal Irish Academy*, lxxix (C) (1979), p. 22.
68 T.W. Moody and J.G. Simms (eds), *The bishopric of Derry and the Irish society of London, 1602–1705* (2 vols, Dublin, 1968–83), i, p. 160.
69 Young, *Town book*, pp 17, 19.
70 Bodleian Library, Oxford, Carte MS 1, f. 379.
71 *Cal. S.P. Ire. 1633–47*, pp 341–2, 344.
72 *True relation of acts performed by Robert Lawson*, pp 2, 5.
73 [Roger Pike], *June 8th 1642: a true relation of the proceedings of the Scots and English forces in the north of Ireland* (London, 1642), p. 7.
74 Ibid., pp 7–8.
75 Richard Head, *The English rogue described* (London, 1666), p. 10.
76 Young, *Town book*, pp 16, 23; Benn, *History*, (1877), p. 195.
77 Daniel Harcourt, *The clergies lamentation* (London, 1644), p. 9.
78 George Hill (ed.), *The Montgomery manuscripts* (Belfast, 1869), p. 309n.
79 Young, *Town book*, pp 30–1, 34–7, 40, 41.
80 Ibid., pp 52–3.
81 Ibid., p. 24.
82 Ibid., p. 22. The date is 1642 old style.
83 Benn, *History* (1823), pp 68–70.
84 *Excavations 2001*, pp 1–2.
85 Robert Dunlop, *Ireland under the Commonwealth* (2 vols, Manchester, 1913), ii, p. 666
86 *Excavations 1990*, p. 11.
87 Gerald Müller and Gavin Williamson, 'Fortification of Belfast' in *Irish Sword*, xix (1994–5), pp 306–12.
88 Thomas, *Walled towns*, ii, pp 57–8, 157–8.
89 P.R.O.N.I., D509/43.; Benn, *History* (1823), p. 68.
90 Chart (ed.), *Londonderry and the London companies*, plate 17.
91 The suggestion that this structure was built much later as a formal entrance to Waring's development at the Plantation seems unlikely: see Shannon Millin, *Additional sidelights on Belfast history* (Belfast, 1938), pp 119–23.
92 Young, *Town book*, p. 28.
93 James Hogan (ed.), *Letters and papers relating to the Irish rebellion between 1642 and 1646* (Dublin, 1936), pp 41–2.
94 Bodleian Library, Oxford, Carte MS 8, f. 11.
95 Bodleian Library, Oxford, Carte MS 10, f. 509.
96 Young, *Historical notices*, p. 57.
97 T.C.D., MS 838, ff 3–3v, 5–6v, 7–8, 15–16.

98 Young, *Town book*, pp 14–15, 28, 30, 31, 32, 38, 45.
99 Ibid., pp 28, 44, 240.
100 *A history or brief chronicle of the chief matters of the Irish wars* (London, 1650), sig a4v.
101 Ibid., sig a4v. Benn, *History* (1877), p. 129n, records that evidence of a battle in the York Street area was discovered during the construction of a cotton mill there.
102 Young, *Historical notices*, pp 78–85.
103 Representative Church Body Library, Dublin, GS/2/7/3/27; Benn, *History* (1877), pp 139–42.
104 Young, *Town book*, pp 69–70.
105 Benn, *History* (1877), pp 101, 106.
106 Young, *Town book*, p. 254.
107 Dunlop, *Ireland under the Commonwealth* , ii, pp 11–26, 40, 69, 77–8, 110, 135, 162, 175, 177, 211; *Cal. S.P. Ire. 1647–60*, p. 800.
108 Young, *Town Book*, p. 240.
109 St John D. Seymour, *The puritans in Ireland, 1647–1661* (Oxford, 1921), p. 225.
110 Benn, *History* (1877), p. 369.
111 Jean Agnew, *Belfast merchant families in the seventeenth century* (Dublin, 1996), pp 249–50.
112 Ibid., pp 233–4.

4

THOMAS PHILLIPS'S TOWN
1660–95

The inhabitants of Belfast looked on with more than ordinary interest as, from 1658, the Cromwellian regime in Ireland slowly imploded. As General George Monck marched from Scotland into England to inaugurate a process that would lead to the restoration of Charles II, someone scribbled into the corporation book a set of verses saluting Monck as the restorer of a free parliament and looking forward to the time when 'all shall cry God save the king'.[1] Somewhat later, someone copied into the corporation book the future Charles II's 'Gracious declaration' issued from Breda in May 1660, which was to form the basis of the Restoration settlement in Ireland.[2] To ensure that their rights under the declaration were not subsequently ignored, a number of prominent Belfast citizens registered their claims in the corporation book.[3] The corporation was not the only beneficiary from the settlement. By August 1660 Sir Arthur Chichester, created earl of Donegall in 1647, who had spent most of the 1650s propertyless in England, was back in Belfast.[4] In 1668 the family received a confirmation of their property, including Belfast.[5] If anything, the Donegalls' control in the town became more effective after 1660 and it became normal to note in the corporation book that decisions had been made with the consent of the earl which, although required by the charter, had not been noted earlier. To many it seemed that much of the old world had been restored, but at the same time Belfast was on the edge of considerable change.

I

Belfast had survived the wars of the 1640s and 1650s well. Indeed, contrary to the experience of other towns, it had prospered. While the numbers returned as liable for the poll tax of 1660 are not figures for total population, they provide at least some measure of the relative size of the town. These estimates suggest that Belfast had grown rapidly in the previous two decades. The civilian taxpaying population of the town, at 589, was considerably larger than that of Carrickfergus, which had only 315 civilian taxpayers, although Carrickfergus's garrison more than doubled that number. However, Belfast still lagged behind the 1,052 taxpayers that Derry was able to muster. Whereas in the 1630s Belfast had been little bigger than Bangor or Newtownards in County Down, it was now five times as large as those settlements. Moreover, its taxpaying population outstripped that of the towns with which it was connected along the Lagan Valley, such as Lisburn, Lurgan and Armagh, by almost 50 per cent.[6] In the area of trade Belfast had consolidated its position in the 1650s. In the early 1660s about 3 per cent of Irish customs were passing through the town, which ranked it as the ninth largest port in Ireland. It was still greatly surpassed by Dublin, Galway, Drogheda and Waterford but it had drawn even with Derry.[7] The fabric of the town was also in good condition. In 1666 the French traveller Jorevin de Rocheford, travelling towards Carrickfergus from Dundalk, noted:

> I arrived at Belfast, situated on a river at the bottom of a gulf, where barks and vessels anchor on account of the security and

Down Survey of 1657 for the barony of Belfast. The view of the town is a very schematic one but the castle and the larger buildings along Waring Street are clear even by this date.

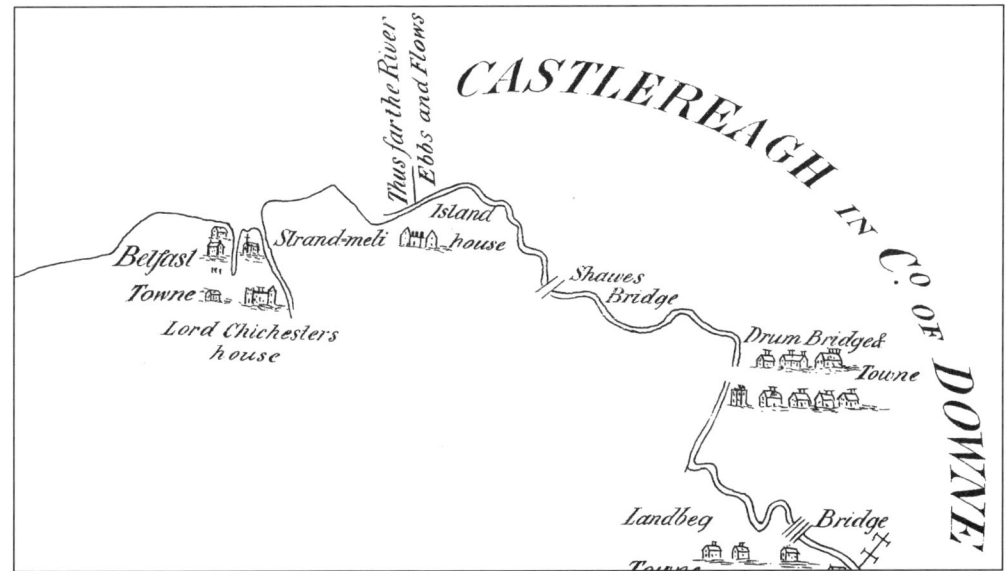

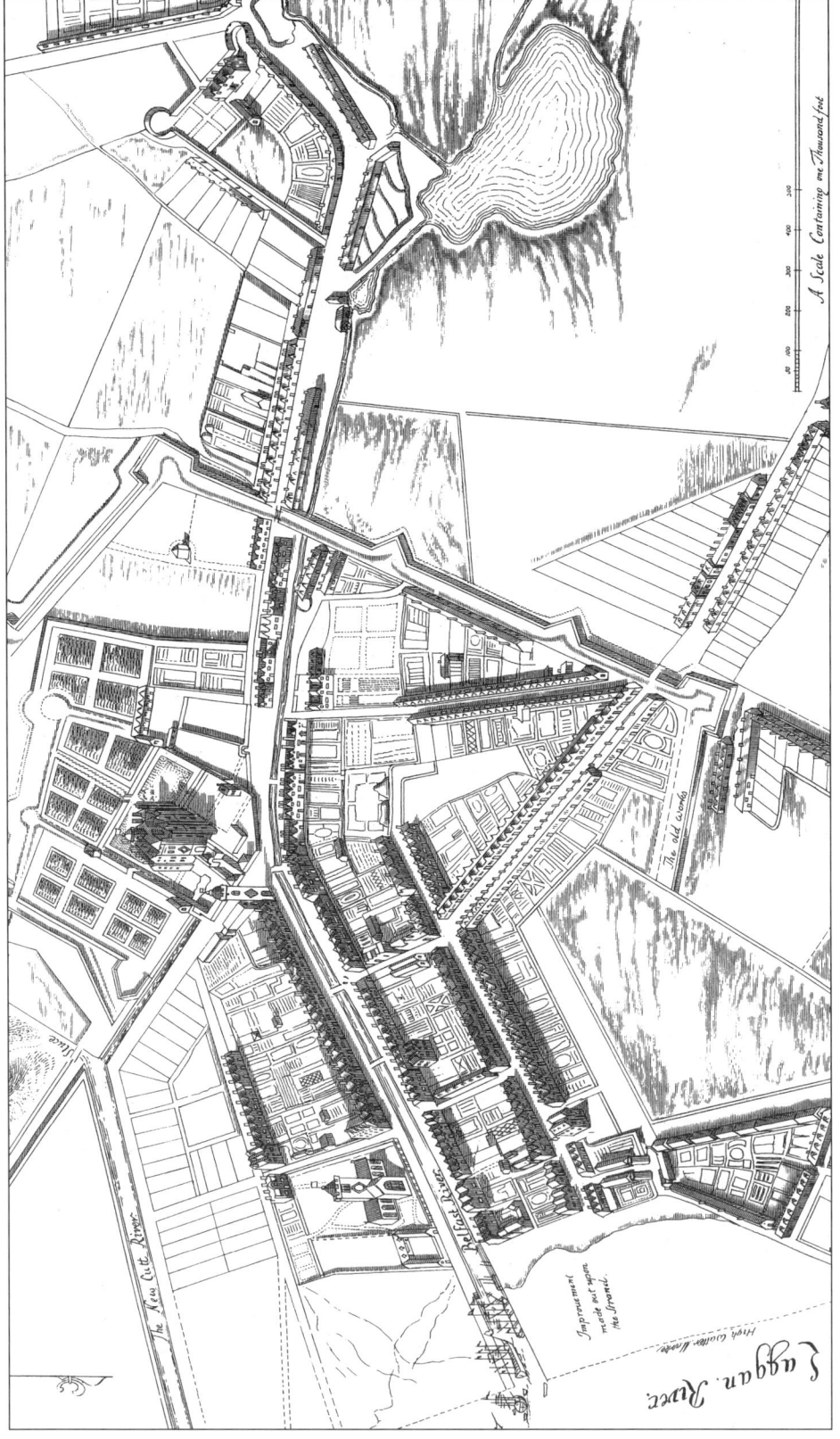

Laggan River.

A Scale Containing one Thousand feet

The New Cut River

Sluice

High Water Mark

Improvement made out upon the Strand.

Belfast River

The old works

goodness of the port; wherefore several merchants live here who trade to Scotland and England, whither they transport the super-fluities of this country. Here is a very fine castle, and two or three large and straight streets as in a new built town. One may often procure a passage here for Scotland[.][8]

De Rocheford described the settlement of Belfast at the beginning of great change. The map of the town prepared as part of the Down Survey of 1657, although admittedly rather crude, shows the church and castle to the south side of the Farset. The three large buildings it shows representing the main area of the town are all in the Waring Street area, suggesting little substantial development outside the core of the early seventeenth-century town. Thus the streets to which de Rocheford referred were probably Waring Street, High Street and North Street, which formed the core of the town. Waring Street had been well established since Belfast's beginnings, while High Street first appeared in a deed of 1656 and North Street first produced property deeds in the 1660s.

Reconstructing some of the detail of the urban topography of the town in the years after the Restoration is possible because of the survival of a number of maps of the town drawn by the military surveyor Thomas Phillips about 1685 as part of a survey made for the improvement of the fortifications of Irish towns. Four Belfast maps in all were made by Phillips. The first, dated 1685, is a bird's-eye view of the town with the viewer located on the slopes of the Cave Hill, giving rise to the peculiarity that north is at the bottom of the map rather than the more usual orientation. The perspective drawing is an alluring but difficult source. Its main elements are clearly accurate, although there are some discrepancies between this map and other evidence. Again, the cartographer has used a wide range of conventional symbols for houses and other features and it is easy to be led astray by cartographic custom as opposed to reality.[9] The other three maps are more conventional plans with only occasional buildings, such as the church or the market house, shown as perspective drawings. There are slight, but mainly insignificant, differences between the three conventional plans. Despite their problems, the maps by Thomas Phillips provide a detailed and vivid point of entry into the world of late-seventeenth-century Belfast.

Opposite: Thomas Phillips's perspective view of Belfast, 1685, redrawn from the original.

It is easy to see in Phillips's maps much that is familiar. The town still lay mainly within the rampart constructed in the early 1640s and the main topographical elements of the early seventeenth century are all identifiable. The dominant urban feature was the castle, which was built on a scale unlike any other building in the town. In 1708 Thomas Molyneux, travelling through Ulster, noted:

> it stands separate from the rest of the houses [...] in the midst of courts and gardens, which are an extremely noble old improvement [...] those improvements are all enclosed in a kind of fortification, being designed for a place of strength as well as pleasure and is a lasting monument of this kind of greatness of its founder.[10]

According to the ground plan on one of Phillips's maps, the castle was nearly a square, each side being 120 feet long, with a central courtyard. There were projections at each corner and a profusion of chimneys and windows. The chimneys were all located around the edge, suggesting that the centre of the building, although roofed in with a cupola on top, may have been left open as a grand entrance space. There is good reason to believe that the castle depicted on Phillips's map of 1685 had already assumed this form by 1660. Certainly by the 1690s it was noted that the castle 'is not of the newest model', suggesting it may have been built a long time previously.[11] There are also other reasons for thinking this. First, the hearth-money rolls of 1666 record a large number of hearths. The castle had 40 hearths, the same number as the Chichester house at Carrickfergus, which implies that it was a substantial structure of similar size to that depicted in 1685.[12] The second reason for surmising that the 1685 structure was complete by 1660 is the sophisticated planning of the gardens around the castle. Gardens of some complexity were common at large gentry houses at this time and examples have been revealed by excavation at Lisburn and Newtownards.[13] The expenditure roll for the earl of Donegall in the 1660s suggests that elaborate gardens were already present at Belfast. The roll describes a cherry garden, an apple garden and a bowling green. There are references to the growing of strawberries, currants and gooseberries, as well as payments for rolling, cleaning, weeding and wheeling in ashes and cinders for paths.[14] In the 1690s a fishpond was recorded.[15] All this would seem to suggest that the castle depicted in 1685 was already there before 1660 and to confirm its position in the town as dominant, yet shielded from urban life by its gardens, surrounding walls (including the rampart of 1642) and complex entrance leading from Cornmarket.

The second topographical element from the early seventeenth century, the church, also appears prominently on Phillips's plans. While this had been damaged in the 1650s as a result of its conversion into a military barracks, most of that damage had been repaired by the middle of the 1650s. In 1679 an episcopal visitation reported that the church was in 'good repair'.[16] In the 1670s a gallery was added to part of the church. At one level this was a practical solution to the problem of accommodating a growing population, yet it is not immediately clear that the Church of Ireland population of Belfast, as opposed to its Presbyterian counterpart, was increasing. As Bishop King of Derry noted in 1698, 'the people of Belfast are very refractory, and do many irregular things; [...] they will not consent to enlarge their church lest there should be room for all their people'.[17] The practical explanation of the building of a gallery as additional accommodation is also weakened by the fact that the owners and builders of at least one gallery seat (the family of Isaac Macartney) were Presbyterians and therefore not likely to use it. In fact, Isaac Macartney had sublet it to one of the officers of the customs house although in 1705 he was concerned that the bishop might somehow confiscate 'our property'.[18] The concern here was clearly not about practicalities, but about display. The building of galleries became fashionable after 1666 because London churches reconstructed after the great fire included them. In the 1670s and 1680s Dublin churches in the process of rebuilding also included galleries for fashionable as much as practical reasons. The church was being remoulded to fit the needs of a new, fashion-conscious merchant class emerging in late seventeenth-century Belfast.

The third main urban element from the early seventeenth century, the Waring Street development, is shown in some detail on Phillips's map. The street is shown running east–west, with its western edge where it had been in the early part of the seventeenth century. As far as Skipper Street, Waring Street is portrayed as a

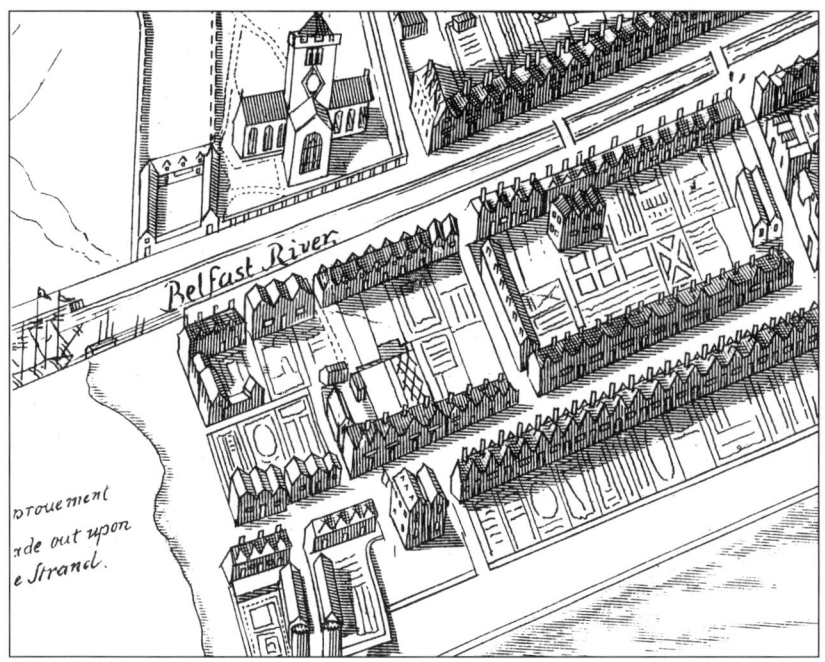

Waring Street as it is represented on Thomas Phillips's map of 1685.

fairly homogenous unit. Houses are aligned with the street, with considerable gardens behind them. These were clearly substantial structures, although the schematic way in which they are depicted on the map means that little can be deduced on that basis alone. There are relatively few leases that would flesh out this picture. One 1656 lease of property in High Street hints at substantial building by requiring that the tenant build 'a good and sufficient house of brick and lime with good and sufficient oaken roof, well slated' and that premises be enclosed by hedges. In 1692 other houses in High Street were said to be of brick.[19] As timber came to be in shorter supply in the late seventeenth and early eighteenth centuries and brick became more fashionable, timber-framed houses were replaced by brick-built ones. This clearly had many advantages, not least among them being the greater resistance to fire. Phillips's map shows most of the Waring Street houses as single-storey structures with dormer windows above them, indicating the use of the roof spaces as rooms, and long gardens extending behind them. All this is probably correct. A lease of 1670 stipulated that a single-storey house be built in Church Lane 'conformable to the buildings in Belfast', which suggests single-storey buildings were the norm.[20] This might also be supported by the fact that most of the Belfast

94

houses in the hearth-money roll of 1666 paid tax on only one hearth, which is probably more a reflection of the size of the houses than the actual number of hearths.[21] On the Phillips map there are twice as many chimneys as doors on Waring Street, suggesting that each house had two chimneys.

Despite the fact that none of these houses has survived it is possible to reconstruct a little more of the detail of these houses on the basis of analogies with elsewhere.[22] The Belfast picture of terraced single-storey houses with dormer windows and two chimneys corresponds closely to the sort of buildings constructed at Coleraine in the early seventeenth century.[23] One of these survived into the early nineteenth century, when it was recorded by the Ordnance Survey. Like the Belfast houses, this was of frame construction and part of a terrace. It had a central doorway with an entrance hall and rooms to left and right. One of these rooms may well have served as a shop for those engaged in the emerging retail industry. Stairs rose from the rear of the entrance hall to the dormer level, which also had two rooms. There were two hearths at either end of the house with fireplaces at both levels. One difference between the Coleraine houses and those at Belfast was their width. Building plots at Coleraine, at about 12 feet, were much narrower than even a half-burgage share at Belfast. This would have given the Belfast houses a more elongated appearance than those at Coleraine. These houses were not the only type available in Belfast. The Down Survey map, though basic, depicts a number of larger buildings in the Waring Street area. The will of Thomas Waring, who lived there in a house of four hearths, suggests that his house was at least two storeys tall, since he mentions two rooms over a kitchen.[24]

Of some importance in the development of the town was the east end of Waring Street. In comparison to the uniformity of the western part this area, roughly from what is Skipper Street to the Strand, was less regularly laid out. This may represent an eastward extension of the original seventeenth-century planned town. There is little doubt that there was considerable activity in this area after 1660. Excavations at what is now Cotton Court, which would have lain in this area, found seventeenth-century structures, property boundaries, drainage gullies, pits and pottery of the same date

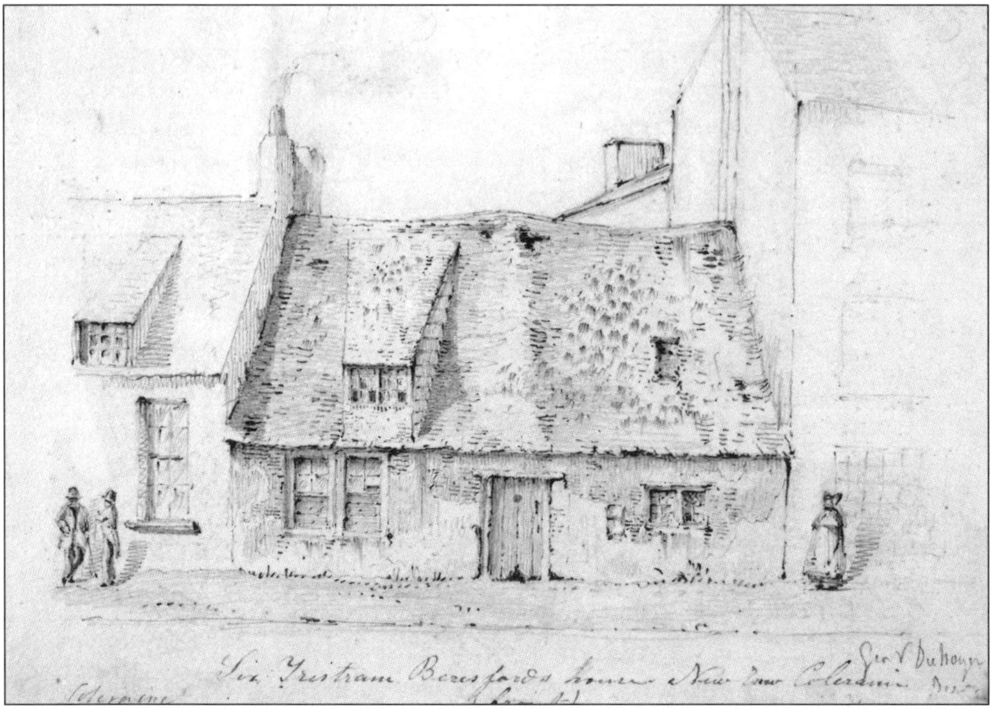
Sir Tristram Beresfords house New Row Coleraine
Coleraine
Geo V Du Noyer

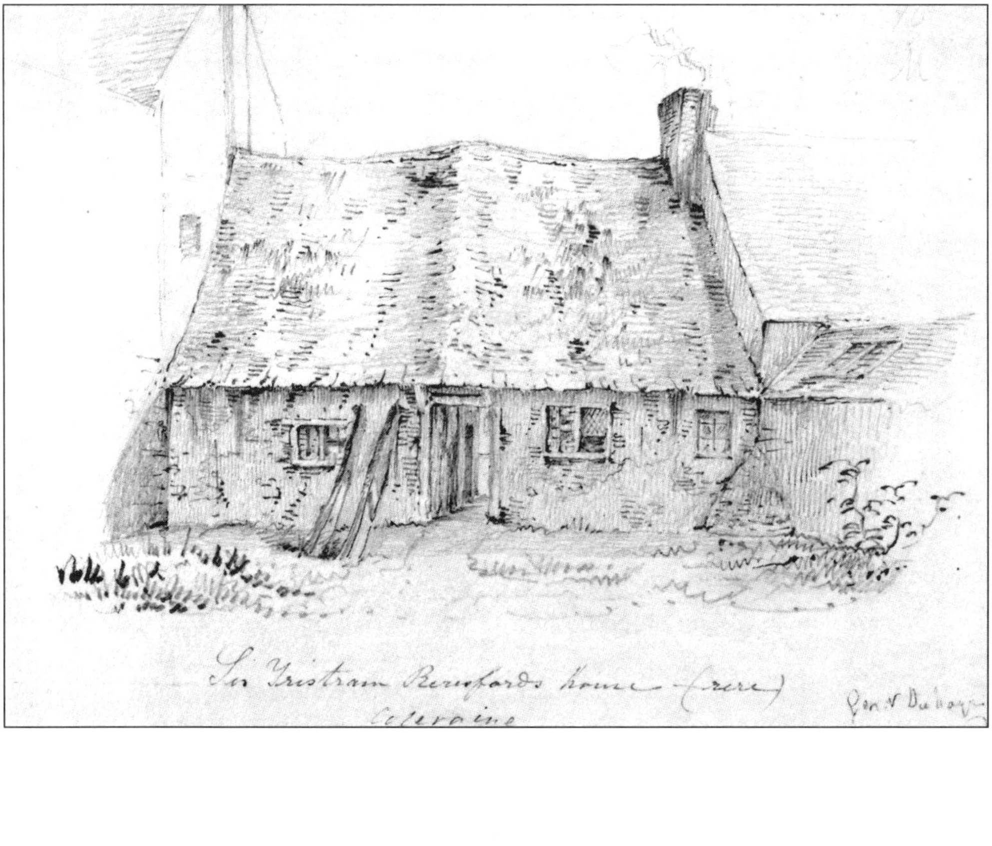
Sir Tristram Beresfords house (rere)
Coleraine
Geo V Du Noyer

(including English, French, German and Dutch pottery as well as local wares), a halfpenny of 1694 and a range of garden deposits.[25]

There were clearly two types of activity at the east end of Waring Street and southwards onto High Street. The first was the development of the port. In the early seventeenth century port facilities appear to have been rather rudimentary. The 1613 charter had allowed the creation of one wharf or quay that seems to have been located at the lower end of High Street, roughly from Skipper Street to the River Lagan. Before the 1630s there was no customs house at Belfast and probably little in the way of warehousing. How much trade passed through the port is uncertain. The only surviving port book for Carrickfergus, that for 1614-15, in which Belfast trade should have been registered contains neither references to the town nor the names of any merchants who can be linked to Belfast.[26] Clearly it required some time for a critical mass of economic activity to develop at Belfast. As trade expanded in the latter part of the seventeenth century there was increasing demand on the port facilities; therefore greater levels of organisation were needed to make the port work. Some innovations were fairly minor. In 1663, for instance, it was complained that empty and full barrels were being left on the street, presumably because of lack of storage space.[27] Other matters were more serious, like keeping clear the channel from the Lagan into the port and the repair of the quay, which was necessary by 1671. By 1675 the demands had changed: the old quay was now to be enlarged substantially, carrying it from the north bank of the Farset to the south bank as well.[28] While the town quay was certainly enlarged, according to a sketch map of Belfast in 1696 another quay had been established by that date on the south side of the river in front of the church.[29] Further work was carried out in 1681 when a number of quarrymen were admitted to the freedom of the town on condition that they provided stone for work at the quay.[30] The response to these problems was to develop the area to the west of Skipper Street as a port area. The buildings on the river front opposite the church are all shown as being without chimneys (apart from the final block). There are also several chimneyless buildings at the Waring Street end of this block. A row of chimneyless

Oppposite: Front and rear views of Tristram Beresford's early-seventeenth-century house at Coleraine, as drawn by the Ordnance Survey in the 1830s. This provides a good model for what the houses in Waring Street may have looked like in the early seventeenth century (Royal Irish Academy, 12 T 6 (40–1)).

Belfast River

Improuement
made out upon
the Strand.

The late seventeenth-century quay at the east end of High Street, Belfast, together with warehousing along the quay and what is probably the customs house (with flag) on Waring Street, from Thomas Phillips's map of 1685.

buildings also appears along Skipper Street, with what appear to be dormer windows, which may be attics for storage or hoists for raising goods. It seems highly likely that these buildings represent warehouse space for the port. Furthermore, this was the location of the customs house. A rough map of Belfast in 1696 also locates the customs house in this area: it may be the large free-standing double-gabled building on the north side of Waring Street that would seem to mark the limit of residential housing. In all probability this was a converted warehouse that was operating as a customs house by 1676. By 1682 this was fully equipped with a beam and scales, tables and an iron chest for money.[31]

The second reason for the growth of this area at the end of Waring Street was the emergence of an industrial quarter here in the late seventeenth century. Unlike in the main body of the town, many of the buildings shown on Phillips's map have outbuildings, which may suggest an industrial function. Excavations in this area, particularly on Hill Street to the north of Waring Street in the late 1980s, revealed rather unusual results. In contrast to the gardens that one might expect to find behind houses and that were recovered by excavation in High Street, there was an area of waste ground on which had accumulated the rubbish of surrounding industries. Much of this was animal bone, predominantly skulls, which seem to have been the by-product of local tanning.[32] Further excavations on Gordon Street recovered quantities of cattle bone, more by-products of tanning, which were subsequently dumped on the Strand.[33] Again, some excavation at Cotton Court suggested that eighteenth-century yards overlay a series of tan pits.[34] There is good documentary evidence for this development in the form of William Waring's activities in this area. William's father Thomas had come to Belfast in the early 1640s as a tanner and by the 1660s, on the basis of the lay subsidy, was one of the richest men in the town. By 1670 he had acquired two tenements from Lord Donegall on Waring Street, probably near Skipper Street. Moreover, he had acquired property on the north side of the street, including tan pits.[35] On this property he was to build houses and, according to a lease of 1701, a 'large brick house' had been constructed on the tan-pits site. This was clearly a substantial industrial location, the 1701 lease stating it to be 228 feet broad by 126 long.[36] This sort of activity may well account for the buildings behind the Strand Gate and those nearly opposite what may be the customs house. This site, therefore, may represent Belfast's earliest industrial complex.

The market house, Cornmarket, directly opposite the castle entrance, as it is represented on Thomas Phillips's map of 1685.

If there is much that is familiar about Phillips's depiction of late-seventeenth-century Belfast, there is also much that is new. A number of buildings, some of considerable significance, had appeared since the 1650s. Of some importance was the new market house and town hall, shown at the junction of High Street and Cornmarket. As discussed in the previous chapter, Belfast had some form of town hall by the late 1630s, probably in or near the marketplace at Bridge Street, but this was probably not a purpose-built structure. By 1663 it had been badly damaged, probably by the Cromwellian garrison in the 1650s, and a cess was to be raised to repair it. This did not prove feasible and in 1663 the sovereign of the town and one of its principal merchants, George Macartney, sublet a new site, which he held from Lord Donegall, to the corporation for a market house and town hall. The lower part of the building was said to be 'cellars', which probably means that it was used for storage. Macartney was said to have 'upon his own charge made a pair of stairs to the house', implying that the upper parts had not been accessible before. This may mean that what was adapted was primarily a warehouse rather than a domestic building. The interior of this upper room was fitted out with benches and the royal arms, the cost of which was levied on the town. In 1668 a new plush cushion was added to the stock of the fashionable accessories of urban government.[37] By 1738 the building was described as 'a very handsome town house, with a charge for the merchants to meet, with a fine room over it where the sessions are held or the town meet together when summons'd by the sovereign on their own affairs'.[38]

It is clear from Phillips's map that much more was spent on the building than the corporation book records. The new town hall was not simply a converted shed. A large tower was built at the corner of High Street and Cornmarket and this was to dominate the town, as is clear from a view of High Street on a token of c. 1730. If Phillips's sense of perspective was correct this was at least as high as

View of Belfast c. 1730, from a token issued by W. Johnston. The view appears to be west along High Street with the sluice bridge at the bottom right. The building with the large tower in the centre is the parish church and the smaller tower to the left is the market house.

the tower of the parish church. It was surmounted by a cupola and appears to have been open on the ground floor. The tower was part of a building plot that ran north–south, as shown on the nineteenth-century maps marking the location of the market house, but the tower does not appear to have been connected to the adjoining building on Cornmarket. None of Phillips's maps shows the feature connected to surrounding buildings, which suggests that this was not a draughtsman's aberration. Towers attached to market houses were becoming fashionable in Ireland during the late seventeenth century. The rebuilding of the tholsel in Dublin between 1676 and 1682 had included such a tower, with cupola, which was 44 feet high, and this had set the standard for other towns.[39] At Derry the 1691 design for a market house included a tower and cupola and at Lisburn in 1708, after the fire, the market house was said to have 'a handsome steeple'.[40] In the case of Belfast, the construction of the tower was not merely fashionable – it also had a practical function. The tower included a ring of bells, which were used to communi-cate with the inhabitants of the town in the same way that church bells did. By the early eighteenth century the bells in the market house were rung for the funerals of prominent citizens and they were probably also used to announce the beginning and end of trading on market days.[41] In 1726 the sovereign assembled the inhabitants of the town for the reading of a letter 'by ringing the town bells'.[42] At Belfast the building behind the tower, which later became known as the market house, was two storeys tall and with-out chimneys, suggesting that it may indeed have originally been a warehouse and probably represents the building leased by Macartney. This building was demolished in 1811 but a single tim-ber dated to the early mid-seventeenth century was recovered from the site during excavations in 2003 and this may indicate the date when the original warehouse was constructed.[43] Those responsible for constructing the market house clearly wanted to make a state-ment in the townscape about the importance of the Restoration corporation of Belfast.

While the architecture of this new building was important, its location was even more so. It was situated opposite the western end of the Waring Street development and hence on the western edge of the built-up area. It is clear that it was built on a green-field site and, apart from the two long buildings without chimneys that appear to be warehouses, Phillips's map shows almost no development to the south of this building. It was also said to be 'next the market place'.[44] This need not mean that the only marketplace in the town was located here. The Bridge Street area, the early seventeenth-century marketplace, is still shown on Phillips's map as an open space with a central two-aisled chimneyless building (which may be interpreted as a warehouse), suggesting the area may still have been used for markets. In the late seventeenth century new market locations were growing up in the town and Cornmarket may have been one of them. Indeed, it may have become one of the main markets for the town. When the contents of the market house were inventoried in 1690 they included the standard measures used for portioning quantities of goods sold in the market.[45] This suggests that this was by then the main trading area. Clearly the market house's location helped to promote the development of such a market in this part of the town. Most importantly, the market house was located directly opposite the main entrance to the castle. The long axis of the building faced the castle, according to a later lease of the site. While the frontage on High Street was 34 feet, that on Cornmarket, opposite the castle, was 91 feet.[46] This marks a shift in the locus of civic authority, and to a lesser extent economic activity, away from the early seventeenth-century core of Waring Street. The tendency, probably linked to the rise of a new merchant community after 1660, was to reassemble an axis of significant buildings on the south side of the Farset from the parish church to the market house and castle, close to the site of the medieval settlement. Such a development was by no means inevitable and in Newtownards, across the Lagan in County Down, at this time the market was moving away from the landlord's house. In 1636, when the market house and market cross were built, they were some way from the landlord's house, whereas the older fair green was beside it.[47]

The erection of an impressive market house and the development of a marketplace at Cornmarket shifted attention onto the south bank of the River Farset and the town began to spread south from its earlier core of Waring Street. By the 1680s, as depicted by Phillips, there were houses similar to those on Waring Street lining this bank of the river, many of which were probably recently built in contrast to the older Waring Street side. Excavations on the gardens at Pottinger's Entry, for instance, produced material that seems to indicate a late-seventeenth-century date for the buildings here.[48] One lease of 1670 may point to the sort of buildings being put up in this area, for example along Church Lane. Church Lane clearly had storehouses – storehouses are mentioned on the lease and represented by small buildings on Phillips's map. On this site of 31 feet frontage (not the normal size of a Belfast burgage plot, which implies that this was a late development) was to be built 'one good handsome English like house with brick or stone or lime walls with oaken roof, [one] storey high conformable to the buildings in Belfast, the said house to be covered with slate, tiles or shingles'.[49] Developing this side of the Farset clearly gave rise to problems caused by flooding from the Blackstaff. Corporation records reveal a much greater concern with the River Farset, and in particular the connections between the two sides, at this time than they had shown before. Such concern is clear from 1664, when the corporation ordered that the banks along the Farset were to be built up with stone, presumably in an attempt to prevent flooding. In the same year Hugh Eccles asked for permission to build a bridge across the Farset to his new house, presumably on the south side of the river.[50] By the time of Phillips's maps four or six bridges – depending on which of the maps is consulted – existed across the Farset. Remains of three of these bridges, built of stone, have been identified and it is possible that the others may have been timber structures.[51] Most are not named but a few, such as Eccles's Bridge and Chads' Bridge, bore the names of prominent Belfast merchants, which suggests that they were responsible for the erection of the bridges.[52]

The arms of the Chads family from the bridge that they constructed across the River Farset (Royal Irish Academy, Du Noyer ix (19)).

The second new feature of late seventeenth-century Belfast's urban life that the Phillips maps cast light on is the emergence of suburbs on the northern and eastern margins of the town. This was not an unusual development as suburbs were developing in Carrickfergus and Derry at the same time. The expansion of these towns took a variety of forms. Firstly, there emerged linear extensions outside the town gates along the roads approaching the towns; and secondly, areas between the walls and the main body of the town that had originally been left as open space were filled in. Both these developments took place at Belfast. Outside the rampart, Phillips's map shows development around the North Gate and at the Mill Gate. Development around the Mill Gate was already under way by 1685, when a lease to George Macartney reveals that houses had already been built there and new tenements had also been 'staked out'.[53] Macartney appears to have sublet one large lease, which he held from Donegall, in a number of standard units measuring 42 feet by 140 feet.[54] However, he did not include any building terms in the subleases and as a result the buildings erected were of rather variable character. Phillips's map depicts a row of houses with gardens, similar to those found in the main town, immediately outside the Mill Gate, while on the other side of the road and beside the terrace are buildings that seem to be more cabin-like, with no gardens and fewer windows and chimneys. A similar variety of buildings is shown outside the North Gate, but

Extramural housing outside the Mill Gate as it appears on Phillips's map of 1685. The manor mill is to the right.

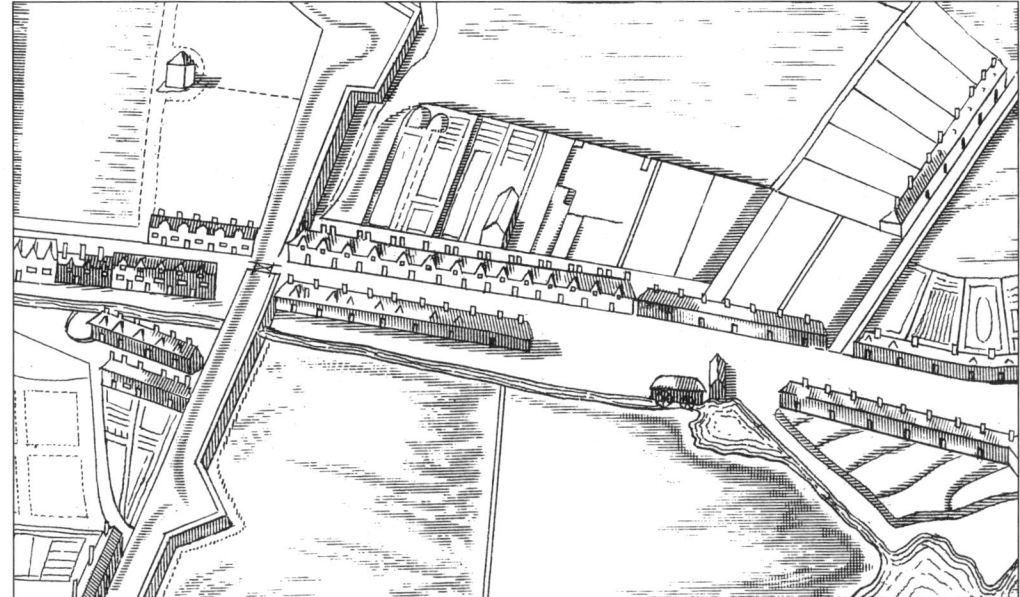

these have much smaller gardens than those associated with houses inside the town. Phillips's depiction of regular, well-laid-out plots here suggests that this, like the development at the Mill Gate, was a planned project rather than random urban sprawl.

The second sort of development occurred inside the rampart. The rampart's construction in 1642 had provided an edge to the town, but a good deal of space had been left between it and the core of the settlement, probably for defensive reasons. Some of this space was important for industrial activities that required large areas of land. Rope making, for instance, depended on being able to lay out long rope walks; these had developed on open land at the edge of Belfast by the 1690s. In other cases, the empty land was used for dumping or butchery. The open area between the east side of North Street and the North Gate was used as a dump and for butchery in the late seventeenth and early eighteenth centuries.[55] In the latter part of the seventeenth century some of this open space was filled in. At the Mill Gate, but inside the rampart, Phillips showed a row of houses constructed in the middle of the wide street, and buildings to the east of Castle Place, which became known as the 'back of the river'. The most significant private development inside the rampart was that of William Waring, who constructed houses on the area behind his tannery, which became known as the Plantation and is represented on Phillips's map as a triangular space with a single entrance from the

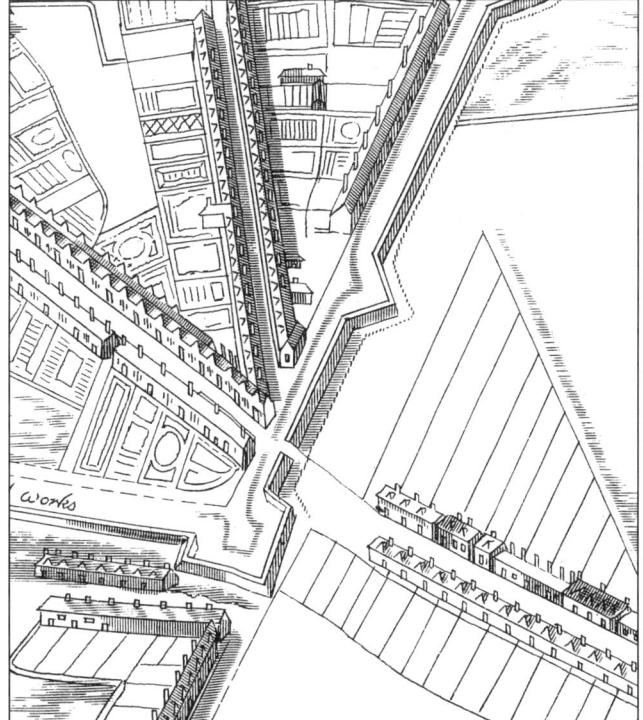

Extramural housing outside the North Gate, 1685

105

Housing filling in the space between the rampart and the beginnings of the
town proper just inside the Mill Gate. This is now represented by the lower end
of Castle Street. There is a variety of styles and types of housing, pointing to the
fact that this was not a planned development.

north. The houses, rather smaller than those of the main town, are
arranged around the space, giving the impression of a self-contained
development.

II

A town of the size Phillips depicted required a much larger and
more sophisticated infrastructure than had been necessary in the
early seventeenth century. It needed fuel, food and building materials on a much greater scale than hitherto. The forges of the smiths
who appear in the freemen's lists needed to be supplied with fuel, as
did private houses. One obvious source of supply was turf from the
surrounding countryside. There was clearly profit to be made in this
trade and in 1674 there were complaints of turf being sold in short
measure by those who brought it into the town.[56] However, relative
to the needs of an expanding settlement, Belfast's hinterland had little in the way of turf or timber for burning, so Belfast depended on
imported coal. Coal was certainly the most common cargo on ships
coming into Belfast in 1685 with almost half the ships entering the
ports carrying coal. According to a 1683 list of imports almost all of
the town's coal came from Scotland, probably Glasgow, although
somewhat more than 10 per cent came from England, either from

Chester or (more likely) from Whitehaven, which was then developing a coal trade with Dublin.[57] Belfast also had to be supplied with food. Archaeological evidence suggests a wide range of meat was eaten, from beef steaks to cheaper cuts suitable for soup and stock. Sheep and rabbit bones have also been found in the High Street excavations.[58] Some of these may have been the by-products of butchers, who are well attested to in the town in the late seventeenth century, preparing meat for export to France, Flanders and Spain. However, more was probably for domestic consumption.

Food came into the town from a number of sources. Locally produced food was sold in the Belfast markets. The original burgage shares in Waring Street and High Street carried with them allocations of land in the town fields, which lay to the south-west of the town, and continued to be mentioned in leases until the eighteenth century. While there is no direct evidence for this, it seems likely that the inhabitants of the town used these lands for the raising of cattle for food. There were also food sales by merchants who purchased supplies in the wider hinterland of the town. From the trade statistics that survive from the 1680s it is clear that the town exported considerable quantities of tallow and hides, both tanned and salted. Beef was also exported, especially to the American colonies.[59] Much of this beef seems to have been brought into the town from the surrounding area of the Lagan Valley and butchered there, the hides and tallow being extracted. Certainly the regulation of butchers' activities was a frequent and contentious matter in the late seventeenth century.[60] The availability of meat for the export trade suggests that some certainly made its way into the domestic market. Analysis of the cattle remains from the excavations at Gordon Street, much of which was dumped by butchers in what was the river shore in the late seventeenth century, suggests that the animals slaughtered in Belfast were of two types. First, there were the remains of young cattle (aged two to three years), which would have produced prime meat, probably for local consumption by the rich. However, the largest group of animals represented were those over ten years old, which provided cheap meat for local use as well as for salting and exporting as barrelled beef.[61] Finally, there was food imported into the city from abroad. Much of this material fell into the class of 'luxury' food items. The port books from Bristol and Chester for the late 1670s and early 1680s reveal a lively trade in such items between those towns and Belfast. Ships imported exotic and expensive wares such as aniseed, figs, currants, raisins, nutmeg and English refined sugar, despite the fact that Belfast had its own sugar refinery by that date. For the discerning not wishing to drink the local beer (made with imported hops), cider was also specially imported.[62] The trade returns of the 1680s confirm this patchy port-book evidence with imports including wine, sugar, raisins, spices and oranges and lemons, all clearly destined for the dining tables of the merchants and gentry of the town. In addition coastal trade from Dublin, in particular, probably brought further luxuries to the town. The growth of the infrastructure for selling food is clear from the proliferation of food markets. In the early part of the century almost everything was sold in the market on Bridge Street. By the 1680s trade had grown to such a scale that meat and other goods were being sold along the streets and new specialist butchers' shambles had to be established in Castle Street.[63] Clearly, moving cattle from the Bridge Street market made living in the centre of Belfast a good deal more tolerable and healthy. By the 1690s hides and tallow were to be sold only on Castle Street, implying that other items were sold elsewhere.[64]

Food and fuel were only two of the products that the town needed. A supply of clean drinking water was a necessity. Some seventeenth-century Ulster towns, such as Derry and Downpatrick, solved this problem by using local springs. Others were less fortunate. At Moneymore the landlords, the Drapers' Company, had ambitiously installed an expensive piped water supply for their small town by 1616 but it had limited effect.[65] In 1676 Lisburn had also explored the possibility of establishing a piped water supply.[66] Belfast, like Carrickfergus, was situated on salt water. By 1648 Carrickfergus had solved the problem of a water supply by channelling water in wooden pipes from the surrounding countryside to a town pump.[67] As long as Belfast remained small, *ad hoc* arrangements could be made. There were several springs close to the town, such as one described by Richard Dobbs in the 1680s:

in the west suburbs of Belfast, in a back side, between

the mill and the common pond, was a small weak spring
which I have drank of […] it looked like white wine and
had not the taste of water.[68]

As the town grew and pollution of surrounding streams became a
problem a more effective water supply was required. In 1678 two
Belfast merchants, George Macartney and Robert Leathes, proposed
to establish a piped water scheme for the town.[69] The proposal
involved taking water from the tuck-mill dam, which lay at the east
side of Barrack Street, and piping it 200 Irish perches (1,280 metres)
to the Great Bridge of Belfast, now the site of the Boyne Bridge.
Wooden water pipes made in sections of 10–14 inches with a diam-
eter of 4.5 inches have been excavated in this area. The pipes were
joined by inserting the end of one length, which had been tapered,
into a socket in the second length. The socket was strengthened by
bands of iron whose inner edge had been sharpened. The joint was
then smeared with white lead.[70] At the Great Bridge of Belfast there
was to be a common conduit that ran into the town. All this, it was
estimated, would cost £250 and would be paid for by subscription.
The scheme as it evolved provides a little more detail. The wooden
pipes, bound with iron, carried the water underground from the
dam to a water house; then three conduits 'standing in the streets'
delivered the water into the town, all of which cost £175.
Subscriptions fell short and the scheme had to be funded by an
assessment on the town.[71]

The development of this physical infrastructure was paralleled by
the need for a more effective form of urban government to manage
the growing town. The charter of 1613 remained the framework for
urban government but it had been designed for a modest settlement
controlled by a landlord, not a rapidly expanding town. Moreover, it
was now clear that Belfast had overtaken its rival, Carrickfergus, and
was now the most important town in County Antrim. Such anom-
alies were recognised by some in the Dublin administration. In 1675
Lord Lieutenant Essex mentioned 'the trade and condition of some
towns here being now very much altered from what they were at
the time of the granting of their former charters, as particularly
Belfast and some others'.[72] The sort of problems resulting from the
expansion of the town that had to be dealt with were numerous.

One example was the problem of representation on the corporation. The number of burgesses had been limited by the charter to
twelve and they were to serve for life. This meant that there were
few opportunities to rise to this level. Between 1660 and 1669 the
unusually high number of nine new burgesses were appointed while
in the three succeeding decades four, seven and seven appointments
were made. With the number of freemen increasing in the town a
smaller proportion could aspire to the rank of burgess of the town.
This was little to do with representative government and everything
to do with the display of wealth and status by the newly rich mercantile community of Belfast. To persist in excluding those who
regarded themselves as an elite for local administration would create
problems for the future.

Possibilities for reform were offered in 1666, when government
proposed to issue new charters to towns, and Belfast began raising
money to promote a new charter for itself.[73] In the event nothing
came of the proposal, although Carrickfergus also wished to sur-
render its charter, but that did not prevent Belfast Corporation,
apparently with Lord Donegall's agreement, drawing up ten proposals for reform of the charter in 1671.[74] Many of the issues
addressed here were familiar ones that could be traced back to the
early seventeenth century. The problem of the provision of an
income for the corporation surfaced as a request for charges to be
levied on shipping using the quays of the town, as in other places
such as Drogheda, to provide an urban income. Corporation finance
was a problem of long standing but it was made even worse in 1667
by the allocation of grand-jury fines from the corporation to the
sovereign, thus eliminating one of the few sources of income the
corporation had possessed.[75] In other cases existing customs providing income, such as the payment of gate tolls for the market, made
possible by the building of the walls and gates in the 1640s, and customary duties from butchers, were to be confirmed. However, most
significant was the request for the creation of a grand jury of the
corporation to inquire into misdemeanours and to deal with roads
and bridges within the corporation-controlled area. This was tanta-
mount to a request that the town be removed from the jurisdiction
of the grand jury of County Antrim and established as a county

structure in its own right. Part of the explanation of this demand was that Belfast was probably aping Carrickfergus, which was a county with its own jurisdiction, both criminal and civil. In reality, however, what was being asked for was a legitimation of existing practice. In the 1640s a grand jury of Belfast is first mentioned in the corporation book and the idea was revived in the 1660s.[76]

The scheme to issue new charters to towns was never carried into effect and the problems identified by the corporation remained. However, at least some of the proposals of the corporation did produce a result. In 1674 Lord Donegall in his capacity as water bailiff granted the same office to the sovereign of the town. The associated table of the duties of the water bailiff made it clear that the corporation now had the right to levy charges on ships using the port but equally had a duty to create a port infrastructure.[77]

One other agent of local administration emerged in the late seventeenth century, partly as a result of the economic expansion of Belfast: a system of guilds. While in most towns the guild system was much weakened in the late seventeenth century it appears only to have been established in Belfast and Carrickfergus at that point. Carrickfergus had a shoemakers' guild by 1674 and a tailors' and glovers' guild by 1680.[78] It is more difficult to be precise about developments in Belfast but by 1674 it is possible to see the tailors in the town acting together to defend their trading rights.[79] This may indicate some early form of guild activity. By 1722 there was a well-organised guild structure in Belfast. In that year funeral cloaks were hired from the Presbyterian church by 'the captain of the tailors, the captain of the bakers and the captain of the shoemakers'.[80] It is likely that these sort of occupational associations emerged in the late seventeenth century as trade grew and became more specialised within the town.

III

The growth of late seventeenth-century Belfast was not dependent on the initiative of the Chichester family as landlords of the town. Indeed, the evidence points to the fact that the family was becoming increasingly mired in debt, with little surplus capital to support its burgeoning offspring. The estate had been undercapitalised from

the beginning but the actions of the first earl of Donegall compounded the problem. At his death in 1675, and after three mar-
riages, he was survived by one daughter and a grandson by another
daughter. The earl chose not to leave his property to his nephew,
who inherited the title, but divided the estate among his daughters
and their children and also made generous provision for his friends.
The second earl immediately contested the will and after he died in
1678 his son took up the legal fight, which was not resolved until
1692. The settlement was an expensive one, even apart from the
legal costs incurred. The second earl had also left a costly will, antic-
ipating success in the legal battle. At the beginning of the eighteenth
century debts incurred in the 1670s remained unpaid.[81] The family
had little time or money to invest in the development of Belfast.

When it did come, funding for Belfast's development was not
from the landlord but from mercantile capital. While some seventeenth-century Belfast merchants such as Thomas Knox and
William Anderson invested the profits of trade in Irish landed
estates, most did not. Before the 1690s little Irish land came on the
market and one Belfast merchant, Robert Johnston, had to acquire
a plantation in the exotic location of Antigua.[82] A few others, such
as the Legg family, acquired what can only be described as large
farms, in Legg's case at Malone, from the Donegall family, on which
they built splendid houses. This ensured that, unlike that of Cork,
the Belfast merchant community was a cohesive body whose mem-
bership changed little over time. Despite this there was a good relationship between landowners and merchants and the latter often
recruited apprentices from among the younger sons of the former.[83]
Mercantile profits, in the main, had to be utilised in other ways and
a portion of these went into the town. In the case of the merchant
George Macartney, some resources went into urban improvements
such as the market house or the provision of piped water for Belfast.
Motives were not always philanthropic, however. A prosperous-
looking and well-appointed town encouraged trade in a way that a
run-down one did not. There were also practical reasons for diver-
sification. Most of the Belfast trade was highly seasonal. The butter
trade, for instance, ran from the spring to the autumn while the barrelled beef trade concentrated on the cattle killing season in
the autumn. To deal with this situation Belfast merchants had to

diversify their interests into others branches of trade and into other economic spheres. Moreover given the very stable nature of the merchant community in Belfast investing in the town was the same as investing in one's family, who could be presumed to remain in town for several generations.

It is possible to trace the rise of other new industrial activities in the town, all funded by mercantile money. Shipbuilding, for instance, had probably been carried on in the town in a small way in the early seventeenth century but by 1663 four substantial ships trading from the port had been built there. More common were the small gabbards of 6–16 tons, used to offload goods from ships anchored at the pool of Garmoyle, of which there were 11 operating in the port in 1663.[84] It was not unknown for even these small ships to put to sea and in 1691 such gabbards were transporting horses from Belfast to Scotland and they were probably also used in the coastal trade with Derry and Dublin.[85] Shipbuilding presumably developed in the late seventeenth century and material to outfit a ship being built at Belfast was imported from Ayr in 1680.[86] Very prominent in this world of industrial activity was George Macartney. The geographical and financial scale of Macartney's trading operations allowed him to diversify into a wide range of activities. It was Macartney, for instance, who established the sugar works at the west end of Waring Street, probably on or near what became known as Sugar House Entry in the eighteenth century.[87] Macartney was also responsible for the development of milling. By the 1690s he had established four mills along the line of the Farset on Mill Street. All four were corn mills, presumably set up to grind flour for local consumption. A tuck mill had previously stood on the site and a new one was to be constructed, suggesting that the manufacture of wool was taking place, possibly financed by Macartney, in or near Belfast.[88]

What funded most of this industrial and infrastructural development was the expansion of Belfast's trade in the late seventeenth century. Before the 1630s Carrickfergus had been the main port in the south Antrim area and controlled the customs. This, according to a note by a resident of Belfast in the 1630s, led to considerable inconvenience:

When Carrickfergus was constituted a port in this kingdom there was hardly a house in Belfast except Lord Chichester's castle. Afterwards his lordship coming there to live, several British families did come to settle, upon which, for the good of the English interest his lordship did prevail with King James of blessed memory who gave it a charter. It had few or no merchants trading beyond seas. Now by the encouragement of the earl of Donegall that now is and the industry, with God's blessing, upon the endeavours of the merchants of this corporation the trade exported and imported at Belfast is at least 7 parts of the whole customs and excise that are taken at the port of Carrickfergus. But the customs house at Carrickfergus being eight long Irish miles distant from Belfast the merchants and traders to Belfast are much discouraged to trade, for at the arrival of any ship or boat, be it never so small, the master and merchant must go from Belfast to Carrickfergus, to present the ship and to make entry of the goods and pay the duty there, which occasioned great loss of time, beside the hazard of the ship, which the master must leave to perform that duty which the law enjoins him to do. This causes delays often of two or three days.[89]

In 1638 Lord Deputy Wentworth forced Carrickfergus Corporation to sell the customs rights back to the government.[90] At some point after this, but certainly before 1662, Belfast acquired the right to collect its own customs.[91] This privilege undoubtedly encouraged ships to use the port and this, combined with a dramatic improvement in economic conditions in the late seventeenth century, created a trade boom in Belfast. The scale of the expansion is clear from comparing the Carrickfergus port book of 1614–15 with that for Belfast in 1685. In the year 1614–15 forty-four vessels entered the port of Carrickfergus while 247 entered Belfast in 1685, of which eighty-two totalling 3,228 tons were said to be from the town.[92]

The expansion of trade occurred on a number of levels. First, Belfast emerged as a local market for the surrounding area that was undergoing an economic boom. Since towns can only survive when a surplus is available in the surrounding countryside the growth of agricultural output in the area around Belfast made the growth of the town possible. The trading area can be measured in a number of ways. Belfast apprentices, for instance, came from a wide area. The grandson of Andrew Rowan at Clogh in Antrim was apprenticed to a Belfast merchant in 1708 and Rowan himself certainly visited the town.[93] More revealing are the merchants' tokens found in excavations in High Street in the 1850s. These came from Carrickfergus (2), Holywood (1), Bangor (1), Lisburn (4), Antrim town (3), Lurgan (1), Dromore (2), Dungannon (1), Monaghan town (1), Drogheda (1), Waterford city (1) and Dublin (1).[94] Late seventeenth-century Belfast tokens have also been found in Carrickfergus.[95] This points to a wide local trading role for Belfast. At least some of the goods gathered as a result of the local role were then internationally traded. By the 1680s Belfast's export trade was larger than that of any other Ulster port and was based mainly on butter, beef and hides. In the late 1690s William Sacheverell commented of Belfast that 'the quantity of butter and beef which it sends into foreign parts is almost incredible. I have seen barrels piled up in the very streets.'[96] This substantial trade was carried on not with only England and Scotland but with continental Europe and the North American colonies. In fact, the vast bulk of the beef and butter exported from Belfast went to France and Flanders, with Spain next in importance. Some may not have gone directly. The French ship *Mary* in 1700 called at Belfast for tallow and hides before proceeding to Scotland to complete the cargo before sailing to Bordeaux.[97] More than half the vessels leaving Belfast were engaged in the European or North American trade, again perhaps using an English port to clear before sailing to the colonies.[98] In 1675 the Belfast merchant Lewis Thompson identified tanned leather, skins, beef, butter, tallow, salmon, wool and linen cloth as being Belfast's main exports, being shipped to London, Bristol and Ostend as well as ports in Spain, Flanders, Scotland, Holland, Virginia and New England.[99]

The port books of Bristol, Liverpool and Chester from the late 1670s and early 1680s reveal that in exchange for agricultural produce, skins and linen-yarn imports were brought back to Belfast in the small ships that took the town's exports to those ports. Some of those imports were purely practical. The barrelled-beef trade on which Belfast depended for its livelihood needed salt, and that was not made locally before the 1750s. Thus large volumes of salt imports, mainly from Liverpool, became an important part of the trade.[100] Equally significant, and with a wider appeal, were the quantities of 'English earthenware' that were carried from Chester and Bristol to Belfast. Excavation evidence from Waring Street confirms the importance of pottery from the hinterland of these ports in the life of the town. North Devon ware, Bristol ware and Blackwares from Buckley (to the south-east of Chester) made up the bulk of the pottery found on excavations, although some French and Dutch ware was also recorded.[101] As well as pottery, glass was imported in varying forms, reflecting the lack of a local source. Imports of English bottles, drinking glasses and chests of window glass, which reveal the demand created by the significant building activity in Belfast, are all represented among Belfast imports in the port books.[102]

Imports sucked into Belfast with the growth of trade affected almost every aspect of daily life and shaped the appearance of the town. People wore clothes made of imported fustians, cambrics, calicoes or fine holland linen and men wore imported stockings. They used whips, bridles and bellows, ate from imported pewter and hunted with gunpowder or shot that had all been imported into Belfast from Bristol or Chester. However, what is most striking about this growth in the volume and range of imports is the high level of luxury goods in the trade, reflecting the growing prosperity of Belfast and its hinterland. One example is the high volume of manufactured silk (mainly for clothes) and raw silk that was being brought into the town.[103] Among the most significant of these luxury goods was tobacco, which had to be imported since it could not be produced locally. Belfast and its hinterland consumed large quantities of this expensive luxury, mainly imported through Bristol. In 1678 alone Bristol ships carried almost 160,000 pounds of tobacco into Belfast.[104] Some of this was then distributed across Ulster by provincial merchants or even pedlars and a number of 'chapmen' are noted as becoming free of Belfast in the 1670s.[105] From 1675 tobacco spinners became increasingly common among the freemen of Belfast. Much of the imported tobacco was smoked in Belfast. With the tobacco hundreds of thousands of clay pipes for smoking it were imported into the town and these have been found in excavations, suggesting that they were used there.[106] For some at least in the late seventeenth century Belfast was an affluent provincial town.

This expansion of Belfast's trade was linked to developments in other areas. It had an adverse effect on Carrickfergus – in 1678, in an attempt to reverse the decline in trade there, the corporation agreed that no tolls would be collected at the Carrickfergus fairs.[107] But by contrast, the towns along the Lagan Valley that acted as feeders for the port of Belfast benefited from its growth in trade. By 1679 Belfast merchants had established agents at Lurgan, Moira and Dromore to buy butter for export.[108] From Antrim the notebook of Rev. Andrew Rowan at Clogh shows that butter was traded from this area to Belfast and sugar and chairs were acquired in return.[109] One of the greatest beneficiaries of the growth of Belfast's influence was Lisburn. In 1660 Lisburn returned 357 poll-tax payers, perhaps representing a population of 900. By 1725 there were 787 houses in the town, probably representing some 3,935 people.[110] Measures of economic activity such as token issues or market tolls also show significant increases in the late seventeenth century.[111] Not all of this can be attributed to the prosperity of Belfast but as George Macartney wrote to George Rawdon, the landlord's agent at Lisburn, 'if our town prosper your town of Lisburn certainly must, for one depends on the welfare of the other'.[112] Scottish merchants from Belfast were certainly said to have encouraged the trade at Lisburn in 1679 and excavations at the castle gardens there have found pottery from England, Germany and Holland in a late seventeenth-century context, all of which probably came through Belfast.[113] Further down the Lagan Valley, Lurgan also benefited from the marketing structures provided by Belfast. Here population also grew dramatically, with a significant surplus of baptisms over burials; consequently, rents in the town increased and plots were subdivided to accommodate more residents. Like in Lisburn, some of the economic activity here was fed by local influences, especially the landlord Arthur Brownlow, but the stimulus provided by Belfast merchants was also important.[114]

The expansion of this trade made effective communications more important than hitherto. As trade volumes increased packhorses became less satisfactory as ways of moving large volumes of goods and carts became more common. For carts, and larger wagons, fords were not very suitable for crossing rivers and hence in the late

The Long Bridge, from a sketch by Mary Delany, 1755. The tower to
the left is that of the parish church and the buildings are part of Isaac
Macartney's development at Hanover Square including the new customs
house, discussed in the next chapter (National Gallery of Ireland).

seventeenth century the Lagan Valley and its surrounding area saw
an explosion of bridge building with stone bridges, such as that at
Shaw's Bridge built near Belfast in the 1650s, replacing older
fords.[115] In that context the main weakness in Belfast's communications network was the link to County Down, then served only by
the main ford and perhaps some smaller crossing points. Settlements
had developed around the ford – most obviously the town of
Belfast, but probably also on the ford's southern side. The 1616 will
of the north-Down landowner Sir James Hamilton had bequeathed
money for the establishment of a number of schools, including one
'at the ford of Belfast'. This can only be understood to relate to the
County Down side of the ford, where Hamilton's lands lay and
where some sort of settlement presumably existed.[116] However, the
ford posed a problem for shipping. One alternative was a ferry service between Ballymacarret and Belfast, which had been established
by 1624.[117] This proved of limited value in moving goods and in
1680 George Macartney proposed that a bridge should be built

across the Lagan linking Antrim and Down. The earl of Donegall was keen on the proposal but the earl of Clanbrassill on the County Down side was not, presumably because it would interfere with the ferry rights. The grand jury provided £500 for the bridge, which would cost £1,600, leaving the remainder to be raised by subscription among the gentry of Antrim and Down.[118] The resulting structure was a 21-arched bridge spanning the River Lagan at 2,562 feet. To understand the significance of this edifice it is worth comparing Belfast with other towns that were separated from part of their hinterland by significant rivers. In the case of Waterford there was no bridge across the River Suir to link the town with County Kilkenny until 1794, and at Derry no bridge crossed the River Foyle until 1789–91. Only Limerick with its 13-arched medieval bridge comes close to the sort of structure that was built at Belfast. The Long Bridge was thus a very early example of bridge building on this scale, a fact that highlights its importance to the evolution of the town. The bridge was influential in another way, since it ensured that ships even modest in size could not proceed any further upstream on the tidal Lagan. As such it served to concentrate the activities of the port around the mouth of the Farset, promoting the building of further quays in this area in the eighteenth century.

IV

In the late seventeenth century Belfast grew prosperous. Much of that prosperity was created by Scottish merchants who, because of their Presbyterian background, were uneasy with the Dublin administration and the established Church of Ireland. As the earl of Arran commented in the 1680s, the town was 'as fanatic a one as any in Ireland'.[119] Moreover, as Irish towns rushed to congratulate Charles II for surviving a series of plots in the early 1680s, Belfast refused to do so. The town's Presbyterians regarded Charles's Catholic sympathies with great suspicion.[120] However, in February 1685, as a new Catholic king – James II – ascended the throne, Belfast Corporation relented. They sent him a loyal address signed by the sovereign, the burgesses and 126 inhabitants of the town.[121] Not all were pleased with the arrangement and one man in Belfast tore down the proclamation of James's accession, although he later claimed to have been drunk at the time.[122] James initially tried to conciliate his new Protestant subjects. Others, notably the new lord deputy, the earl of Tyrconnell, moved the regime onto a more radical footing. The army was becoming increasingly Catholic and Catholic soldiers were billeted to Belfast. In 1687, along with other Irish towns, the charter of Belfast was called in – a move resisted by the corporation, but to no avail. A new charter was issued, to take effect in October 1688.[123]

For some, the new charter had attractions including the breaking of the Donegall family's power over the corporation. Others were more ambivalent. Of the 35 burgesses appointed 18 were Catholic; of the remainder 11 or 12 were Presbyterian, including some of the old corporation. For those excluded, perhaps the most satisfying act of the dying days of the old corporation was the refusal of a request that the Catholic soldiers in the town should have the use of the Donegall schoolhouse beside the parish church for the celebration of Mass.[124]

The new corporation, which took control of the town in 1688, had a difficult task ahead. Economic problems combined with a political crisis in England (in which William III ousted James II) meant that conditions in Ireland were degenerating rapidly. During 1688 merchants began to flee Belfast to Whitehaven in England and to Scotland.[125] Until the middle of 1689 James II continued to issue proclamations urging them to return.[126] Later allegations were made against many members of this new corporation, especially the sovereign, the Presbyterian Thomas Pottinger, claiming that they had supported the Jacobite regime in its last days. In reality, what they had attempted to do, with much success, was to minimise the local disorder evident in many parts of Ulster and to maintain the fabric of the town.[127] As James II and his army arrived at Derry in April 1689 and the second siege began, it seemed that Ulster was lurching towards civil war. Most of those in Belfast had little doubt on which side their sympathies lay and they declared for William III. The Belfast merchant Henry Chad, then in Glasgow, supplied the Williamite loyalists at Belfast with arms through the spring and summer of 1689.[128] While the Jacobite force withdrew from Belfast, it continued to occupy nearby Carrickfergus. In August 1689, when

a Williamite force under the command of Marshal Schomberg finally landed near Bangor, Belfast was a well-established Williamite centre. Given his need to capture Carrickfergus, the local strong point,
Schomberg quickly established his main base at Belfast.
Carrickfergus fell after a short siege on 28 August 1689 and the following day Schomberg and his forces entered Belfast.

The attention the Williamite forces brought on Belfast was not
necessarily welcome. While some of the merchants who had fled in
1688 may well have returned, the town did not have the resources
to quarter a considerable military force. Grain, for instance, had to
be imported into Belfast from Glasgow in some quantities in 1690
to feed both the army and civilian population.[129] Moreover, armies
brought disease as well as disruption and the establishment of the
military hospital at Belfast placed the town at considerable risk. The
Williamite army chaplain George Story remembered that at Belfast
he had 'sometimes stood on the street and seen ten or a dozen
corpses of the townspeople go by in little more than half an hour'.
In all, he reckoned 3,762 men died there in the winter of
1689–90.[130] Disease, combined with the normal activities of soldiers
encamped with limited occupation, made the winter of 1689–90 a
difficult one in Belfast. With the spring, however, came the opening
of the campaigning season. In June 1690 William III himself arrived
at Carrickfergus, from where he travelled to Belfast. There, according to one account, 'the streets were filled with bonfires and fire-
works'.[131] After four days in Belfast he pressed southward with the
army toward the final defeat of James II at the battle of the Boyne
in July. To celebrate the return of normality the town clerk copied
the charter of James I to Belfast into the corporation book, under-
lining the fact that it had triumphed over the abortive charter of
James II.[132]

V

Belfast, in contrast to other towns, survived the Williamite wars well.
Newry had been virtually flattened and in 1706 the damage caused
by the siege at Derry could still be seen.[133] Belfast's trade was gradually re-established after the war, with the customs yield from
exports growing from £201 in 1689 to almost £770 in 1693 and

to £874 by 1709.[134] Perhaps the most severe structural damage was that to the Long Bridge. In 1738 one man recalled a story that had been told to him of one John Egan of Rush, coming over the bridge with a cart of sand to sell in the town:

> as he came to the seat of the first arch, the arch fell behind him and so on, as he got from one arch the arch fell in behind him and so on for seven. This happened in the year 1692/3, for a little before this Frederick, duke of Schomberg, landed at the time of the late Revolution. He marched from thence to Belfast drawing his canon [sic] over the bridge. Soon after a ship drove against it and shook these arches which I suppose was the occasion of this odd story.[135]

Apart from this mishap Belfast thrived. One commentator in the 1690s was able to observe that 'Belfast is now counted the second place of trade in Ireland yet the Scotch merchants are spread unto all other trading places of that kingdom and are made magistrates in their turn'; another noted that the town was 'rich and numerous' and certainly by the late 1690s trade had recovered to the levels of the mid 1680s.[136]

That prosperity, even in the wake of war, was built on the foundations of the expansion of trade in the late seventeenth century. In the 1630s the tithes of the parish of Shankill, in which Belfast lay, were reckoned to be worth £50, while by 1713 the income was said to be worth £180 a year.[137] The physical growth of the town and its infrastructure also provides powerful evidence for its increasing wealth. This does not mean that it was a pleasant place to live. It was an active and busy port. The corporation complained about the dirt of the streets and the dangers associated with the timber and empty barrels that littered the quay and attempts were made to make people sweep the area in front of their houses.[138] Trading goods also brought unwelcome visitors. The Belfast merchant Isaac Macartney advised one Lisburn customer not to bring his cheese to Belfast until it was ready for export as it would be 'much abused by rats which are very numerous here all the town over'.[139] Ships might bring other unwelcome visitors as in 1666, the year after the outbreak of plague in London, when Lord Donegall forbade the unloading of a ship from Ostend for fear that the plague then raging there would be brought to Belfast.[140] However, there were initiatives to make town life endurable. The expansion of Belfast in all directions and the arrangements for feeding, heating and providing drinking water all point to the increasing wealth and sophistication of its inhabitants. Yet, that wealth did not appear by magic. Belfast's prosperity was the creation of a merchant community who began to identify with the town in which they lived, becoming part of its government and investing in its appearance. In that sense the late seventeenth century saw the emergence of a community as much as a merchant group.

NOTES

1 Young, *Town book*, p. 79.
2 Ibid., pp 85–7.
3 Ibid., pp 87–8.
4 *Cal. S.P. dom, 1660–1*, p. 174.
5 Young, *Historical notices*, pp 127–38.
6 Séamus Pender (ed.), *A census of Ireland c. 1659* (Dublin, 1939), pp 5, 8, 20, 25, 29, 93, 94, 145.
7 *Cal. S.P. Ire. 1663–5*, pp 460-1; *Cal. S.P. Ire. 1666–9*, pp 672–3. In both cases the customs figures are ascribed to Carrickfergus but since Belfast had replaced Carrickfergus, as discussed below, this must be seen simply as administrative inertia and the return should be read as relating to Belfast. A similar situation exists with English port books of the late seventeenth century which record Carrickfergus when Belfast is meant.
8 Falkiner, *Illustrations*, p. 422–3.
9 For a commentary on these maps, see *Belfast atlas*, p. 37.
10 Young, *Historical notices*, pp 155–6.
11 William Sacheverell, *An account of the Isle of Man ... with a voyage to I Columb Kill* (London, 1703), p. 125.
12 Trevor Carleton (ed.), *Heads and hearths* (Belfast, 1991), pp 37, 51.
13 *Excavations 1998*, pp 33–4; *Excavations 2003*, pp 8–9. For further context see Terence Reeves-Smyth, 'Irish gardens and gardening before Cromwell' in *Medieval Ireland: The Barryscourt lectures i–x* (Kinsale, 2004), pp 121–31.
14 Benn, *History* (1877), p. 292.
15 Sacheverell, *Account of the Isle of Man*, p. 125.
16 P.R.O.N.I., DIO 4/23/1/4.
17 Richard Mant, *History of the Church of Ireland from the Revolution to the Union* (London, 2840), pp 97–8.
18 Agnew, *Belfast merchant families*, p. 64, note 12; P.R.O.N.I., D501/1, p. 196.
19 P.R.O.N.I., D509/13; Registry of Deeds, Dublin, 7/305/2456.
20 P.R.O.N.I., D509/25.
21 Benn, *History* (1877), pp 741–5.

22   Fragments of some of these buildings may have survived into the nineteenth century as outhouses. One photograph of 1896 of McGlades yard in North Street (P.R.O.N.I., T1129/295) shows a timber-framed structure at the lower level of one building. This was demolished shortly afterwards.

23   Philip Robinson, 'Some late survivals of box framed "plantation" houses in Coleraine, Co. Londonderry' in *U.J.A.*, 3rd ser., xlvi (1983), pp 129–36.

24   Benn, *History* (1877), p. 250.

25   *Excavations 1999*, p. 2; *Excavations 2002*, pp 4–5.

26   Leeds District Archives, Leeds, TN/PO7/1/1(3).

27   Young, *Town book*, pp 97–8.

28   Ibid., pp 119, 134.

29   *Belfast atlas*, map 6.

30   Young, *Town book*, p. 286.

31   Benn, *History* (1877), pp 329–31; *Cal. treasury books, 1693-6*, p. 781.

32   Mallory and McNeill, *Archaeology of Ulster* (Belfast, 1991), pp 316–17.

33   Ó Baoill and Logue, 'Excavations at Gordon Street', p. 133.

34   *Excavations 2001* p. 2.

35   Benn, *History* (1877), pp 283–4; Agnew, *Belfast merchant families*, pp 249–50.

36   P.R.O.N.I., T811/1, p. 546.

37   Young, *Town book*, pp 100–03, 113.

38   Paterson, 'Belfast in 1738', p. 119.

39   Raymond Gillespie, 'Describing Dublin; Francis Place's visit, 1698–1699' in Adele Dalsimer (ed.), *Visualising Ireland* (Winchester MA., 1993), p. 110.

40   Brett, *Court houses*, pp 33, 86.

41   Benn, *History* (1877), pp 580, 581.

42   Young, *Town book*, p. 329.

43   *Excavations 2003*, p. 3.

44   Young, *Town book*, p. 101.

45   Benn, *History* (1877), p. 224.

46   Benn, *History* (1880), p. 118.

47   Trevor McCavery, *Newtown: a history of Newtownards* (Dundonald, 1994), pp 58, 80.

48   Ann Hamlin and Chris Lynn (eds), *Pieces of the past* (Belfast, 1988), p. 80.

49   P.R.O.N.I., D509/25.

50   Young, *Town book*, p. 99.

51   Grainger, 'Results of excavations', p. 113.

52   For Chads' Bridge see Young, *Town book*, p. 187. A stone with an inscription describing it as Chads' Bridge is now in the Ulster Museum.

53   Benn, *History* (1877), p. 285.

54   P.R.O.N.I., D271/2.

55   Cormac McSparron, 'Excavations at Church Street, Belfast' in *U.J.A.*, 3rd ser., lxiii (2004), p. 118; Young, *Town book*, p. 97.

56   Ibid., p. 133.

57   British Library, Add. MS 4759, ff 1–14.

58   Hamlin and Lynn, *Pieces of the past*, p. 81.

59   British Library, Add. MS 4759, ff 1–7.

60   Young, *Town book*, pp 97, 136–7, 154, 181, 185.

61   Ó Baoill and Logue, 'Excavations at Gordon Street', pp 32–3.

62   T.N.A., E190/1138/1, ff 34v, 189; E190/1324/10, f. 53; E190/1139/3, ff 56, 65–6; E190/1344/6, ff 14v, 15, 18, 19v; E190/1345/13, ff 4v, 11, 14v; E190/1341/3, ff 11v, 19v; E190/1140/3, ff 7, 10v, 64, 74.

63   Young, *Town book*, p. 154.

64 Ibid., p. 186.
65 T.W. Moody, *The Londonderry plantation* (Belfast, 1939), pp 302–6.
66 Raymond Gillespie, 'George Rawdon's Lisburn' in *Lisburn Historical Society Journal*, viii (1991), p. 33.
67 Robinson, *Carrickfergus*, p. 12.
68 Hill, *The Macdonnells of Antrim*, p. 383.
69 Young, *Town book*, pp 138–9.
70 A. McI. Clelland, 'Old wooden water pipes' in *Irish Naturalists' Journal*, vi (1937), p. 261, Pl. 16.
71 Young, *Town book*, pp 149–52.
72 *Letters written by his excellency Arthur Capel, earl of Essex* (London, 1770), pp 32–3; *Cal. S.P. dom. 1675–6*, p. 50.
73 Young, *Town Book*, p. 107.
74 P.R.O.N.I., T707, p. 92; Young, *Town book*, pp 118–9.
75 Young, *Town Book*, p. 148.
76 Young, *Town Book*, pp 40, 100, 117, 148, 172, 189.
77 Young, *Town book*, pp 12–17.
78 Gillespie, *Colonial Ulster*, p. 183, note 66.
79 Young, *Town book*, p. 128.
80 Jean Agnew (ed.), *Funeral register of the first Presbyterian church of Belfast, 1712–36* (Belfast, 1995), p. 25.
81 Peter Roebuck, 'Landlord indebtedness in Ulster in the seventeenth and eighteenth centuries' in L.A. Clarkson and J.M. Goldstrom (eds), *Irish population, economy and society: essays in honour of the late K.H. Connell* (Oxford, 1981), pp 141–3.
82 *Calendar of treasury books 1685–9*, p. 521.
83 Agnew, *Belfast merchant families,* pp 44–59.
84 Benn, *History* (1877), p. 310. Of course, ships built in Belfast could trade from elsewhere. For an example of a Belfast-built ship trading from Coleraine in the 1680s see *Calendar of treasury books 1685–9*, p. 521 and for others in the 1680s see T.N.A., E190/1345/134, f. 7v; E190/1138/1, f. 72.
85 *Reg. P.C. Scot., 1691*, pp 309–10
86 National Archives of Scotland, E72/3/6.
87 Benn, *History* (1877), pp 332–3.
88 Ibid., pp 359–61.
89 *Cal. S. P. Ire. 1647–60*, p. 336.
90 William Knowler, *The earl of Strafforde's letters and despatches* (2 vols, London, 1739), ii, pp 103, 205. Carrickfergus Corporation duly entered the transaction in their book: P.R.O.N.I., T707, pp 59–60.
91 *Cal. S.P. Ire. 1660–2*, pp 526, 593. As early as 1660 there were petitions for the appointment of customs officers at Belfast, see Bodleian Library, Oxford, Carte MS 154, ff 30v, 32.
92 Robin Sweetnam and Cecil Nimmons, *The port of Belfast, 1785–1985* (Belfast, 1985), pp 87–8. The 1685 port book is in P.R.O.N.I., HAR/1F/1/1
93 Raymond Gillespie, 'The world of Andrew Rowan: economy and society in Restoration Antrim' in Brenda Collins, Philip Ollerenshaw and Trevor Parkhill (eds), *Industry, trade and people in Ireland, 1650–1950: essays in honour of W.H. Crawford* (Belfast, 2005), pp 15–16.
94 Grainger, 'Results of excavations', pp 114–15, 118–19.
95 Miskimmin, *Carrickfergus*, p. 375–6.
96 Sacheverell, *Account of the Isle of Man*, p. 125.
97 *Cal. S.P. dom. 1700–2*, p. 46

98 British Library, Add. MS 4759, ff 1–14, *Acts of the Privy Council (Colonial series), 1680–1720* (London, 1910), p. 86 . For a more detailed examination of the trade see Agnew, *Belfast merchant families.*

99 Henry Roseveare (ed.), *Markets and merchants in the late seventeenth century: the Marescoe-Davis letters, 1660–1680* (Oxford, 1981), pp 388–9.

100 T.N.A., E190/1345/13, ff 9v, 10, 12v, 14, 23; E190/1343/2, pp 8, 13–15, 24, 28, 31; E190/1341/3, ff 3, 8–11, 17v; E190/1341/24, ff 3v, 4, 6v.

101 T.N.A., E190/1344/6, f. 45; E190/1343/2, pp 15, 18; E190/1341/3, ff 7v, 11v, 12, 19v; E190/1138/1, f. 27; E190/1324/10, ff 52v, 53; Ó Baoill and Logue, 'Excavations at Gordon Street', pp 121–7.

102 T.N.A., E190/1324/10, f. 53; E190/1138/1, f. 34v; E190/1139/3, ff 7v, 15, 19v; E190/1140/3, ff 7, 10v, 74v (window glass); E190/1138/1, ff 35, 71–72, 190; E190/1139/3, ff 13v, 27; E190/1140/3, f. 8 (glass bottles); E190/1138/1, f. 72; E190/1344/6, ff 20, 45; E190/1341/3, ff 4, 11v, 12 (drinking glasses).

103 T.N.A., E190/1345/13, ff 11, 11v, 14; E190/1343/3, p. 55; E190/1341/3, ff 4, 19v; E190/1344/6, ff 45, 45v; E190/1139/3, f. 65; E190/1138/1, f. 34v; E190/1324/10, f. 53.

104 T.N.A., E190/1139/3.

105 Gillespie, 'World of Andrew Rowan', pp 24–5.

106 T.N.A., E190/1139/3, f. 20; E190/1344/6, ff 19v, 24, 45; E190/1138/1, f. 35; E190/1324/10, ff 53, 53v; E190/1341/3, ff 4, 9v, 10v, 11v, 12; E190/1140/3, f. 64; E190/1343/2, pp 9, 18; E190/1343/3, p. 55; E190/1345/16, f. 20v; Ó Baoill and Logue, 'Excavations at Gordon Street', pp 134–5.

107 P.R.O.N.I., T707, p. 106.

108 *Cal. S.P. dom. 1679–80*, pp 282–3.

109 Gillespie, 'World of Andrew Rowan', pp 16, 24.

110 Pender, *Census*, p. 5; P.R.O.N.I., T808/15260.

111 Gillespie, 'George Rawdon's Lisburn', pp 34–5.

112 *Cal. S.P. dom. 1679–80*, p. 456.

113 Ibid., p. 298; *Excavations 2003*, pp 8–9.

114 For Lurgan see Gillespie, *Settlement and survival.*

115 Peter O'Keeffe and Tom Simington, *Irish stone bridges* (Dublin, 1991), pp 47, 228–30; P.R.O.N.I., D3113/7/227.

116 Lowry (ed.), *Hamilton manuscripts*, p. 50.

117 Ibid., pp 55–6n; Young, *Historical notices*, p. 130.

118 *Cal. S.P. dom. 1679–80* , p. 455.

119 *Cal. S.P. dom. July–Sept. 1683*, p. 268.

120 Tim Harris, *Restoration: Charles II and his kingdoms* (London, 2005), pp 393, 404.

121 Benn, *History* (1877), p. 153.

122 T.C.D., MS 1178, f. 20.

123 Young, *Town book*, pp 156–65.

124 Ibid., pp 166–7.

125 *Correspondence of Sir John Lowther*, pp xxxiv–xxxv; *Cal. S.P. dom. 1690–1*, p. 434; *Reg. P.C Scot., 1686–9*, p. 390.

126 Benn, *History* (1877), pp 163–4.

127 For the Jacobite corporation see Agnew, *Belfast merchant families*, pp 82–91.

128 *Reg. P.C. Scot., 1686-9*, pp 537.

129 *Reg. P.C. Scot., 1690*, pp 22, 26–7, 88.

130 George Story, *A true and impartial history of the most material occurrences in the kingdom of Ireland* (London, 1693), p. 50.
131 *Exact account of his majesty's progress.*
132 Young, *Town book*, pp 172–8.
133 Young, *Historical notices*, p 159.
134 Benn, *History* (1877), pp 325, 327.
135 Paterson, 'Belfast in 1738', p. 111.
136 British Library, Sloan MS 2902, f. 218, *Cal. S.P. dom. 1691–2*, p. 73.
137 Joy, *Historical collections*, pp 84–5.
138 Young, *Town book,* pp 97–8.
139 P.R.O.N.I., D501/1, p. 5.
140 P.R.O.N.I., Mic 19/1, 22 Aug 1666 George Macartney to William Wall.

5

JOHN MACLANACHAN'S TOWN
1695–1750

Late seventeenth-century Belfast had been a boom town. This was reflected in the comments of visitors at the end of that century. In 1693 the Williamite army chaplain George Story described it as a 'very large town', the greatest for trade in the north of Ireland.[1] A few years later William Sacheverell recorded it as being 'well built, full of people and of great trade'.[2] In 1708, when Thomas Molyneux visited Belfast, he found it a 'very handsome, thriving, well peopled town, a great many new houses and shops in it.' He went on, 'The folks seemed all very busy and employed in trade, the inhabitants being for the most part merchants.'[3] Belfast's growth meant that it outstripped its neighbours. By 1725 Belfast and its parish was one of the most densely settled areas of east Ulster, with 2,093 houses. Newry, by contrast, had 1,063 houses, Lisburn 787 and Carrickfergus 546.[4] Indeed, by 1712, of the 500 freemen of Carrickfergus, some 140 actually lived at Belfast.[5]

Over the course of the early eighteenth century that situation was to change. Perhaps the best way to chart the outline of Belfast's story in the early eighteenth century is to follow the fate of the life blood of the town: the ships that carried the goods to and from the port. In 1700 382 ships passed through the port of Belfast. By 1710 that had risen to 445 but by ten years later the number had fallen significantly to 263. By 1740 the number had not yet recovered its 1700 value, with only 336 ships passing through the port. In 1750 434 ships used Belfast, which pointed to a recovery in trade, but all was not as it seemed. Whereas in 1700 the ships using Belfast represented almost 14 per cent of all Irish shipping, 50 years later that had fallen to under 9 per cent, indicating a relative fall in Belfast's trading position. Measures of the tonnage of Belfast shipping

suggest a similar picture. Over the first half of the eighteenth century, ships using Belfast more than doubled in average size but still
remained well below the mean tonnage of an Irish ship in 1750. As
a result Belfast's share of the tonnage of Irish ships fell from 5.5 per
cent to 4.9 per cent between 1700 and 1750.[6] Some of the luxury
goods, such as raisins and wine that these ships carried could not be
sold for want of money in the town and had to be shipped on to
Dublin.[7] All this points to the decline of the trade that had underpinned late seventeenth-century Belfast's expansion and to the
emergence of a problem that would have to be tackled by the early
eighteenth-century town.

I

One way of exploring the changes in Belfast's fortunes is to look
through the eyes of John Maclanachan, who mapped the town in
1715. Changes in the topography from that of Thomas Phillips's
town provide at least some clues about the reasons for Belfast's
decline. A second map of the town, made in 1757, provides a view
of Belfast when it lay on the edge of being transformed by the
Donegall family, and hence it is possible to chart some of the
changes taking place in the early eighteenth century. The appearance of two estate maps of the town within 40 years, when the only
pre-existing survey (that of Thomas Phillips) had been made for
military purposes, is not coincidental. It betrays a new interest in the
townscape as a whole by the earls of Donegall, who commissioned
the maps. In the seventeenth century the Donegalls had used the
lease to manage individual properties rather than controlling the
townscape as a whole. In the eighteenth century, however, the wider
perspective of the whole townscape set out in maps was being
adopted. Therefore, both maps showed not just properties but ter-
races of houses and proposed fashionable squares that were never
begun or, in one case, started but never finished. The imposition of
order became the key to understanding the town. This was also
reflected in the rise of Classical architecture, with its sense of proportion and order, by the middle of the eighteenth century.

Using the two maps it is possible to fix the main topographical
points in the town that have already been discussed. The church as

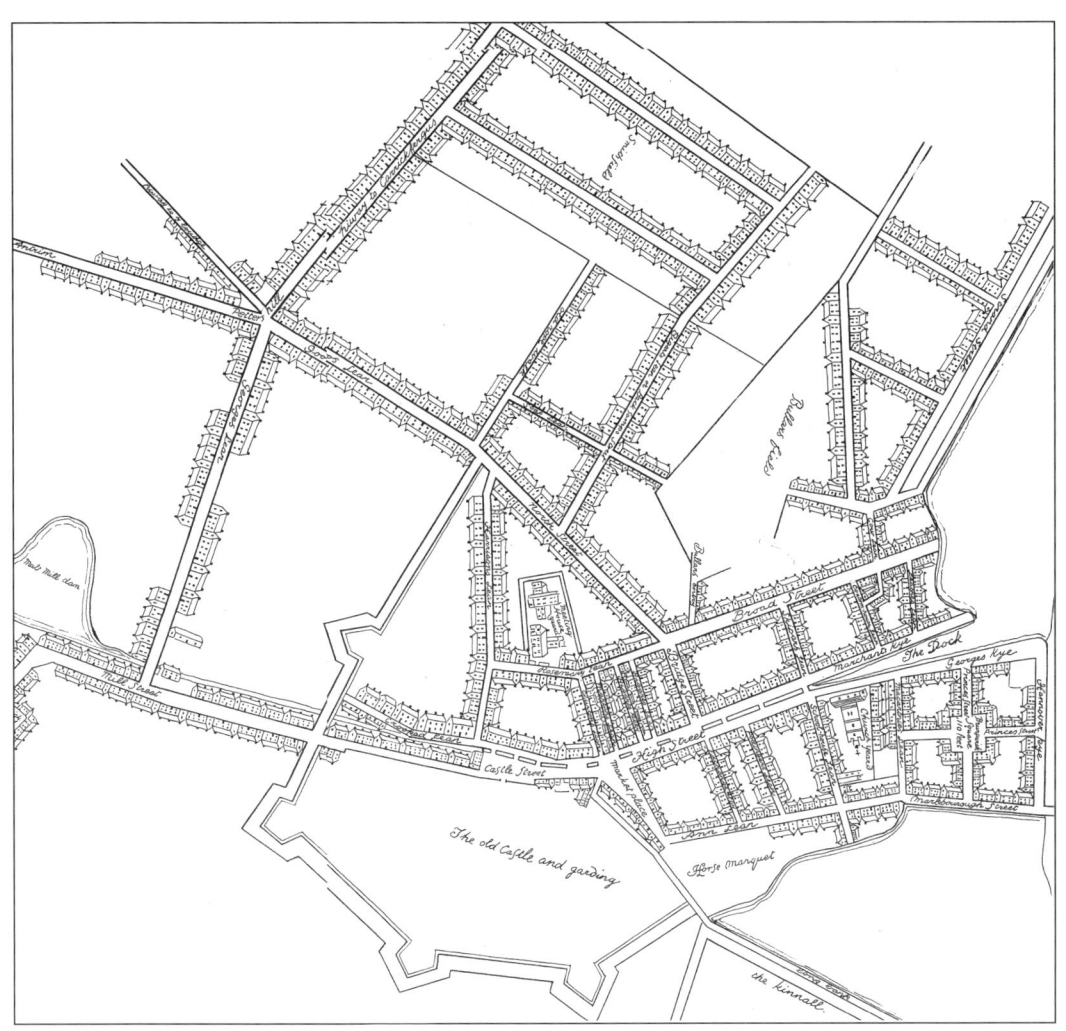

John Maclanachan's map of Belfast, 1715.

Opposite: Map of Belfast, 1757, prepared as part of the beginnings of
the redevelopment of Belfast from the 1750s by the earls of
Donegall. The cartographer was clearly told what the street names
were rather than seeing them written down, since 'Wern Street' is
the Belfast dialect form of 'Waring Street'.

depicted on both maps provides a fixed point to link the eighteenth-century topography to the earlier urban layout. The church
appears in both the 1715 and 1757 maps but it is increasingly
hedged in by buildings, especially on the southern and western side
of the churchyard. A token of *c.* 1730, which is the oldest known
view of Belfast, shows the church still dominating the skyline, but
with other buildings crowding around it. The fabric of the church

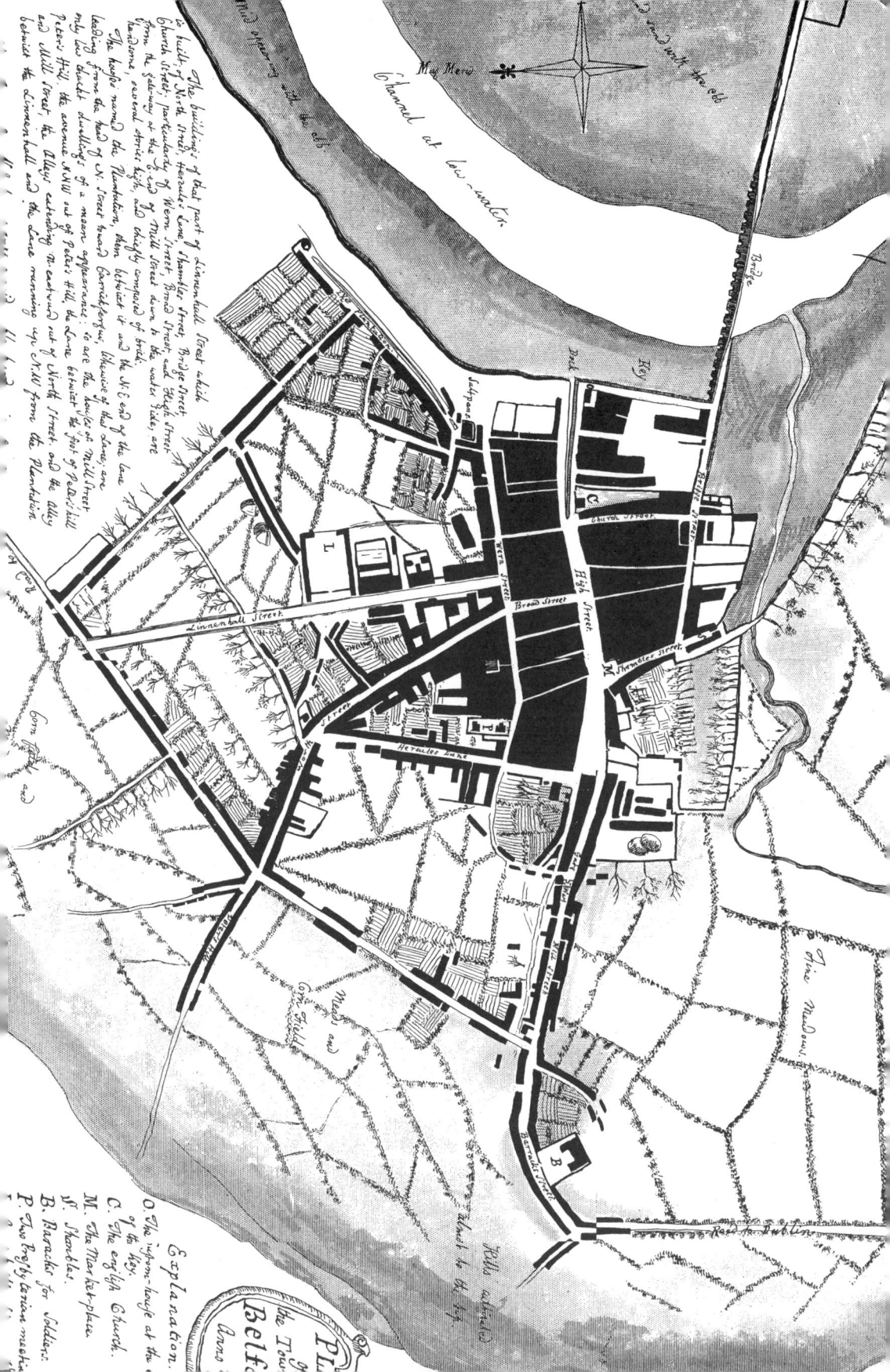

The buildings of that part of Linnenhall Street which is built of North Street, Hercules Lane, Chamber Street, Bridge Street, Church Street, particularly of Wern Street, Broad Street and High Street from the gateway on the top of Mill Street down to the water side, are handsome, several stories high, and chiefly constructed of brick.

The houses named the Plantation, then between it and the N.E. end of the lane leading from the head of W. Street toward Carrickfergus, likewise of that shore, are only low thatched dwellings of a mean appearance; to see the houses of Mill Street between NWW and of Peters Hill, the lane between the foot of Pedeers Hill and Mill Street, the avenue NWW out of North Street, and the Alley which street, the Alley extending W. eastward out of North Street from the Plantation behind the Linnen hall and the Lane running

May Mew

Channel at low water

Bridge

Key

Dock

Skipper's Lane

C

Church Street

Wern Street

High Street

Broad Street

Linnenhall Street

L

K

Shambles Street

M

Mercer

P

W

Hercules Lane

BELFAST

Meads and Corn Mills

Mill Street

Barrack Street

B

Road to Dublin

The Meadow

Fields cultivated

Explanation.

O. The infirm-house at the of the Key.
C. The english Church.
M. The Market-place.
S. Shambles
B. Barracks for soldiers.
P. Two Presbyterian meetin

PL
the Tow
Belfa
Anno

itself was beginning to show signs of disrepair. In 1738 it was noted that 'the church was very old but lately repaired' and a new set of bells was cast as part of its refurbishment.[8] Attempts such as this to patch up the fabric were not enough. In 1754 Richard Pococke, visiting the town, observed that the church was 'a very mean fabric for such a considerable place'.[9] New churches in the surrounding area, such as that at Knockbreda, built in 1747 in the latest Classical style, served only to highlight the dilapidated state of the church in Belfast. Funding was a problem. A proposal was made in 1753 to build a poorhouse in the town funded by a lottery and 'whereas the church of Belfast is old and ruinous and not large enough to contain the parishioners, and to rebuild and enlarge the same would be an expense grievous and unsupportable by the ordinary means of public cess' it was proposed to rebuild that also from the lottery.[10] The lottery collapsed without having raised any significant sum of money. Perhaps more promising was the approach made to Lord Donegall in 1765 by the merchant John Black, suggesting that a new church and poorhouse be built by the landlord. Nothing came of this in the short term.[11] By 1773 it was clear that the old church was unsafe and plans were drawn up for a replacement. Despite fears that a lack on money would stall the project the seventeenth-century building was demolished in 1774 and a new church constructed in Donegall Street by the earl of Donegall, partly funded by selling seats in the new building.[12] The graveyard of the old parish church continued to be used for burials until 1800, when it was closed and part of it was sold.

By the early eighteenth century the parish church was no longer the only element in the religious make-up of the town and Maclanachan's map shows a number of churches in Belfast. It thus becomes possible to talk about a religious topography of Belfast in a way that was not applicable before. Perhaps the most prominent feature of the town's religious topography was the absence of Catholic places of worship. According to the poll tax of 1660, 'Irish' (who might generally be equated with Catholics) made up almost a third of the town's population.[13] By 1708 the sovereign of the town, George Macartney, wrote to the Privy Council:

I have made the constables return a list of all the inhabitants with-

> in this town and we have not amongst us in the town above seven
> papists and by the return made me by the High Constable there
> is not above one hundred and fifty papists in the whole barony.[14]

The town had no parish priest in 1704, the cure being served by a
priest resident in the nearby parish of Drumbo.[15] A similar process
of attrition seems to have taken place among the Church of Ireland
community. On the basis of surnames, Belfast *c.* 1640 was fairly
evenly divided between settlers of English origin (who may be
roughly equated with adherents to the Church of Ireland) and
Scots.[16] By the 1740s, on the evidence of Archdeacon Pococke,
there were about 60 churchgoing families, perhaps 300 people, in a
town of around 8,000.[17] Other dissenting groups, such as Quakers,
had made no impression on the town by the early eighteenth century.[18] What had happened in the late seventeenth century was that
the immigration of Scottish Presbyterians into Belfast had dwarfed
the position of other religious groups. However relations between
the various Protestant groups in the town were good and the custom of taking apprentices across Church of Ireland and Presbyterian
boundaries was well established by 1700.[19]

The earliest Presbyterian congregation had been formed in the
town during the 1640s as a result of its capture by Robert Munroe.
It seems very likely that it met in the parish church since, according
to the Presbyterian minister Patrick Adair, Church of Ireland services were not held during this period.[20] Belfast certainly had a
Presbyterian congregation after 1660 and a meeting house by 1674,
but where it was located is not known. A nineteenth-century tradition placed it somewhere near the top of North Street, possibly near
the North Gate.[21] However, by the 1690s a Presbyterian church had
been constructed on the site of the present Presbyterian church at
the west end of Rosemary Street (which terminated near that site
at the time). As such the church was built on the edges of the existing town. If the earlier church was near the North Gate, that would
also fit with this location. The emergence of Presbyterian churches
on the edges of Ulster towns was a common feature in the late seventeenth century. At Derry the first Presbyterian church that can be
located was built in 1690 in Magazine Street, just within the walled
town. The position of the early eighteenth-century Presbyterian

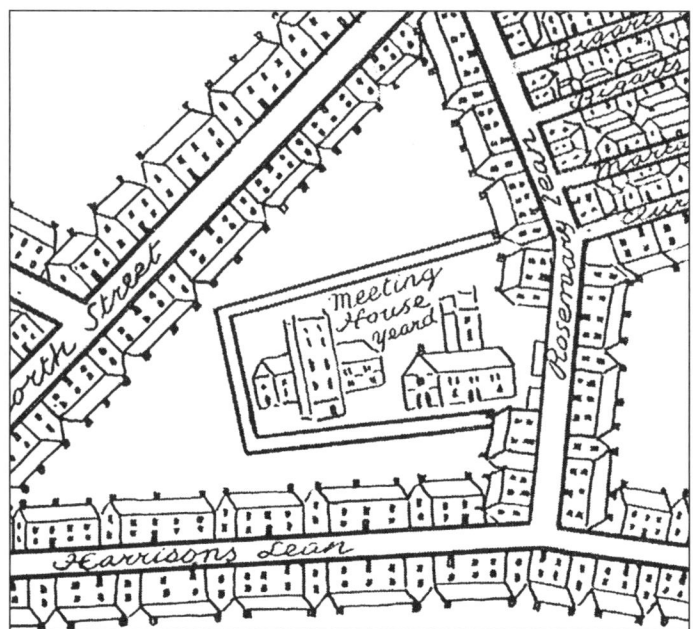

First and second Presbyterian churches, from John Maclanachan's map of Belfast of 1715.

Below: First and second Presbyterian churches, from the 1757 plan.

church at Carrickfergus was similar, being located at the end of North Street, close to the walls and in Armagh in 1676 the Prsbyterians set up their church on the northern edge of the town.

As the size of the Presbyterian community in Belfast grew the site was subdivided among a number of churches. By 1707 the first Presbyterian church was too small for its congregation and a second church was built on the same site in Rosemary Street and by 1712 the first church was being referred to as the 'old meeting house'. In

1708 the second congregation had 120 families.[22] By 1722 both churches were full and a third church had to be constructed behind the others. Relatively little is known about the physical appearance of these churches. Maclanachan's map of 1715 contains a sketch of two of them. Both were long, two-storey structures. They are shown with what appear to be attached towers but the presence of such towers seems very unlikely. This may be an attempt to represent what appears on the 1757 plan — two T-shaped buildings that would be more typical of Ulster Presbyterian churches. The church of the third congregation, opened in 1722, was described by Benn in the 1820s as having small windows, a projecting front, a steep roof and being 'devoid of all external ornament'.[23] Little is known about the churches' internal arrangement. Given that they were two storeyed, presumably there were galleries inside. All the churches were pewed and, as in the parish church, pews were owned by families and could be sold by them.[24] As well as the churches there were ancillary buildings on the site. A school under the control of the Presbyterian minister John McBride had been established in the town by the 1690s and there the Killyleagh merchant James Traill was educated.[25] Although its location is unknown, it was presumably on the same site as the church. In addition, residences were required for the ministers. Maclanachan's map shows a large house within the boundaries of the church site, which is a manse attached to the first Presbyterian church, a fact confirmed by a lease map of 1767. By the early eighteenth century it is appropriate to think not of an isolated Presbyterian church on the edge of the town but of a complex of buildings located there that were owned and managed by the church.

In contrast to the flourishing of buildings associated with religion in Belfast, the castle suffered an unfortunate fate. By the time of Maclanachan's map the castle had gone from the town. It had been destroyed by fire on Sunday 25 April, 1708 killing three daughters of the earl of Donegall.[26] A more detailed account of that 'melancholy providence' was provided by the devout Killyleagh merchant James Traill. Traill described how the fire, started by accident, spread across the wooden beams and staircases of the house and how the floors collapsed as a result. The three girls, with two servants' children, could be heard 'screeching' in their room. Rather than jumping from their window to a shed that was six feet below, they fled to another part of the castle – into a morass of collapsing floors – and were buried. They probably died of smoke inhalation since Traill recounted, 'I don't remember that any of them was burnt to ashes' and 'some of their bodies were not much burnt'. The heat was so intense that help could not get close enough to the castle until it was almost destroyed. One servant escaped by climbing onto the roof and lowering herself by way of a waterspout onto an adjoining building.[27]

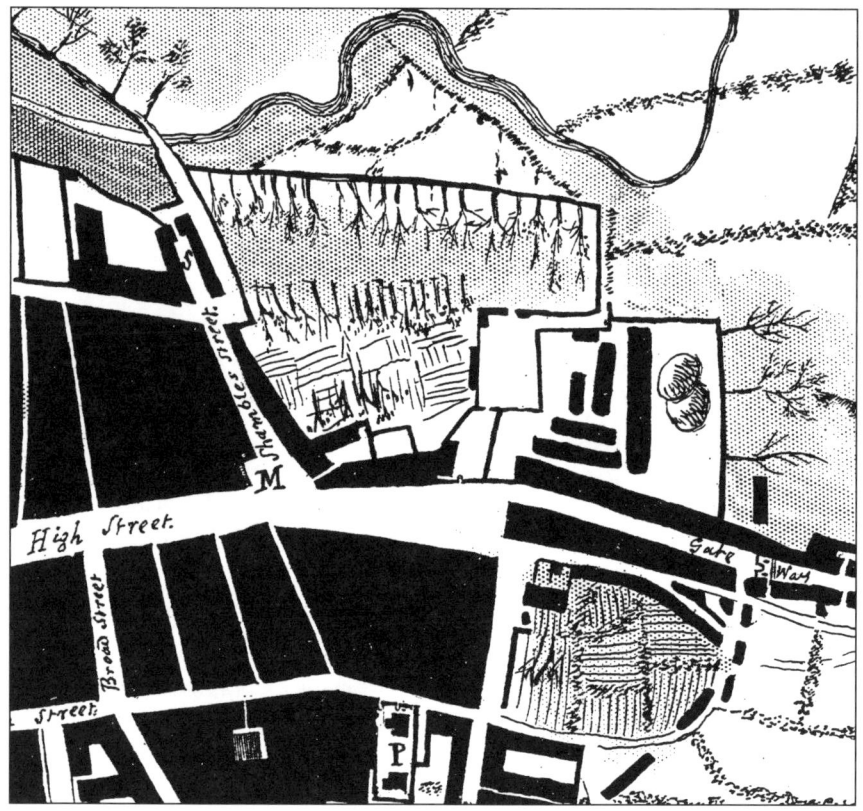

The site of the castle in 1757. There are still some remains of the old buildings but most have been cleared and the ground mainly left undeveloped. Some new buildings have been added. The houses around the edge of the castle at Cornmarket were known as New Buildings.

After the burning of the castle the Donegall family, beset by other problems (discussed below), left the town and the site on which the castle stood remained vacant, although the family did continue to keep a house in the town.[28] The castle site was rented out on a series of leases, the earliest of which suggested that the Donegalls might rebuild it, since it included a clause that the property would be surrendered if the castle were rebuilt. By 1717 that clause had disappeared and the salvageable bricks, timber and lead were being sold.[29] By 1757 the site was still shown as an open space beside Castle Street. This failure to rebuild the castle was an important development for the town, since it removed an important focus for Belfast's urban topographical development and allowed new areas to be opened up, most particularly the lower end of Ann Street.

The final topographical element that can be traced in the evolution of the town is the commercial area of Waring Street.

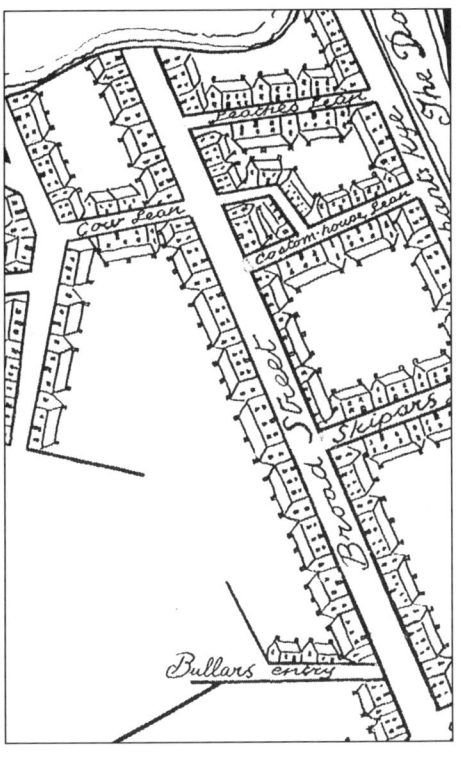

Waring Street as it is shown on John Maclanachan's 1715 map of Belfast. Compare this with figure on page 94, which shows the same area 30 years earlier, and notice the growth in the scale of housing.

Maclanachan's map depicts most of the houses in the Waring Street area, and indeed over much of the town, as being two storeyed. The evidence from the middle of the seventeenth century suggests that most of the houses of the town were of one storey, so if Maclanachan is correct his depiction implies that the town was considerably rebuilt in the late seventeenth and early eighteenth centuries. This may be so, given Molyneux's comment about 'a great many new houses' in the town in 1708.[30] Certainly most timber-framed buildings of the early seventeenth century had come to the end of their useful life by the end of that century and some of the more successful merchants had built more fashionable brick houses in High Street and Castle Street, probably with slate roofs.[31] Moreover, the houses being built in Belfast were growing taller. In the middle of the seventeenth century single-storey houses were usual. By the early eighteenth century two-storey houses were the norm and advertisements in the *Belfast News-Letter* for letting houses suggest that three-storey buildings were common the middle of the eighteenth century. A drawing made *c.* 1715 for a house for Captain Chichester beside the customs house at the east end of Waring Street shows a house with a frontage of almost 40 feet, which was the normal size of a burgage plot. To the left of the entrance hall was an office for business and a pantry, while to the right was a parlour and drawing room. The dining room was presumably on the first floor and accessed by a staircase at the rear of the building. In plan this was similar to, but rather grander than, the houses that already stood on Waring Street but it differed in being free standing and not part of a terrace. The large courtyard behind

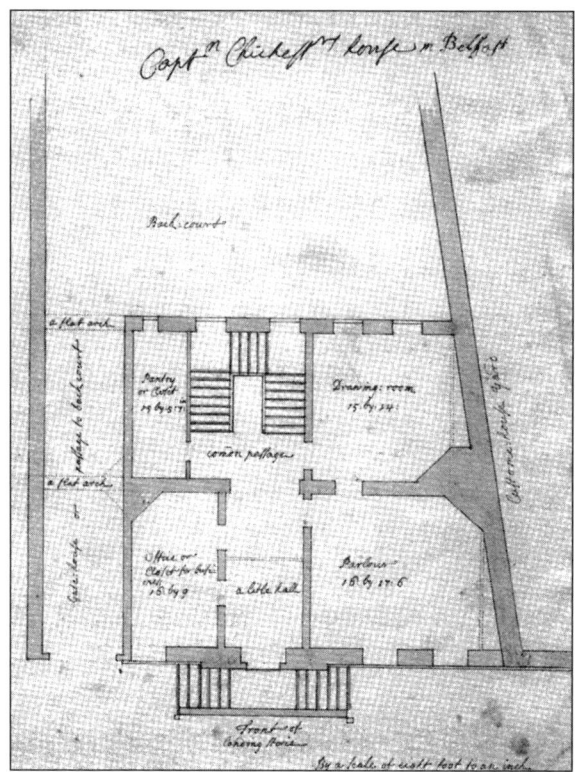

An early eighteenth-century drawing by Samuel Waring of Waringstown, County Down, of a house to be built for a Captain Chichester in Waring Street (private collection). I am grateful to Toby Barnard for his help with this illustration.

it was accessed by a passage along the side of the build-ing with an arched gate-house. Here, presumably, were the stables, attached to another house adver-tised in the same area in 1758.[32] All this suggests a substantial and fashionable townhouse. However, this needs to be set against the large number of timber structures with thatched roofs that still existed in the town. In 1686 the corporation had required that the inhabitants of Belfast provide 'cupple poles' to pull down burning thatch or timber buildings and prevent the spread of any fire that might break out.[33] Such buildings were becoming much less com-mon by the early eighteenth century.

The development of an industrial zone at the east end of Waring Street was discussed in the previous chapter, particularly as regards its association with the tanning trade. In the early part of the eigh-teenth century the signs of industrial activity in this area intensified. Excavations and chance finds of many eighteenth-century pot-sherds, including wasters, along Hill Street and into Gordon Street point to a significant new development in this area. On Hill Street large quantities of pottery, both imported and locally made, were found that were not arranged randomly, with parts of pots grouped together. These finds clearly reflected the presence of an organised pottery.[34] Little additional archaeological evidence for the pottery has been found, nor has its site, but there is other evidence that allows its activities to be understood. Thomas Molyneux, travelling through Ulster in 1708, commented that at Belfast 'here we saw a very good manufacture of earthen ware which comes nearest delft of any made in Ireland and really not much short of it. 'Tis very clean and pretty and universally used in the north, and I think not so much owing to any peculiar happiness in their clay but rather to the manner of beating and mixing it up.'[35] This suggests that by 1708 the pottery was well established, and indeed thriving, since its products were widely used in Ulster. William Sacheverell commented in 1698 that 'the new pottery is a pretty curiosity set up by Mr Smith, the present sovereign, and his predecessor Captain Leathes, a man of great ingenuity'.[36] In reality it may have been a happy conjunction between mercantile capital and the availability of expertise. It seems probable that the skill required for the establishment of a pottery was provided by a London potter, Mathew Garner, who had fled London for debt about the same time that the Belfast business was established.[37] By 1700, when the lease for the premises was taken out, four Belfast merchants were involved: David Smith, his

The pottery and associated buildings, from the 1757 plan. The pottery is the large free-standing building behind Waring Street and the other buildings represent the 'pot-house tenements', which accommodated the workers in the pottery. By the date of this map the buildings had ceased to function as a pottery. the site marked 'L' near the bottom of the extract was the old linen hall, demolished to build St Anne's Church.

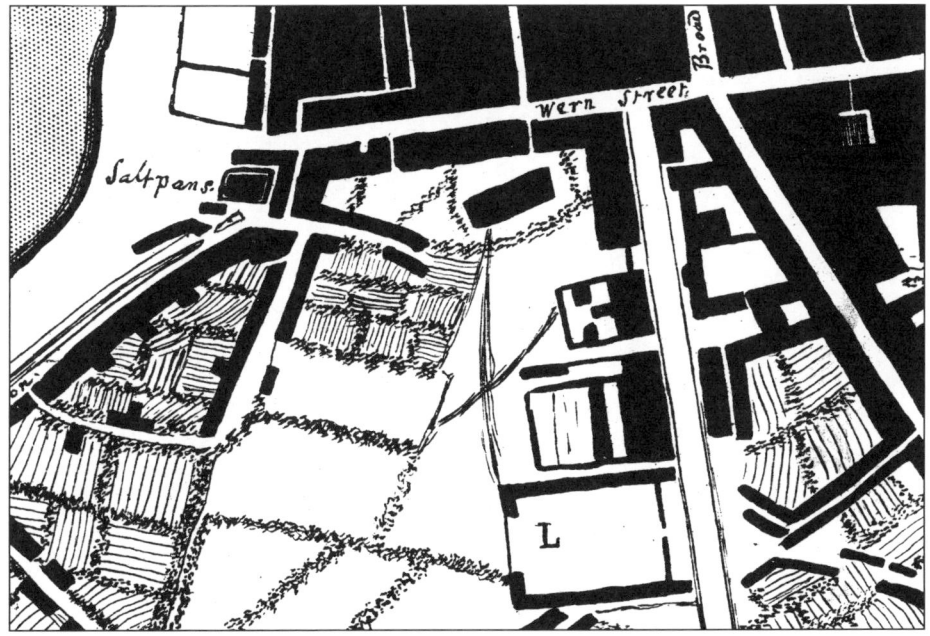

brother Patrick Smith, their brother-in-law Thomas Crawford and Henry Chads.[38] David Smith died in 1705, leaving his brother to manage the business. The following year the Belfast merchant Isaac Macartney commented of Smith:

> what judgement he has in managing a pot-house I know not further than he was concerned in this house and was frequently looking after the workmen and burning the ware when I took any friends thither to see it and he says he has good knowledge and can by overseeing and directing make three or four men do as much as ten men.[39]

It is clear from the surviving fragments of pottery from excavation and elsewhere that this was very high-quality delftware, imitating Dutch and London models and bearing comparison with delftware produced anywhere in England at this time.[40] This suggests that the developers of the pot-house may have had the English market in mind as much as the local one. While craftworking in the early seventeenth century had concentrated on the clothing trades, mainly for local consumption, growing trade and commercialisation in the late seventeenth century encouraged the production of material for much wider markets. The development of the pottery makes this trend clear and it would grow in the eighteenth century as trade in primary products survived. However, by 1725 the pot-house had closed, probably having become the victim of the economic downturn and increasing English competition in the early eighteenth century.

The development of the pot-house clearly made a major contribution to this industrial end of Waring Street. It occupied a large and significant site — which later in the 1750s would house an iron foundry — along what is now Hill Street. Large buildings on the site are depicted on the map of 1757 in the middle of Bullar's Fields. These must have been the pottery itself and are set back from the main line of Waring Street to avoid the smoke and other pollution generated by the pot-house. There may also have been a soap-making business on the site, although no separate building is marked for this on the 1757 plan. Finally, as part of the complex there were houses — the pot-house tenements — which were presumably intended for those employed in the business. The tenants of these properties were recorded on several of the leases of the pot-house.[41]

At Cotton Court, for instance, excavations have revealed a brick-and-stone terrace overlying the late seventeenth-century structures and fronting onto Waring Street. These have been interpreted as houses for industrial workers.[42]

The pottery had a significant impact on the industrial life of Belfast. One indication of this is the decline in imported ceramics into Belfast over the working life of the pottery when locally produced products filled the market.[43] Equally important, but of longer duration, was the introduction of printing into Belfast in the 1690s.[44] Of course, that does not mean that there were no books in the town before that date. Books, both legal and suppressed, were part of the normal trade of the town. In the 1630s one Belfast merchant had primers and horn books among his stock, intended for those learning to read. In the 1660s pamphlets were being smuggled into Belfast from Scotland and in the 1680s a ship arriving from Scotland contained Bibles, psalm books and pamphlets. In 1698 Bibles were being imported from Holland.[45] Belfast had a stationer by 1661 and a bookbinder by 1684.[46] The first printer in the town was Patrick Neill, who came from Glasgow, probably in 1694, and had been invited to Belfast by the sovereign, William Crawford, who was also involved in the establishment of the pottery.[47] What induced Neill to come to the town is a matter of speculation but, given that his early productions were all of a religious (and specifically Presbyterian) nature, it is probable that he was invited to act effectively as a printer to the Presbyterian community. In the early 1690s a religious controversy had erupted between Bishop King of Derry and the Ulster Presbyterians and they had found themselves unable to state their position effectively for want of a local printing press. This would have acted as a powerful incentive to establish such a press. That Belfast was chosen is an indication of how important the town had become as a distribution centre for imports and locally manufactured goods. The establishment of the press was thus linked to Belfast's pre-eminence in trade.

Unlike the pottery, the printing press survived the economic dislocations of the early eighteenth century, although it operated at a low level. Some 34 titles can be identified from surviving copies as having been printed in Belfast before 1750. Less is known about the length of print runs. Some indications of what these may have been is provided by the subscription lists printed in a number of Belfast books before 1750. A 1730 subscription list contains subscriptions for 477 copies; a second of 1741 has 121, while a list of 1747 has 344. Some lists, such as those of 1745 and 1746, record many fewer copies subscribed for − 118 and 130 respectively in these two cases.[48] It seems likely, therefore, that print runs were small, probably about 500 for a popular work. Neill, however, and his successor James Blow, were not full-time printers. They probably supplemented their printing activities with other related employments such as bookselling and the stationery business. Belfast printers certainly had links with Dublin booksellers, to whom they sold stock and, presumably, acquired books for sale in Belfast.[49] A number of early-eighteenth-century Belfast printed books contain advertisements for titles which, it was claimed, were printed there. In reality, though, these were probably imported and sold by the printers acting as booksellers.[50] A good example of this sort of activity is the Belfast printer Francis Joy, who began his working life as a tailor, moved into the stationery business and then moved into printing. He constructed printing presses for others and established paper mills. In 1737 he founded the first newspaper in Belfast, the *Belfast News-Letter*.[51] Such a move reflects the growing merchant community's need for information, much of it culled from English news sheets. It also reflects local commercial expansion, since a good deal of the space of this newspaper comprised advertisements. In themselves these advertisements were important, for they informed Belfast's residents of changing fashions, insuring them against both falling behind in displays of status and neglecting opportunities for consumption.

While the industrial activity of the pottery was concentrated at the end of Waring Street the topography of the print trade was rather different. An advertisement in the 1700 edition of *The psalms of David in metre* identifies Neill's shop as being in Bridge Street. When Neill's business was inherited by James Blow he kept the Bridge Street premises. By 1713 there was a second printer in Belfast, Robert Gardner, but the location of his business is not known. In 1733 one Samuel Wilson, printer, was based at the Stone

Bridge, or Bridge Street.[52] By the 1740s, on the evidence of imprints, James Magee also seems to have established himself in Bridge Street, 'near the Four Corners'. This would place him at Bridge Street's northern end, perhaps near the corner of Waring Street. This highlights the commercial importance of printing, since it was established in the trading area of the town. It also suggests that Bridge Street was an area in which suitable premises were available. This may be result of the relocation of the main marketplace of the town to Cornmarket and Castle Street, near the market house, which allowed new property to be constructed in the old market-place, changing it from a triangular space to a more normal street space as it appears today.

The biggest topographical problem that the town had in the early eighteenth century was that of space to expand. As late as 1757 it was still shown as largely contained within the rampart constructed in the 1640s. By this date the rampart had ceased to have any defensive meaning; indeed, parts of it were planted with trees.[53] To the east the River Lagan constrained growth and northward space for expansion was limited by the mountains that swept down to Belfast Lough. The most likely way in which the town could grow was westward and there are distinct signs of this taking place in the early eighteenth century. The groundwork for this had been laid in the late seventeenth century with the expansion outside the Mill Gate and the North Gate and the colonisation of the empty space behind the rampart. Perhaps the most significant development in this area was the construction along the older routeways of Durham Street and Carrick Hill, which Maclanachan depicts as being well built up with two-storey houses in 1715. The map of 1757, on the other hand, indicates a rather lower density of houses, suggesting that Maclanachan's view of this area may be rather optimistic. What was clearly aspirational on Maclanachan's depiction of this area is the large square of one- and two-storey houses called Smithfield, shown to the west of Carrick Hill. This scheme reflects the emergence of Classical town planning in Belfast, mirroring the squares then being created in Dublin and later in Limerick. In Belfast, however, the scheme depicted by Maclanachan was never carried out.

More substantial than such hopes was the spreading of the town

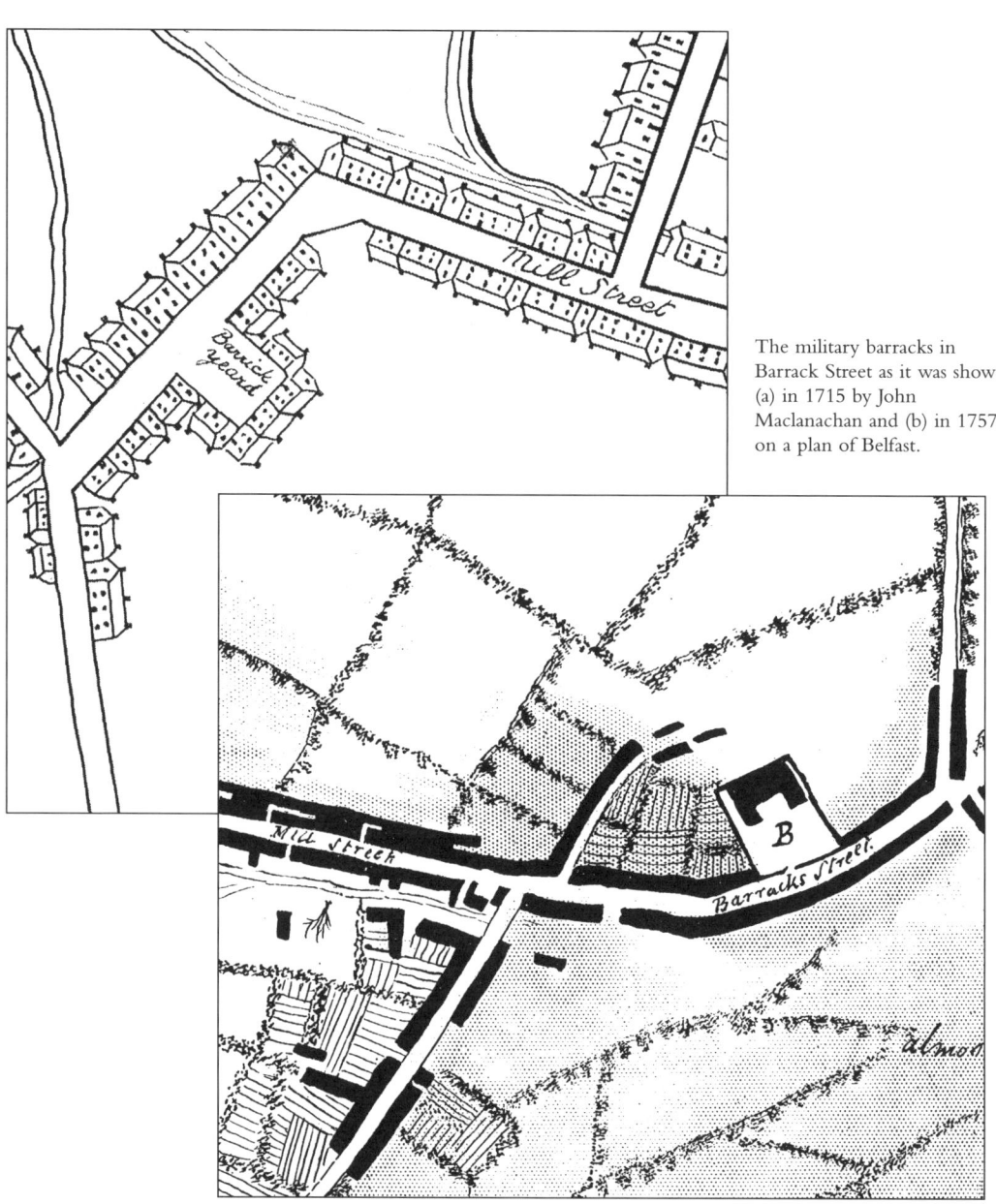

The military barracks in Barrack Street as it was shown (a) in 1715 by John Maclanachan and (b) in 1757 on a plan of Belfast.

westwards along what is now Castle Street towards the town mill on Mill Street, which is shown on both Maclanachan's map and the 1757 plan as more built up than it had been in 1685. The laying out of Mill Street, linking Carrick Hill with Castle Street, was of considerable importance since it created a second edge to the town to the west of the rampart into which subsequent building could spread. Moreover, if Maclanachan is to be trusted, the buildings in this expanding western end of the town were substantial two-storey houses, whereas Phillips in 1685 had shown small one-storey cabins along Castle Street. The creation of these may in part have been the effect of the building leases that the earl of Donegall was issuing for Mill Street. These required new tenants to construct houses of better quality than before, with oak roofs covered with tiles or slates.[54] While thatch and shingles certainly continued to be used in Belfast, slate was becoming more common and by 1683 slate from north Down was being shipped into Belfast for roofing.[55]

The construction of a barracks to the south-west of the town by the 1690s, which moved to Barrack Street in 1715, gave this area greater importance. A garrison had been established in Belfast during the wars of the 1640s and after the Restoration it had been maintained. There are certainly references to troops in the town in 1667 and 1677 and by 1717 two companies of foot were garrisoned there.[56] Phillips's plan shows a substantial building on the site of the early eighteenth century barracks in 1683 but on the 1715 and 1757 plans the building looks very different and it had been reconstructed at least once, in 1739.[57] The plan of 1757 show a main square surrounded by buildings in a U-shaped formation, as was normal for barracks constructed by the Barrack Board.[58] In the 1760s it was recorded that the wing on the right had four rooms for officers and that that on the left had six rooms on each level for enlisted men. The main block contained the infirmary, coal yard and administrative offices.[59] This undoubtedly encouraged westward development along Castle Street as far as the barracks. This was important in establishing a solid population in this area, which had not previously been built up. Both Maclanachan's map and that of 1757 show significant development around the barracks. The parish register from the middle of the eighteenth century highlights the importance of the army garrison based in the barracks at Barrack Street. The number of soldiers' children listed as baptised in the register varied from ten in 1749 and eight in 1760 to one in 1752, 1758, 1759 and 1761, with an annual average of just over three.[60]

Within the town a long street, Hercules Street, linking the North Gate and the upper end of High Street, developed at right angles to the east–west orientation of the town. This had been established as Michael Harrison's Lane (later represented by Hercules Street on

The earliest phase of the development of the Belfast 'entries' in 1715, built at right angles to the main streets to maximise the use of building land. The houses here are smaller than those on the main streets. Note the names of prominent Belfast merchants attached to these laneways, suggesting they were the developers.

the line of the present Royal Avenue) by the 1670s, but is shown as incomplete on Phillips's map. By the time of Maclanachan's plan it is shown as complete, forming a western edge to the built-up town. The construction of the Presbyterian church on Rosemary Street in the late 1680s or early 1690s had promoted the extension of this street from where it had finished in the 1630s to a junction with the new street. This extension followed the line of High Street, which bent with the Farset, giving Rosemary Street a dog-leg appearance.

Expansion westward, however, was less than ideal. Those who settled in the west of the town were some distance away from its core commercial activity, the port. An alternative was to expand the town southward, but here too there were limits. The River Blackstaff, which frequently flooded, posed a problem. In the late seventeenth century some attempt was made to make land to the south of the town more usable. Instead of entering the Lagan at what is now Victoria Square, the Blackstaff was diverted to enter the Lagan at a point just opposite where Ormeau Avenue now runs. The diversion is already shown on Phillips's map of 1685, where it is described as the 'New Cut', and it appears on Maclanachan's map as 'the kinnall'.

Along this line a stone sea bank, the so-called 'Long Walk', was constructed. Other measures were taken to drain this area, including the walling of the Farset and the 1697 requirement that the river be cleaned every year 'to prevent overflowing'.[61] All of this was of considerable importance in allowing the building up of the south side of High Street in the late seventeenth century. In the early eighteenth century it also allowed the construction of houses along Ann Street and into what is now Victoria Square, which previously had been subject to flooding from the Blackstaff.[62]

Given the constraints imposed by the topography of the town, those who wished to develop property had two main options: to use what land existed within the rampart more intensively or to reclaim land into the Lagan. Both techniques were resorted to as the housing stock of Belfast grew from the 530 houses listed on the hearth-money roll of 1663 to some 2,000 estimated from Arthur Dobbs's hearth-tax returns in 1725.[63] By the beginning of the eighteenth century those holding the large tenements characteristic of the town began to build on what had previously been gardens, or to sublet those gardens for others to build on. By 1709 one lease for property on the south side of High Street described that property as a 'dwelling house, cellar, gardens and premises now in the possession of the said William Rainey, situated in the backside of the house now in the possession of Moses Richardson, watchmaker'.[64] Another lease of the following year spoke of a 'passage or courtyard leading to the tenement' in High Street, which suggests the process of constructing buildings behind each other.[65] Such development implied that access would be needed to the rear of houses and this resulted in the laying out of lanes at right angles to the main streets. Maclanachan's map of 1715 shows this technique being deployed between the northern end of High Street and the southern part of Rosemary Street. The names of these new streets, Biggar's Lane and Clugston's Lane, are those of prominent Belfast merchants Alexander Biggar and John Clugston, which suggests that they may well have been involved as developers. As Ann Street attracted new residents, further lanes were added between it and High Street. Pottinger's Lane, shown on Maclanachan's map, is also named after a Belfast merchant. These were the origins of what came to be known as the Belfast 'entries', which, grew in number and in population density in the eighteenth century.[66] Richard Pococke, visiting the town in 1752, described it as consisting of 'one long broad street and of several lanes in which the inferior people live'.[67] This is supported by the depiction of houses on Maclanachan's map. While the buildings on High Street are shown as having two storeys, those in the lanes between High Street and Rosemary Street are depicted as one storey, cabin-like structures without chimneys. Newspaper descriptions of houses to let in these areas, while confirming the main elements of the depictions on the map, present a slightly more favourable picture. In 1756 an entry off High Street was said to have a kitchen, a parlour, a cellar, a loft, a garret, a shop and a coal hole. Another house in Post Office Entry was said to have a kitchen, a parlour and garrets.[68]

The process of land reclamation in Belfast was already under way in the late seventeenth century, with the channelling of the Blackstaff into its new course, though this had limited impact. A more popular option was to begin reclaiming land from the river. As early as 1685 Phillips's map noted that there was 'improvement made upon the strand'. A lease of 1692 described the reclamation of land east of Schoolhouse Lane and another lease, also from 1692, of property at the end of Waring Street mentioned 'all that parcel of land as it is now gained from the sea and built with good brick houses'. This lease described the reclamation process as land being 'fenced from the sea with posts and pales'. 'Good brick houses' were built here to form the outline of what would become Quay Lane.[69] Excavations at the junction of Gordon Street and Victoria Street, which on Phillips's map of 1685 would have lain on the Strand, revealed eighteenth-century building foundations resting on lough-shore deposits, dumps of stones and roughly circular wooden post piles driven into the silt. At another part of the site dump deposits of domestic and industrial rubbish containing seventeenth- and eighteenth-century material provide evidence of attempts to reclaim land in this area.[70] By 1757 further reclamation had been carried on in this area and a salt works had been established on the reclaimed land. More sophisticated was the construction of sluice bridges in the Long Bank, built to hold back the Blackstaff from the

Ann Street area in an effort to regulate water levels, but this was ineffective and the ravages of the sea kept breaching the Long Bank.[71]

The most important of these land-reclamation projects was that of the Belfast merchant Isaac Macartney. By 1711 he had acquired a lease of unreclaimed land between the church and the River Lagan.[72] On this he laid out a new residential development of Brunswick Square and a new quay, Hanover Quay, depicted on Maclanachan's map. That project was described in 1738 by a Captain Cobb, who recorded:

> in 1710 Isaac Macartney esq. obtained of the Lord Donegall a lease of all the marshy ground between the churchyard and the low water mark, on which he built a fine quay for ships to take their loading or unload with great ease, and was finished in 1714, soon after his majesty's accession to the throne and in honour of the royal family and to show his zeal for the Protestant succession, called it Hanover Quay, on which are now erected many good buildings and amongst the rest His Majesty's Custom House is no mean building. There are all conveniences above stairs and weigh-house and warehouses below which is a great convenience for the merchants and trade of the town.[73]

The technique Macartney employed here was the building lease, the use of which had been pioneered in Belfast by the Donegalls. Leaseholders in this area were required to build houses of stone or brick with slate roofs in the development, in return for which they were granted a rent-free period.[74] By 1720 work was well under way in the development but it was not yet finished.[75] While Maclanachan's map shows the development as complete, with a central Brunswick Square and four radiating streets, it seems that this was aspirational. The 1757 plan shows only the northern part of the square as complete with a single block on the south side. Of this northern development the most substantial structure was the new customs house on the north-west corner of Brunswick Square, which Maclanachan shows as a large four-storey building, on a site leased by Macartney to the Commissioners for Customs and Revenue. Two other buildings of this development still survive in part – the former Telford's ships' chandlers on Donegall Quay and

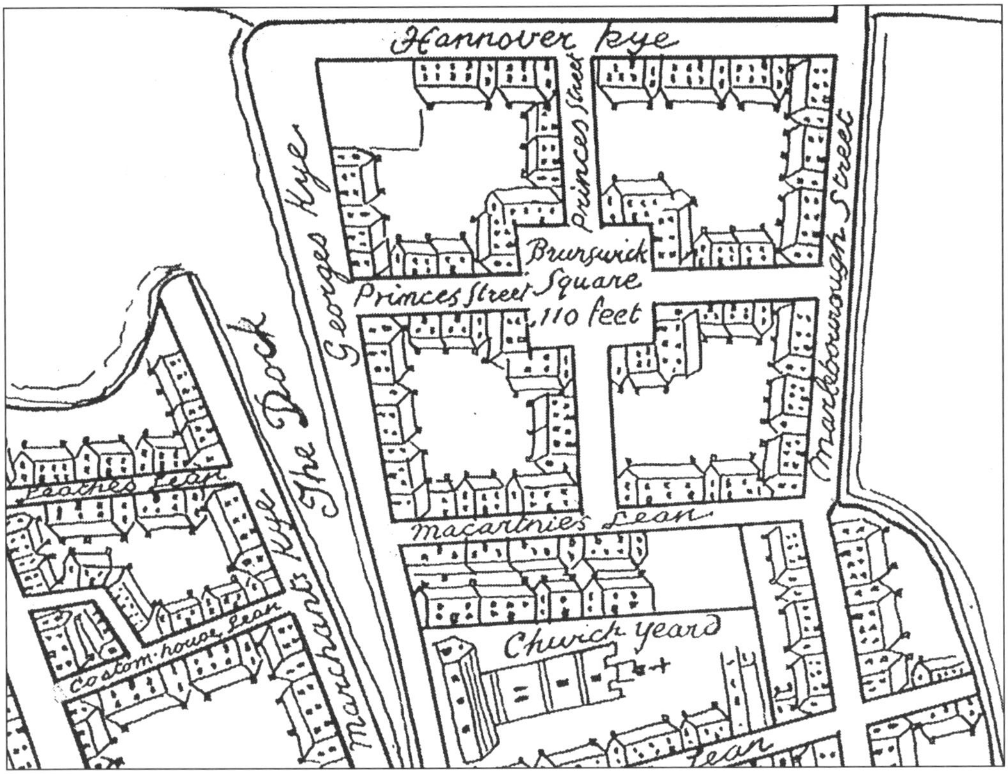

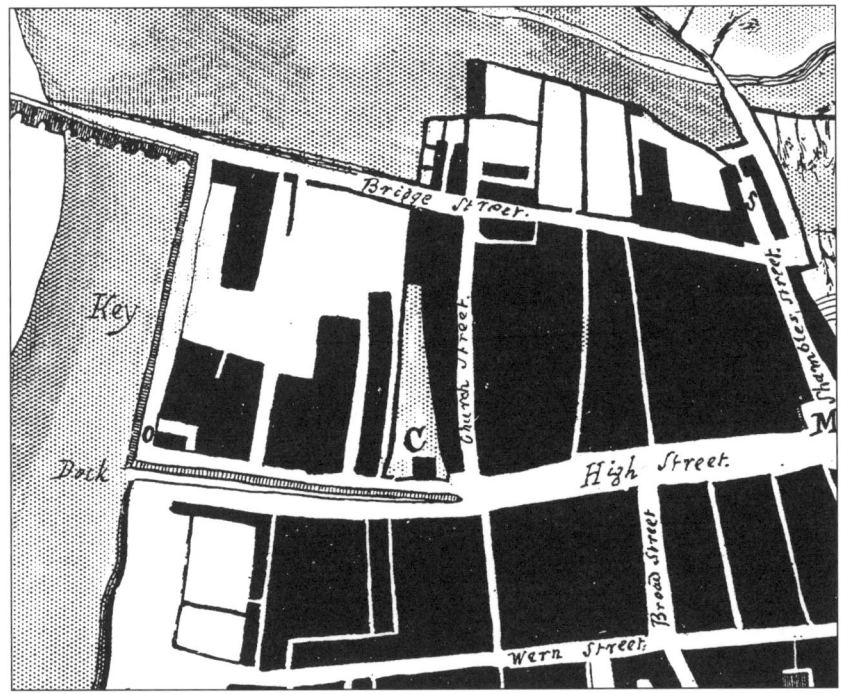

Isaac Macartney's development at Hanover Square as it was depicted (a) in 1715 by John Maclanachan and (b) in 1757 on a plan of Belfast.

McHugh's bar on Queen's Square. While the scheme may not have been completed, it was still profitable and by the 1720s Macartney was clearing £400 a year from his property, including the venture. This may have encouraged others to attempt to emulate his success. In 1716 Westenra Waring, the son of the tanner and merchant William Waring who developed part of Waring Street, obtained a lease of the 'waste and unsettled ground' on the Strand, to the south of Macartney's development and within the area bounded by the Long Bank.[76] Part of this land reclamation scheme may be represented by the grid iron of stone walls with a river wall encountered in excavations on Victoria Square, although further reclamation work was carried out here in the 1760s and 1790s and these walls may belong to that later development.[77] If Waring intended a building programme like Macartney's, it never materialised.

Most of Macartney's profit may have come from the quays and the customs house, which were constructed along the river as part of the development. Since at this stage it was Revenue Commissioners' policy to lease rather than build customs houses, Macartney's scheme was welcomed by officialdom. The new customs house and quays were considerably more convenient than the old town quay at the end of High Street. He proposed to levy a tax of 3½*d*. a ton on goods loaded or unloaded. In this he was frustrated by Lord Donegall's agent on the grounds that it would discourage trade. After a period of haggling with the merchants a fee of 2*d*. a ton was agreed with the merchants. This was clearly a profitable tax, since when Macartney sold it in 1738 he got ten years' purchase for it, rather more than a landed estate would have realised at that point in time.[78] This profitability signalled the importance of land reclamation as the way in which the town would expand over the next century.

II

The factors that lay behind the problems Belfast exhibited in the early eighteenth century are difficult to untangle. It is clear that general economic conditions in the years after 1700, as the Irish economy generally moved into recession, took their toll on the town. More significant were the local problems of the Donegall family, the landlords of Belfast. Three near-simultaneous family crises had long-lasting repercussions for the town. Firstly, the burning of the castle in 1708 had a powerful psychological effect on the family. As the Killyleagh merchant James Traill expressed it, what a 'surprising shock must the news of this give the poor lady their mother that was bereaved of three hopeful children at one stroke'.[79] Moreover, this was not the countess's first bereavement. The second crisis was the death of the third earl of Donegall, who was killed in 1706 in Spain while serving with the duke of Marlborough's army there, leaving a minor as his heir. The impact of this on the town was considerable, since it affected the estate's financial solvency. The merchant Isaac Macartney wrote in 1706 of 'nothing being more sure than that there is not estate enough to answer for jointures, life rents and interest of the money' so that 'some of the creditors will suffer for the present'.[80]

The third crisis revolved around the relationship between a weakened Donegall family and an increasingly powerful merchant elite in the town. The first signs of tension here appeared under the guise of religion. In 1704 the Test Act had imposed the requirement on mayors that they receive the sacrament according to the rite of the Church of Ireland. In Belfast, where Presbyterians held control of the corporation, this was not possible and that year's sovereign, David Buttle, resigned. If the same situation were to continue it would clearly debar from office most of the wealthiest inhabitants of the town despite their protestations of loyalty to the state in loyal addresses to the lord lieutenant.[81] The restrictions of the Test Act coincided with another crisis in 1703 over the issue of the corporation's power to levy money on ships docking at the quay. In reality this tax was the result of a shortage of corporation funds to improve the quay. However, it was represented by William King, bishop of Derry, as a Presbyterian conspiracy, since the vicar of Belfast was experiencing problems around the same time in collecting his house money, the urban equivalent of tithes.[82] These poor social relations within Belfast formed the context for the most important confrontation between the Donegalls and the corporation over the election of an MP for the town in 1707. A group of Belfast merchants proposed one candidate, the Presbyterian Samuel Ogle, while the countess of Donegall espoused the cause of

Alexander Cairnes. Ogle triumphed at the polls but Cairnes challenged the election on the grounds of irregular behaviour by the sovereign of Belfast. Parliament judged in favour of Cairnes and declared that all the burgesses of Belfast were required to take the sacramental test. Lady Donegall, having broken the corporation's power, ensured that her own will would prevail in future by replacing the non-conforming Presbyterian burgesses with her own nominees, members of the established church[83] Any feeling that the corporation still held any residual power was firmly quashed in 1709 when the corporation's attempt to promote a bill in the Irish parliament, perhaps emulating the Cork harbour act of 1704 and attempts to pass a similar bill for Dublin port, entitling it to collect tolls in the port was firmly put down by Lady Donegall.[84] This did not mark the end of political disputes in Belfast. In 1728, for instance, Lord Barrymore wrote to the town's MP about 'the disputes in relation to the magistrates of Belfast being adjusted' and in 1739 there were further disputes but these are poorly documented episodes.[85] However the trial of strength between the Donegall family and the merchant oligarchy had certainly gone the way of the Donegalls and for the most part the corporation remained compliant throughout the early eighteenth century.

These three crises all combined to ensure that the Donegalls no longer felt comfortable in the town of Belfast and they departed for their estates in England. They would not return until the 1760s. The loss of a substantial employer had an immediate impact on the town. As the vicar of Belfast, William Tisdall, put it in 1720:

> the unhappy effects [of the Donegalls' departure] descended to all the inferior ranks of people, especially to the poor of the parish insomuch that some tradesmen were obliged to leave the town, others fell into great want whilst a number of common poor were reduced to the last necessity, all this for want of that employment and of those charitable supplies which they usually had from that great and numerous family and their dependencies.[86]

Underlying all these immediate problems for the inhabitants of the town there were more were profound ones created by structural weakness in the Donegall family's finances. The dispute over the first earl's will had been settled by the third earl in an agreement in 1692 but that had been expensive. The third earl had made long leases in return for high entry fines to fund it. When he died in 1706 the estate was deeply in debt. He was succeeded by the fourth earl – a minor. That was only the beginning of a series of disasters for the family. During the minority of the fourth earl, the family was involved in a series of protracted disputes over the property and as a result of the earl's manifest mental incapacity (which the countess had tried to conceal by an unsuitable marriage) the estate was administered by a set of three trustees. Initially the trustees quarrelled and pursued their own policies towards the estate, the actions of one negating the efforts of another.[87] The trustees exercised a much greater degree of control over the estate and its expenditures than hitherto but they were limited in a number of ways. First, the leaseholding structure of the town was much the same as it had been in its early years, with most of the property in the hands of a number of large leaseholders. A rental of 1719 reveals that the town was divided into only 95 holdings and that two thirds of these were very substantial ones. The entire town brought in an annual rental of only £671, since rent levels had been sacrificed to the immediate gain of entry fines.[88] Secondly, the trustees were limited in the length of leases that they could grant. Leases were limited to 41 years, and this had the effect of discouraging leaseholders from repairing their buildings or investing in their property. In 1726 the agent for the family, Robert Greene, suggested that a private act of parliament be obtained to allow longer leases to be made, 'which will be of great advantage and profit to this town and country', but this came to nothing.[89] Not surprisingly, the situation gave rise to unease and uncertainty. Pococke, writing in 1752, observed that many of the residents were 'very uneasy that they cannot get new leases to build, all of them being near expiring'.[90] Other expressions of concern took on a more dramatic turn. The earl of Massareene, Lord Donegall's nephew, exclaimed, 'I live in the neighbourhood of Belfast and know it to be in a ruinous condition and will lose both its trade and inhabitants if it is not speedily supported by proper tenures.'[91] Clearly by the 1750s Belfast was a town with considerable problems, whose future was uncertain because of absentee and inadequate landlords.

Those problems were perhaps most acutely felt in the area of the town's infrastructure. The accounts for the early eighteenth century, during the minority of the earl, reveal that the family spent almost nothing on the town but still drew their rents from it. Those rents had risen substantially based on the town's good fortune in the seventeenth century. In 1630 the town and manor had yielded the family £400 a year but by 1706 this stood at £2,175 14s. 2d. and by 1715 had reached £2,335 10s. 6d.[92] However while many Ulster landlords, such as Arthur Brownlow of Lurgan, drew a substantial portion of their rental from towns, Belfast, like Strabane, represented a small proportion of the total Chichester rental because of the size of their estates.[93] Thus the family had less interest in Belfast than they might have had. They did continue to support a number of developments in the town. At the time of the Restoration the family had established a school in Belfast, located behind the parish church.[94] After 1700 they continued to pay the salary of the master and repair the schoolhouse and the area around it.[95] In addition they repaired the bridge at Cromac a number of times in the early eighteenth century, enclosed their deer park and undertook occasional repairs to a few houses, known as New Buildings, built facing Cornmarket, on the site of the destroyed castle.[96] In all it was a modest investment for the substantial return. For more complex problems the family resorted to tried, if not necessarily effective, means to provide the town with the amenities required for everyday life. The water supply was a case in point. In 1738 it was noted:

> the town was very ill watered. Tho' a river runs through the town, and a large one at the need of it, yet good water was not to be had, but at a dear rate in the summer, for all the filth of the town emptied itself in one and the other brackish a great way up the river.[97]

Clearly the attempt by Macartney to establish a piped water supply in the 1680s did not keep up with the needs of an expanding town. The Donegalls attempted to solve this problem in 1733 by leasing to William Johnston of New Forge for 41 years all the water supply around Belfast, including the wells at Fountainville and Sandy Row, on condition that he supply water to the town. The scheme was an ambitious one. Initially it went well, with a comment in 1738 that Johnston had undertaken 'to bring good water into the town at a certain rate per house, which he perfected and they have now plenty of most excellent water'.[98] This did not last and in 1753 it was proposed to let the waterworks and by 1755 the scheme was a loss-making one, one later lessee claiming that the amount received was not enough to pay the rent.[99] The scheme may have been overly ambitious but it does point to the inability of such farming schemes, on which the Donegalls relied for the development of the town, to deliver in times of economic difficulty.

III

The problems the Donegall family presented for Belfast were only part of the town's tribulations. Its wealth in the seventeenth century had been built on trade and in the early eighteenth century that trade began to experience problems. In the years after 1700 the customs yield on exports fell, while that on imports increased, marking the emergence of trading difficulties. Most of these stemmed from the collapse of the markets that had been carefully exploited in the late seventeenth century. The butter business, for instance, had been one of the staples of Belfast trade in the 1680s. Almost 34,000 hundredweights of butter were exported from Belfast in 1683. In 1700 the figure stood at 22,103 hundredweights; by 1750 it was about 8,000 hundredweights. The collapse had come in particular areas – the European trade and most especially the exports to France, which had fallen from almost 26,000 hundredweights of butter in 1683 to 420 hundredweights by 1750. This pattern was repeated over all the main staples of late seventeenth-century trading at Belfast. Barrelled beef, for instance, fell from 4,205 barrels in 1683 to 2,700 barrels in 1700, although it recovered some of its former importance due to a rise in the colonial American trade around 1750.[100] The reasons for these changes are not difficult to discern. The decline of the trade can in each case be attributed to a collapse in the trade with continental Europe linked to persistent warfare, French levies on imported butter and general economic instability, in some cases offset by a growth in the colonial trade.

In response to this situation the Belfast merchants looked for new areas in which to do business that would generate profit. In 1726, for instance, a woollen business for the town was being contemplated by Donegall's agent, prefiguring the later successful establishment of cotton in the poorhouse.[101] The wool trade never took off but merchants found other ways of making a profit. The first area that emerged as a potential profit earner was the linen trade. This had grown slowly in the late seventeenth century, principally along the Lagan Valley and centred mainly on Lisburn and Lurgan.[102] By the early eighteenth century the linen trade had spread well outside these bounds to the areas in and around Belfast. Linen weavers were noted in the town in 1729 and between 1712 and 1736 the funerals of 22 Belfast weavers were noted in the register of the first Presbyterian church, most of whom had been living on the edges of the town.[103] In 1744 Walter Harris reported of Newtownards, to the east of Belfast, that 'the principal and most beneficial trade of it is the linen manufacture, and especially in repute for the sales of great quantities of fine diaper linen'.[104] Given the geography of the trade, and especially its origins in the Lagan Valley, it might be expected that Belfast would act as the main port of export of fine linens and that merchant capital would be used to promote the trade. Some Belfast merchants thought so too, especially after the passage of a 1705 act to promote the manufacture of Irish linen. As early as 1675 the Belfast merchant Lewis Thompson observed that linen cloth for sheets and shirting was looked on by other Belfast merchants as the best commodity for trading with Virginia and New England.[105] These possibilities were not immediately fulfilled. Most of the trade in fine Ulster linens was carried on through the more sophisticated Dublin market, and was supported by the capital of the linen merchants there.

The slow rise of the Belfast linen trade in the early eighteenth century was underpinned by a number of developments. Changing fashions may have played a part and in 1730 it was commented that the inhabitants of Belfast had taken to wearing linen scarves at funerals instead of imported French silk as part of a patriotic reaction to luxury imports.[106] In 1729 a yarn market was established in the town and in 1739 a linen hall for the sale of unbleached brown linen was built, partly funded by the earl of Donegall, in Ann Street. The building process was not a easy since Donegall commented in February 1739 'the late conduct of a great number of my tenants at Belfast (who have unreasonably flown in my face and disturbed the tranquility of the town) has induced me ... to suspend building the hall'.[107] It was finished that year and, according to Donegall, was 'conformable to the one erected in Dublin but not quite so large'.[108] The Dublin hall had been constructed only ten years earlier and comprised a series of two-storey buildings surrounding a large open courtyard in which the linen was displayed. The Belfast hall presumably looked similar. The position of the new hall is significant, being on a previously unbuilt area on the south side of Ann Street, which had been subject to flooding from the Blackstaff. In conjunction with the building of the linen hall Donegall improved the sea bank to the south of this area, which was intended to protect it from the worst of the flooding.[109] The area itself had some prospects. Ann Street, for instance, was named by 1712, although it had appeared as unnamed on earlier maps, which suggests that it was taking on a new importance.[110] Isaac Macartney's new development at the west end of Ann Street had established the commercial potential of this area, especially since the quay and customs house were now located there. By the early eighteenth century the markets had already moved into the area around Cornmarket and after the destruction of the castle there was the possibility of a redevelopment on this site, although this took some time to emerge since in the 1720s there was still open ground around Cornmarket that could be leased.[111]

By 1746 the linen trade of Belfast was said to be 'greatly increased', although it was still weak and somewhat unpredictable, some of the business still being carried on outside the linen hall in the markets.[112] By the 1770s almost two thirds of the linen exported from Ulster passed through the port of Belfast. It is also clear that by the 1750s some Belfast merchants were beginning to enter the trade not simply as dealers in cloth and yarn but as organisers and financiers of the trade. One visitor recorded that Belfast merchants were now 'buying the yarn and giving it to be wove'.[113] In this can be seen the sort of emerging interest in new ways of making money on which the cotton trade would be built in the late eighteenth century.

The second element that the Belfast merchant community identified as a new exploitable area has left less of a topographical trace. In the early eighteenth century one of the growth areas in Belfast's trade was that of people, in the form of emigration to North America. Belfast had well-established trading contacts with the American colonies from the 1680s and in 1731 it was the first town in the north of Ireland to enter into a two-way trade with mainland North America.[114] Emigration from Ulster to North America was already well established by 1718 as Belfast merchants developed contacts with the labour markets in North America. That trade grew significantly in the 1740s and 1750s. In 1765 at least ten emigrant ships left Belfast for North America, with nine departing the following year and at least twelve departing in 1767.[115] Between 1750 and 1775 over a third of all emigrant ships leaving Ulster did so from Belfast.[116] By the time of the American revolution in 1776 many of those who lived in the town had relatives or friends in North America who might have been responsible for channelling radical ideas back into Belfast.

As the Belfast merchants identified new markets to resolve problems in the older ones they also encountered new competition. In the north-west the port of Derry was well placed to be a substantial player in the same Atlantic trade that Belfast was vying for. As a result, in the early eighteenth century Derry boomed, in contrast to Belfast. The population of Derry more than tripled between 1706 and 1788.[117] We can be less sure about the Belfast's population but numbers of houses in the town probably fell between 1725 and 1757. This suggests both a falling population and the dilapidation of the housing stock.[118] To the south of Belfast another rival appeared, this time in the domestic markets. In the late seventeenth century Newry had not been a particularly important port. It was described by travellers as poor and was certainly insignificant compared to Belfast about 1700. In the early eighteenth century, however, Newry began to expand. In the 1730s, for instance, new warehouses were built on the quays, reflecting the growth in trade there. By 1744 Walter Harris noted that it was much improved 'in trade, inhabitants and buildings' since the Williamite wars and was 'now in a thriving condition, being the largest trading town in the county, and still likely to improve further'.[119] By the 1760s new town-planning projects, including the gridiron pattern of streets with squares at the intersections, had been laid out. Newry's prosperity might be gauged by the large number of fine houses of mid-eighteenth-century date that were put up.[120] There are various explanations for this boom. One factor may have been the relocation of the customs house from Carlingford in 1726, but much more important was the construction of the Newry canal, highlighted by Harris as one of the key elements in generating that town's wealth. The idea of a canal had been floated as early as 1703 but it was given new impetus when coal, which could be sold in Dublin, was discovered at Coalisland. By 1731, the construction of a canal of 18 miles connecting Newry and Lough Neagh was under way and it was completed in 1742. This gave Newry merchants water access to the large markets of central Ulster. While the canal's main function was the export of coal, it also allowed the import through Newry of fashionable goods from Dublin. In all this the burgeoning trade of Newry was eating into Belfast's and in the 1780s Newry would construct a linen hall in an attempt to rival Belfast's position in that trade. These developments emphasised to the Belfast merchants the importance of inland communications. Some quickly took advantage of private acts of parliament to establish turnpike roads. In 1733 an act was passed for the construction of such a road from Banbridge to Belfast and in 1739 another permitted the building of a road from Belfast to Antrim that linked to an earlier turnpike to Coleraine, both roads being funded by issuing debentures.[121] In 1757 a new road to Newtownards was constructed, but more significant were early attempts to link Belfast with Lough Neagh by canal. This idea had been mooted as early as 1637 but had never been attempted.[122] In 1753 an act was passed for the building of a canal between Belfast and Lough Neagh to rival that of Newry. Work began in 1756. Within a year six miles had been completed, but it took two more years to build a further mile. Various ways of funding the new project were considered, including a tax on spirits consumed locally but many were not hopeful of progress. As one of Lord Donegall's agents commented in 1772 'what a pity it is that a thing of such consequence to this town in particular ... were not likely to succeed'. Work was slow and fitful for want of funds and the canal was not finally completed until 1793.[123]

IV

The early eighteenth century was a period of difficulties for Belfast. There is a good deal of evidence to support the view that the town by the 1750s was becoming rather run down. In 1738 the market house was said to be 'very handsome' but, while still a prominent building, it was becoming increasingly dilapidated. In 1746 it was said that the balcony was rotten, the roof needed reslating and all the floors required repairs.[124] The proposals made by tenants for new leases in 1757 also highlight the extent of decay of the urban fabric. One North Street tenant's house was two 'thatch'd cabins not to be lived in much longer as the premises in part had fallen down and the rest upon props and coming down'.[125] However, it is important not to exaggerate this problem. In the 1730s and early 1750s new three-storey houses could be found in North Street with slate roofs. The prevailing impression, however, whatever the reality, was of dilapidation.[126]

The physical dilapidation was paralleled by institutional inertia. The series of crises between 1704 and 1707 saw the corporation changing from a merchant oligarchy into a landlord-controlled institution. This was by no means an inevitable drift. At Newtownards in north Down a dispute in 1747 between the former owner of this town and its new owner, Alexander Stewart, over control of the corporation led to the Newtown Act of 1748.[127] This strengthened the power of the corporation and weakened landlord influence over it. The result was a vigorous political and administrative atmosphere at local level as Stewart tried to capture the hearts and minds of the corporation. In Belfast, landlord control stifled rather than expanded corporate power. The burgesses could now be drawn only from the narrow pool of members of the established church. The institutions of urban government no longer worked as well as they had done given the small pool of talent from which the corporation could draw. By the 1720s it was claimed that there were not enough people in the town qualified to take civic office.[128] As always, there were complaints about the financial position of the corporation. In the early eighteenth century the corporation could not afford to make the new larger maces it thought appropriate since the old ones were 'really too small for such a place' and tried to raise private funding from elsewhere. They told one potential benefactor that such expenditure 'will last longer in memory' than anything else. In the 1750s the corporation had raided the poor fund to obtain enough money to make silver freedom boxes given to distinguished men who were made free of the city.[129] For the years after 1707 the town book becomes a very uninformative document, containing only election results and the appointment of burgesses, with no attempt to grapple with the issues facing the town.

However, the absence of a landlord prepared to take the initiative fostered a sense of voluntarism. In 1716, for instance, the main inhabitants of the town established a charity school that had 50 pupils by 1720, run by a committee and financed by private benefactors.[130] Such voluntarism was to characterise Belfast through the eighteenth century. The establishment of the Belfast Charitable Society in the 1760s, after a number of false starts, following the demographic crisis of 1753–4, is one example of that. Through the late eighteenth century the Belfast Charitable Society took on many of the functions a corporation should have fulfilled. It managed the water supply, provided burial grounds and cared for the poor, all on a voluntary basis.[131] It was no accident that political voluntarism in the shape of the Volunteer and United Irish movements for parliamentary reform should have originated in Belfast. All this speaks of a growing self-confidence among the town's inhabitants, fostered by the lack of a guiding hand rather than by the presence of one.[132] Their actions speak of that confidence as eloquently as the surviving portraits of the Belfast merchant classes that appeared in the middle of the eighteenth century. Here were represented families such as those of Thomas Bateson and Thomas Gregg, painted amid the opulent furniture and fittings of their homes and surrounded by globes, maps and engravings of ships as the tools of their trade.[133] By 1750 the difficulties of the early eighteenth century were easing and Belfast was about to reinvent itself once again.

NOTES

1   Story, *True and impartial account*, p. 38.
2   Sacheverell, *Account of the Isle of Man*, p. 125; British Library, Sloane MS 2902, f. 218.
3   Young, *Historical notices*, p. 155.
4   P.R.O.N.I., T808/15260.
5   Miskimmin, *Carrickfergus*, p. 276.
6   Based on T.N.A., Cust 15/3, 14, 24, 34, 44, 54.
7   P.R.O.N.I., D501/1, pp 86, 144.
8   Paterson, 'Belfast in 1738', p. 112. One of the bells cast for this repair, dated 1731, is now in the hands of the Belfast Charitable Society.
9   McVeagh, *Richard Pococke's Irish tours*, p. 38.
10 *Belfast News-Letter*, 6 July 1753.
11 P.R.O.N.I., D719/73–4.
12 P.R.O.N.I., T1893. 16 Jan 1773, George Portis to C.H. Talbot; 26 April 1773, John Alexander to C.H. Talbot, 30 Dec 1773 George Portis to C.H. Talbot.
13 Pender, *Census*, p. 8.
14 W.P. Burke, *The Irish priests in the penal times* (Waterford, 1914), p. 281.
15 *A list of all the names of the popish parish priests throughout the several counties in the kingdom of Ireland* (Dublin, 1704).
16 Young, *Town book*, pp 11–12, 19–20.
17 McVeagh, *Richard Pococke's Irish tours*, p. 38.
18 *A journal of the travels, sufferings and labours of … William Edmundson* (Dublin, 1715), p. 14.
19 Agnew, *Belfast merchant families*, pp 33–4.
20 Adair, *Presbyterian church*, pp 96, 100.
21 P.R.O.N.I., D3113/60; *Historic memorials of the first Presbyterian church of Belfast* (Belfast, 1887), pp 16, 108.
22 P.R.O.N.I., ANT4/1/1, p. 5; Benn, *History* (1877), p. 115.
23 Benn, *History* (1823), p. 116.
24 For Presbyterian pew sales see Registry of Deeds, Dublin, 8/308/2810; P.R.O.N.I., D298/16.
25 P.R.O.N.I., D1460/3; William Tisdall, *Conduct of the dissenters in Ireland* (Dublin, 1712), p. 55.
26 National Archives, Dublin, Sarsfield-Vesey MSS. Printed in Shannon Millin, *Catalogue of exhibits relating to old Belfast* (Belfast, 1939), p. 53 and reproduced in idem, *Additional sidelights*, p. 44.
27 P.R.O.N.I., D1460/3.
28 P.R.O.N.I., T3425/3/11/15–16, 36; T3425/3/14/39/79.
29 Benn, *History* (1880), p. 115; T.N.A., C107/16, pt 1, ff 11v, 13v.
30 Young, *Historical notices*, p. 155.
31 Registry of Deeds, Dublin, 4/2/32/909; 4/392/1068; 4/394/1072; 7/301/2456.
32 *Belfast News-Letter*, 14 July 1758.
33 T.N.A., C107/16, pt 2, p. 15, Benn, *History* (1877), p. 539; Young, *Town book*, p. 155.
34 T.E. McNeill, 'Belfast's first industrial revolution' in *Current Archaeology*, xii, no. 2 (1993), pp 56–7; T.E. McNeill and M.G. Baillie, 'An early eighteenth-century pottery assemblage from Dunbar Street, Belfast' in Gearóid Mac

Niocaill and P.F. Wallace (eds), *Keimelia: studies in medieval archaeology and history in memory of Tom Delaney* (Galway, 1988), pp 349–64.

35   Young, *Historical notices*, p. 156.

36   Sacheverell, *Account of the Isle of Man*, p. 125.

37   Peter Francis, *Irish delftware: an illustrated history* (London, 2000), pp 11–12.

38   Recited in Registry of Deeds, Dublin, 25/203/14741.

39   P.R.O.N.I., D501/1, pp 321–2.

40   Francis, *Irish delftware*, pp 23–33.

41   Ibid., p. 17.

42   *Excavations 2002*, p. 5,

43   Francis, *Irish delftware*, pp 16–17.

44   A.S. Drennan, 'On the identification of the first Belfast printed book' in *The Library*, 7th ser., i (2000), pp 193–6.

45   National Archives, Dublin, RC9/1, p. 40; Bodleain Library, Oxford, Carte Ms 34, f. 397; Benn, *History* (1877), p. 316; P.R.O.N.I., D 1449/13/1, p. 53; Tisdall, *Conduct of the dissenters*, p. 68.

46   Raymond Gillespie, *Reading Ireland: print, reading and social change in early modern Ireland* (Manchester, 2005), pp 86–7. For early eighteenth-century bookbinders see Agnew, *Funeral register* (Belfast, 1995), pp 20, 39, 40, 41.

47   Wesley McCann, 'Patrick Neill and the origins of Belfast printing' in Peter Isaac (ed.), *Six centuries of the provincial book trade in Britain* (Winchester, 1990), pp 125–38.

48   Wesley McCann, 'The distribution of books from Belfast: the evidence of subscription lists' in Gerard Long (ed.), *Books beyond the Pale: aspects of the provincial book trade in Ireland before 1850* (Dublin, 1996), pp 75–85.

49   McCann, 'Distribution of books from Belfast', pp 78–80.

50   Listed in John Anderson, *Catalogue of early Belfast printed books, 1694 to 1830* (2nd ed., Belfast, 1890), pp 6, 8, 13–14, 17.

51   For a short biography see Robert Munter, *A dictionary of the print trade in Ireland, 1650–1775* (New York, 1988), p. 151.

52   Agnew, *Funeral register*, p. 40.

53   Benn, *History* (1823), p. 68.

54   P.R.O.N.I., D509/25, 28, 29; Benn, *History* (1877), p. 588.

55   D.B. Quinn (ed.), 'William Montgomery and the description of the Ards, 1683' in *Irish Booklore*, ii (1972), p. 38.

56   Bodleian Library, Oxford, Carte MS 215, f. 330; *Reg. P.C. Scot., 1676–6*, p. 297; Young, *Historical notices*, p. 156; *Cal. Treasury books, 1699–1700*, p. 265.; *Cal. Treasury books, 1717*, p. 48.

57   P.R.O.N.I., D162/31,32.

58   Edward McParland, *Public architecture in Ireland, 1680–1760* (London and New Haven, 2001), pp 131–3.

59   *Observations made by the commissioners on their view of several barracks: north-east circuit* (Dublin, 1760), pp 18–21.

60   Raymond Gillespie and Alison O'Keeffe (eds), *Register of the parish of Shankill, Belfast, 1745–1761* (Dublin, 2006), p. 25. On the barracks see F.J. Bigger, 'The old barracks of Belfast' in *U.J.A.*, 2nd ser., xvii (1911), pp 74–8.

61   Young, *Town book*, pp 189–90.

62   For these buildings see *Excavations 2004*, p. 7.

63   *Belfast atlas*, p. 10.

64   Registry of Deeds, Dublin, 4/231/908.

65   Registry of Deeds, Dublin, 4/477/371.

66   On the evolution of the 'entries' see Kenneth McNally, *The narrow streets* (Belfast, 1972).

67 McVeagh, *Richard Pococke's Irish tours*, p. 38.
68 *Belfast News-Letter*, 18 Apr. 1755; 6 Apr. 1756.
69 Registry of Deeds, Dublin, 50/338/33264; 7/98/1805.
70 *Excavations 1999*, p. 1; Ó Baoill and Logue, 'Excavations at Gordon Street', pp 112–15.
71 T.N.A., C107/16, pt 2, pp 3, 8, 29, 40.
72 Registry of Deeds, Dublin, 6/429/2479.
73 Paterson, 'Belfast in 1738', p. 112.
74 Registry of Deeds, Dublin, 15/474/8141; 15/103/6900.
75 P.R.O.N.I., ANT/4/1/1, pp 103, 154–5, 293.
76 Millin, *Additional sidelights*, p. 29.
77 *Excavations, 2004*, p. 7.
78 Benn, *History* (1877), p. 479.
79 P.R.O.N.I., D1460/1.
80 P.R.O.N.I., D501/1, pp 340–1.
81 For example P.R.O.N.I., T456/5.
82 Benn, *History* (1877), pp 380–2, 475–7; P.R.O.N.I., D1449/1/13/1.
83 The details of this can be followed in Agnew, *Belfast merchant families*, pp 91–104.
84 Young, *Town book*, pp 200–10.
85 P.R.O.N.I., D572/21/101, p. 51; D562/701.
86 William Tisdall, *An account of the charity school in Belfast* (1720), pp 3–4.
87 W.A. Maguire, 'A question of arithmetic: Arthur Chichester, fourth earl of Donegall, 1695–1757' in Collins *et al.*, *Industry, trade and people*, pp 31–50.
88 P.R.O.N.I., D 2249/61.
89 Young, *Historical notices*, p. 165.
90 McVeagh, *Richard Pococke's Irish tours*, pp 37–8.
91 Benn, *History* (1877), pp 535.
92 T.N.A., C107/16, pt 1, ff 2v, 14.
93 William Roulston, *Restoration Strabane, 1660–1714* (Dublin, 2007), pp 27–8.
94 For its position see Millin, *Additional sidelights*, p. 24.
95 T.N.A., C107/16, pt 2, pp 9, 15, 20, 39, 44.
96 Ibid., pt 2, pp 1, 15, 21, 28, 30, 35, 48, 50, 54, 56.
97 Paterson, 'Belfast in 1738', p. 112.
98 Ibid., p. 112.
99 Benn, *History* (1877), pp 487–8; *Belfast News-Letter*, 2 Nov. 1762.
100 British Library, Add. MS 4756, ff 1–7; T.N.A., Cust 15/3, 14, 54.
101 Young, *Town book*, p. 329.
102 For the emergence of the trade see Gillespie, *Settlement and survival*, pp xxxv–xxxviii.
103 *Tribune* (London, 1729), pp 29–35; Agnew, *Funeral register*, pp 13, 15–17, 22, 28–9, 31–3, 35, 38–41.
104 Harris, *Antient and present state* (Dublin, 1744), p. 56.
105 P.R.O.N.I., D501/1, pp 68, 84; Roseveare, *Markets and merchants*, pp 388–9.
106 *A list of the inhabitants of Ireland and the yearly value of their estates and income spent abroad* (London, 1730), p. 77.
107 P.R.O.N.I., D562/701.
108 Benn, *History* (1877), p. 345; P.R.O.N.I., T3425/11/1–55; T3425/14/39; T3425/15/36–7, 39; McParland, *Public architecture in Ireland*, pp 22–3.
109 P.R.O.N.I., T3425/3/14/42; *Belfast News-Letter*, 17 July 1739.
110 Registry of Deeds, Dublin, 10/172/3374.
111 P.R.O.N.I., D509/48.

112 Benn, *History* (1877), p. 346.
113 McVeagh, *Richard Pococke's Irish tours*, p. 39.
114 Thomas Truxes, *Irish American trade, 1660–1783* (Cambridge, 1988), pp 78–81.
115 Ibid., pp 135–6.
116 R.J. Dickson, *Ulster emigration to colonial America, 1718–75* (London, 1966), pp 229–30.
117 Thomas, *Derry~Londonderry*, p. 10; *Belfast atlas*, p. 10.
118 *Belfast atlas*, p. 10.
119 Harris, *Antient and present state*, p. 94.
120 Jope, *Archaeological survey of County Down*, pp 422–30.
121 David Broderick, *The first toll roads: Ireland's turnpike roads, 1729*–1858 (Cork, 2002), p. 38
122 *Cal. S.P. Ire. 1633–47*, p. 174.
123 P.R.O.N.I., T1893, 28 Sept 1771 Thomas Gregg to George Portis, 23 Nov 1772 John Alexander to C.H. Talbot; W.A. McCutcheon, *The canals of the north of Ireland* (London, 1965), pp 40–5.
124 Paterson, 'Belfast in 1738', p. 112; P.R.O.N.I., D354/999, 1000, 1002–06.
125 Benn, *History* (1877), pp 538–42.
126 *Belfast News-Letter*, 9 Mar. 1739; 24 Dec. 1754.
127 A.P.W. Malcomson, 'The Newtown Act of 1748: revision and reconstruction' in *Irish Historical Studies*, xviii, no. 71 (Mar. 1973), pp 313–44.
128 Young, *Historical notices*, p. 166.
129 P.R.O.N.I., D501/1, pp 501–2; *Letters from Belfast* (Belfast, 1752), p. 12.
130 Tisdall, *Account of the charity school*.
131 Strain, *Belfast and its charitable society, passim*.
132 For this group see W.H. Crawford, 'The Belfast middle classes in the late eighteenth century' in David Dickson, Dáire Keogh and Kevin Whelan (eds), *The United Irishmen: republicanism, radicalism and rebellion* (Dublin, 1993), pp 62–73.
133 Eileen Black, *Art in Belfast, 1760–1888* (Dublin, 2006), p. 4, Pls 1–2.

EPILOGUE

THE TRANSFORMATION
OF BELFAST

In the century before 1750 Belfast had developed quickly. However, that evolution of an urban environment could hardly be described as a transformation. In the Belfast of 1750 there was much that a resident of a hundred years earlier would still recognise. While there had been some land reclamation, the town still lay mainly within the limits of the rampart of 1642. As yet, no one was prepared to consider expanding the town southwards into the damp flood plain of the River Blackstaff, around what is now the City Hall. The main streets remained much as they had been in 1650, with Waring Street at the core of the town. There were also individual buildings and elements in the landscape that were still recognisable from the previous century. In some cases the older fabric had degenerated, either by the passage of time or by accident. The castle, for instance, which had been destroyed by fire, was never rebuilt and by 1750 its site lay as an open plot of as yet undeveloped land; but the site was still immediately recognisable. The seventeenth-century parish church on High Street was still a prominent feature in the urban landscape. Changing economic times had forced changes in the infrastructure of business, especially the docks, but this could hardly be described as transformation either. Belfast remained an intimate town. It was still a place based on face-to-face encounters in which people knew the genealogical matrix within which they operated. The parish register for the 1740s and 1750s, for instance, noted the names of the parents of those buried, even when the deceased were not children, and also recorded the names of their husbands or wives. The town may have been growing but it was still a small world.[1]

By contrast, in the century after 1750 Belfast underwent a process that was indeed a transformation. Not only did the shape of the town change as new streets and public buildings were added to the townscape but the numbers of people living there rose dramatically. The number of houses in the town probably rose threefold between 1660 and 1750 but by the following century it had increased eleven fold. If the merchant John Black in 1766 found Belfast to be a place of 'smoke, hurry, bustle and noise' his successors were even more troubled with the signs of modernity.[2]

The beginning of the transformation in Belfast after 1750 was becoming clear from 1754. In 1752 the trustees of the Donegall estate obtained a private act of parliament to allow them to make leases for the town and in 1754–6 such leases began to be negotiated. Since few new leases had been made in the first half of the century pent-up demand led to 'high offers beyond what could be expected' being made for the property on offer, according to one contemporary.[3] This process of re-leasing, and a later one in the 1760s, was to have a dramatic effect on the layout of the town. The leases that survive from this period all contain building or repairing clauses as a way of improving the run-down urban fabric. Initially, the effect was dramatic. According to a note made on the 1757 map, which was made as part of this process of urban regeneration, the central parts of the town now contained houses that were 'handsome, several stories [sic] high' and built of brick, although some of the areas at the edge of the town from the Plantation to Peter's Hill and along Mill Street were still 'only low thatched dwellings of a mean appearance'. This drive for change in the mid-1750s did not confine itself to rebuilding. It also attempted to alter the townscape. New streets like Berry Street (named after Richard Barry who was one of the trustees of the Donegall estate) were laid out. The most important of the new developments was Donegall Street, which was intended to open up a previously undeveloped area of the town between Waring Street and the road to Carrickfergus. The earl of Donegall also tried to provide a focus for his new initiative by constructing a linen hall for the sale of unbleached linen, later the site of the new parish church of St Anne.

New life was given to this movement for urban development after the death of the fourth earl of Donegall in 1757. The fifth earl took a more active interest in his town, although some Belfast residents thought he was still too preoccupied by his English house and lands at Fisherwick.[4] However, in 1765 he began to make new leases with conditions for rebuilding of Belfast.[5] The leases were all for three lives or 99 years, whichever was the longer, and all carried significant rent increases, up to 50 per cent in some cases. These leases were of four main types. The first was a simple renewal lease, which stipulated only that the property leased be kept in good repair. The second was a repairing lease, which required tenants to repair their own property; and a third type was a building lease, which stipulated that tenants must demolish and rebuild their houses. These leases showed considerable attention to detail, specifying that houses should be built of brick with slated roofs. Sash windows were required and the dimensions of the houses were set out in detail. Even the dimensions of the roof timbers were stipulated. Restrictions were placed on the dumping of rubbish on the property or in front of it, although it was to be 1800 before a scheme for cleaning and paving the whole town was established.[6] The social geography of the town was also regulated. Houses in Castle Place should be 28 feet high, those in High Street 25 feet. Ann Street was to have houses that were 18 feet high and the cabins on Peter's Hill were to be ten feet high. The final type of lease was of new ground, previously unbuilt on. Areas around Donegall Street, for example, were set to property developers such as the architect Roger Mullholland, who laid out further new streets in previously little-developed parts of the town and in the process created Talbot Street, Church Street and Academy Street.[7]

The distribution of the various types of lease was uneven across the town. Along the main east–west axis of High Street, Waring Street and Ann Street, about half of the houses required rebuilding. In the more recently developed areas of Donegall Street, Bridge Street and North Street only a fifth of the leases made were building leases. The impact of the re-leasing was greatest in the suburbs of Millfield, Barrack Street and north of Waring Street, where almost two thirds of the leases called for rebuilding of the property. The scale and relative speed of this re-leasing changed the face of Belfast. Rebuilding meant that it lost much of the older fabric that may have survived into the eighteenth century and it also gave the town

St Anne's Church, built by
the fifth earl of Donegall as
part of his efforts to develop
Donegall Street, from Benn,
History (1823).

an appearance of being formally organised and planned.
In 1766 one Carrickfergus
resident noted that Belfast was
a 'handsome sea port about 2
or 3,000 houses' and Richard
Twiss, travelling through
Ireland in 1775, commented
that 'the town is regularly
built and the streets are broad
and straight' and, as mentioned before, one American visitor went as
far as to record that Belfast was 'a large, populous and beautiful
town'.[8]

If the fifth earl's leasing policy changed the appearance of Belfast,
he also attempted to reorganise its social geography through the
provision of a number of important civic buildings. In 1774–6 he
built a parish church on the site of the old linen hall in Donegall
Street and moved the linen hall to a new site on the opposite side
of the same street. He also provided a site at the top of Donegall
Street for the new poorhouse, opened in 1774, thus closing the vista
along this straight street. Donegall's activities in developing a fashionable new centre in this area indicate the shifting social focus of
Belfast from the east–west line of High Street and Waring Street to
the north–south line of Donegall Street. Not all agreed with the
development, one merchant fretting that the new linen hall had
been placed 'too distant from the town's centre' to make a real
impact on business life.[9] The burning of the castle, and the failure to
rebuild it, had removed the centre of social gravity from the High
Street area and allowed for its repositioning on Donegall Street.
Such a shift would seem to be confirmed by the positioning by the

earl of a new exchange at the junction of Donegall Street and
Waring Street in 1769, to celebrate the birth of his first son. In 1776
a second storey was added to provide fashionable assembly rooms.
This in effect undermined the old market house in Cornmarket,
which had previously been the centre for smart gatherings such as
balls for the king's birthday and celebrations for military victories as
well as more mundane meetings for the relief of the poor and auc-
tions.[10]

   All this suggests that Belfast was a flourishing town in the 1760s
and 1770s. The trades of those taking leases in the 1760s point to a
range of economic activities being carried out in the town but the
most significant activity was that of the town's merchants.[11] Belfast's
revitalisation was underpinned not by manufacturing but by the
revival in trade after 1750. Arthur Young in the 1770s, for instance,
noted the importance of the provision trade and emigration to the
urban economy. The trades listed in the parish register also point to
the importance of the port, with the creation of official posts such
as the surveyor of the port and the tide waiters, as well as the presence of the army in the barracks at Barrack Street. The occupations
in the register also hint at the emergence of a more fashionable element in the town, for example a bookseller, a singing master and a
watchmaker. It is certainly no coincidence that the earliest portraits
of Belfast merchants, displaying the opulence of their possessions,
date from the 1760s.[12] Only rarely do the poor of Belfast appear in
the surviving evidence but the demographic crises of 1751 and
1756–7 provide evidence of a substantial cadre of people in the
town living on the margins of subsistence. Poor harvests and disease
pushed many of these over the edge, resulting in spiralling numbers
of those described as 'poor' being buried in the parish graveyard.[13]

   In the 1780s, for reasons that are not immediately clear but may
be related to the emergence of noxious tanneries in North Street
behind Donegall Street, the earl of Donegall began shifting the
social focus of the town once again.[14] In 1785 he granted land for
a new white-linen hall to be built, on the site of the present city
hall, to confirm Belfast's position in the rapidly expanding linen
trade. Private subscriptions of £17,550 funded the building. At the
same time he laid out Donegall Place, connecting the linen hall with

The white linen hall, built in 1785 on land granted by the marquis
of Donegall, from Benn, *History* (1823).

the west end of High Street. Building here was to be strictly regulated, since this was planned as a high-status residential area. It was
intended that the entrance at the High Street end was to be ornamental and that a canal would be built around the linen hall, which
would be 'eminently useful and ornamental to the thriving town of
Belfast', but most of these works were not completed.[15] However,
Donegall Street remained the 'aristocratic promenade' into the
nineteenth century, although by the 1840s, when it was described as
the 'St James's of Belfast', it was being encroached on by merchants
and traders.[16] What the development of Donegall Street did in the
longer term was to promote the building of fashionable houses
along Chichester Street, an area that had been previously ignored
because of the dampness created by the River Blackstaff, running
nearby. This dampness had led to a view that the area was regarded
as unhealthy. In 1792, on a visit to the town, Charles Abbot
described the houses in this area in approving terms, noting that
they were built of 'good red brick on a modern London plan' and
that one house was 'equal to many in Grosv[eno]r Square'.[17]

Belfast had at last breached the line of the 1642 rampart. As the
urban economy accelerated in the late eighteenth and early nineteenth centuries that expansion would become more marked. The
growth of cotton manufacturing saw large numbers of new workers flood into the town, so that Thomas Gaffikin could write, 'the

people of Belfast in the present generation are principally strangers'.[18] The growth in the population of the town meant that new houses had to be built, which doubled the town's housing stock between 1782 and 1806. These were mainly in the north-west of the town, around Mill Street, Smithfield, which had been formally laid out in 1788, Peter's Hill and Carrick Hill. As industry spread and became mechanised, that development led to further industrial housing around the newly laid-out streets off York Street, which quickly became one of the most densely populated and unsanitary parts of the town.

In the 50 years before 1800 Belfast had been transformed. The social centre had migrated from Waring Street and High Street to Donegall Place, new building had sprung up in almost every part of the town and Belfast's economic focus had shifted from commerce to industry. This was the heritage on which the industrial Belfast of the nineteenth century was to build. The development of ship-building and textiles would provide the wealth to change that town into a modern industrial city. However, none of this should blind us to the importance of the earliest phases of Belfast's development. Many of the patterns laid down in the town's formative years still have resonances and, indeed, traces in the street layout. The town that existed before 1750 still has a significance for the twenty-first-century inhabitant of Belfast.

NOTES

[1]   Gillespie and O'Keeffe, *Register of the parish of Shankill*, p. 40.
[2]   P.R.O.N.I., D719/77a.
[3]   P.R.O.N.I., D354/322.
[4]   For example P.R.O.N.I., D719/77a.
[5]   The topography of this re-leasing can be followed in Brett *et al.*, *Georgian Belfast*.
[6]   C.E.B. Brett, *Buildings of Belfast, 1700–1914* (2nd ed., Belfast 1985), pp 2–4; Brett *et al.*, *Georgian Belfast*, pp 6–7.
[7]   C.E.B. Brett, *Roger Mulholland, architect of Belfast* (Belfast, 1976).
[8]   P.R.O.N.I., D3165/2, p. 113; Richard Twiss, *A tour in Ireland in 1775* (London, 1776), p. 235; Morgan, *American Quaker in the British Isles*, p. 172.
[9]   Quoted in Isaac Ward, 'The Black family' in *U.J.A.*, 2nd ser., viii (1902), pp 178–9.

10   *Belfast News-Letter*, 17 July 1739; 11 Nov. 1756; 7, 14, 17, 31 Dec. 1756; 23, 30 Nov. 1756; 26 Oct. 1759; 11 Dec. 1759; 6 Nov. 1759; 13 Oct. 1761.

11   For the list of trades see Brett *et al.*, *Georgian Belfast*, pp 72–6.

12   Black, *Art in Belfast*, pp 3–7, Pls 1–2. For the emergence of this group see Crawford, 'Belfast middle classes', pp 62–73.

13   Gillespie and O'Keeffe, *Register of the parish of Shankill*, pp 32–7.

14   *Belfast atlas*, p. 23.

15   Benn, *History* (1877), pp 550–1.

16   Gaffikin, *Belfast fifty years ago*, pp 14, 39; Pilson, *History of the rise*, p. 25.

17   T.N.A., 30/9/23, f. 61a.

18   Gaffikin, *Belfast fifty years ago*, p. 42.

INDEX

Abbot, Charles, 172
Academy Street, 169
Adair, Patrick, 73, 133
Albert Clock, 11
Anderson, William, 112
Ann Street, 14, 15, 16, 35, 57, 61, 64, 147, 148, 157, 157, 169
Antigua, West Indies, 112
Antrim castle, 30
Antrim county, 15, 17, 19, 24, 32, 45, 73, 83; grand jury, 110–11
Antrim hills, 4, 11
Antrim plateau, 10, 15
Antrim Road, 1
Antrim town, 115
Ards barony, 44
Armagh, 60, 89
Arran, earl of, *see* Butler
assembly rooms, 171
Auchinleck, Scotland, 83
Aughnabrack, *see* Wolf Hill
Ayr, Scotland, 113

Ballenebraher, *see* Friarstown
Ballycoolcallagh, 15
Ballycullcallaghy, 15
Ballycullo, 7
Ballyfaighnamony, 7
Ballyhenry, 26, 39
Ballymacarret, 14, 118
Ballymartin river, 30
Ballynahatty, 11
Ballynyculnytry, 7
Ballysillan, 7, 35
Ballyutoag, 5, 10
Ballyvaghagan, 5
Ballyvaston, 26; chapel, 38–9
Ballyvicustullie, *see* Greencastle
Ballywonard, 7
Banbridge, Co. Down, 160
Bangor, Co. Down, xiv, 17, 18, 28, 30, 54, 61, 63, 71, 72, 89, 115, 121
banking, 2
Bann river, 45
Bardon, Jonathan, xi
Barr, Robert, 8, 66
Barrack Board, 145
Barrack Street, 109, 145, 169, 171

Barry, Richard, 168
Basset, Arthur, 64
Bateson, Thomas, 162
Beckett, J.C., xi
Belfast castle, 8, 15, 25, 31, 32, 33, 35, 36, 40–3, 45, 53, 54, 69, 70–1, 91, 92–3, 155; burning of, 135–6, 170; gardens, 92–3
Belfast Charitable Society, 162
Belfast Corporation, 67, 68, 72, 79–80, 82–4, 88, 101, 110, 119, 120, 161–2; Corporation Book, 68, 80, 88, 100
Belfast Improvement Act (1800), 16
Belfast Lough, 7, 10, 17–19, 32, 33, 81, 143
Belfast News-Letter, 137, 142
Belfast parish church, 56, 57, 58, 81, 91, 93, 100–01, 120, 129–32, 149, 170; churchyard 16; *see also* Shankill parish; St Anne's church
Belvoir Park, 32
Ben Madagain, *see* Cave Hill
Ben Vadagan, *see* Cave Hill
Benedictine priory, Downpatrick, 27
Benn, George, xi, xiii–xiv, 3, 4, 28, 41, 47, 57, 77, 135
Bernard, saint, 29
Berry Street, 168
Biggar, Alexander, merchant, 147
Biggar's Lane, 147
Bissett castle, *see* Makeon castle
Black Mountain, 3, 5
Black, John, merchant, 132, 168
Blackstaff river, 6, 7, 11, 14, 15, 16, 33, 44, 55, 59, 146, 147, 148, 158, 167, 172
Blow, James, printer, 142
Bog Meadows, 7, 11, 15
booksellers, 142
Bordeaux, France, 115
Boyne Bridge, 15, 16, 109
Boyne, battle of, 121
Braniel, 5
Breadac, *see* Knockbreda
Breda, 88
Brereton, Sir William, 69–70
Brett, C.E.B., xii

Bridge Street, 14, 59, 62, 64–5, 102, 108, 142, 143, 169
bridges, 7, 11, 13, 14, 15, 16, 103, 109, 118–19, 122, 142, 155
Bristol, 115, 116; port books, 108
Broad Street, 58, 59
Brownlow, Arthur, 117, 155
Brunswick Square, 149, 150
Buckley, England, 116
Bullar's Fields, 140
burgesses, 67, 69, 79–80, 110, 120, 162
Butler, James, marquis of Ormond, lord lieutenant, 79
Butler, Richard, earl of Arran, 119
Buttle, David, 152

Calgach, 15, 25
Camlin parish, Co. Antrim, 37
canals, 160
Caol Uisce castle, *see* Narrow Water castle
Capell, Arthur, earl of Essex, lord lieutenant, 109
Carlingford, Co. Louth, 160
Carngraney parish, Co. Antrim, 30
Carrick Hill, 1, 2, 14, 143, 144, 173
Carrickfergus Road, 15
Carrickfergus, Co. Antrim, xiv, 12, 14, 17, 19, 32, 37, 42, 43, 44, 46, 47, 54, 59, 60, 61, 66, 68, 69, 73, 74, 75, 78–9, 81, 82, 89, 92, 108, 109, 110–11, 113–14, 115, 117, 120, 121, 128, 134, 168, 170; bay, 8; castle, 29, 30, 33, 34; Corporation, 68, 114; friary, 40, 46; harbour, 18; port book, 97, 114; suburbs, 104
Castle Lane, 33, 76
Castle Place, 33, 40, 62, 105, 169
Castle Street, 15, 16, 77, 106, 108, 137, 143, 144, 145
Castleconnaugh, 25
Castlereagh hills, 5, 10, 11
Castlereagh, Co. Down, 63, 89; castle, 41–2
Cath Fersde, 12, 24
Catholic church, 132–3
Cave Hill, 3, 4, 5, 10, 24, 30, 91
Chads family, 103
Chads, Henry, merchant, 120, 140
Chads' Bridge, 103
Chapel Lane, 77
Charlemont, ship, 18

Charles I, king, 47
Charles II, king, 81, 88, 119
charter (1613), 67, 68, 83, 88, 109, 110, 121
Chester, England, 18, 72, 107, 115, 116; port books, 108
Chichester family, earls of Donegall, xiv, 54, 67, 111–12, 129, 151–6
Chichester Quay, 13
Chichester Street, 172
Chichester, Sir Arthur, Baron Belfast, 8, 38, 54–84
Chichester, Arthur, 1st earl of Donegall (d.1675), 88, 99, 110, 112, 122, 153
Chichester, Arthur, 2nd earl of Donegall (d.1678), 112, 114,
Chichester, Arthur, 3rd earl of Donegall (d.1706), 145, 152, 153–4
Chichester, Arthur, 4th earl of Donegall (d.1757), 149, 154, 157–8, 168; agent of, 151, 156, daughters of, 135, 152
Chichester, Arthur, 5th earl and 1st marquis of Donegall (d. 1799), 132, 168–9, 170
Chichester, Captain, 137, 138
Chichester, Catherine née Forbes, countess of Donegall, 154
Chichester, Sir John 40
Chichester, Viscount Edward, 70, 74
Chichester, Mary née Digby, countess of Donegall, 82
Church Lane, 94, 103
Church of Ireland, 133, 152
Church Street, 169
Churchill, John, duke of Marlborough, 152
Cinament of Derryvolgie, 37
City Hall, 7, 11, 167
Clanbrassill, earl of, *see* Hamilton
Clandeboy, Co. Down, 5, 36, 43, 44, 47, 55
Clifton Street, xiv
Clogh, Co. Antrim, 114, 117; castle, 33
Cloghcastally, *see* Greencastle
Clowney river, 11
Clugston, John, merchant, 147
Clugston's Lane, 147
Coalisland, Co. Tyrone, 160
coins, 37, 47–8, 97
Coleraine, 33, 44, 54, 59, 62, 67, 71, 73, 77, 78, 95

Colin river, 11, 12
College Square, 76
Comber, Co. Down, 72
Connor castle, Co. Antrim, 33
Connor diocese, 26, 28, 30, 72
Connswater river, 10
Conway, Viscount Edward, 72
Conway, Sir Fulke, 8
Cork, 1, 112, 153
Cornmarket, 7, 35, 41, 61, 93, 99, 100–01, 102, 136, 143, 155, 158, 171
Cornwall, John, 82–3
Corry, John, 66
Costello, see de Angulo
Cotton Court, 95–6, 99, 140–1
Court McMartin castle, Co. Antrim, 33
Crawford, Thomas, merchant, 140
Crawford, William, sovereign, 141
Cromac Bridge, 155
Cromac chapel, 38–9
Cromac Street, 8
Cromac Wood, 8
Cromwell, Oliver, 81, 100
Cross castle, Co. Antrim, 33
Cruithin, 12, 24
Crymble, Waterhouse, 68
Cunningham, Waddell, 2
Cusack, Sir Thomas, lord chancellor, 43
customs house, 62, 97, 98, 118, 149, 151
customs, 114, surveyor of, 19

Danesford, 6
de Angulo family, 37
de Burgh, Walter, 33
de Burgh, William, 'brown' earl of Ulster, 25, 29, 37
de Courcy, John, 28
de Lacy, Hugh, earl of Ulster, 31, 33
de Mandeville family, 34
de Mandeville, Robert, 25
de Rocheford, Jorevin, 89–91
Defective Titles, Commission for 71
Del Rath castle 30
Delany, Mary, 118
Derry, Co. Londonderry, 8, 18, 59, 60, 62, 66, 67, 71, 73, 89, 101, 104, 108, 113, 119, 120, 121, 133; population, 159; suburbs, 104
Devereux, Robert, earl of Essex, 45–8, 53

Devon, England, 71; pottery, 116
Digby, Essex, 82
Divis mountain, 3, 4, 11, 15
Dobbs, Arthur, 147
Dobbs, Richard, 108–09
Donegall estate, 168, see also Chichester family
Donegall Pass, 8
Donegall Place, 171–2, 173
Donegall Quay, 149
Donegall Square, 7, 33
Donegall Street, xiv, 26, 76, 77, 132, 169, 170, 171, 172
Donegall, earls of, see Chichester
Doonbought castle, Co. Antrim, 33
Down county, 7, 8, 10, 11, 12, 14, 15, 17, 19, 24, 28, 45, 118
Down diocese, 26, 27, 28, 30, 72
Down Survey, 75, 89, 91, 95
Downpatrick, Co. Down, xiv, 47, 71, 72, 108; cathedral 27, 28
Drapers' Company, 108
Drogheda, Co. Louth, 89, 115
Dromore diocese, 26, 28
Dromore, Co. Down, 115, 117
Drumbo parish, Co. Down, 133
Drumtarsy castle, Co. Londonderry, 33
Du Noyer, George Victor, 96, 103
Dublin, xiv, 1, 81, 82, 89, 107, 113, 115, 143, 153, 157, 158; tholsel, 101
Dundalk, Co. Louth, 89
Dundonald, Co. Down, 5, 32
Dundrum castle, Co. Down, 33
Dungannon, Co. Tyrone, 115
Dungiven castle, Co. Londonderry, 55
Dunmurray, 24, 39
Durham Street, 15, 143

earldom of Ulster, xv, see also de Burgh
Eccles, Hugh, 103
Eccles's Bridge, 103
Edenderry, Co. Antrim, 32
Edenduffcarrick castle, Co. Antrim, 41
Edinburgh, 8
Edward I, king, lord of Ireland, 27, 30, 31
Edward IV, king, 42
Edward VI, king, 37
Egan, John, 122
Ekenhead Presbyterian Church, 35
Eleanor, queen, 31
Elizabeth I, queen, 47

England, 106, 115, 153
English settlers, 58, 73, 133
Essex, earl of, *see* Devereux, Robert;
   Capell, Arthur, lord lieutenant
exchange, 171

Farset, battle of, 12, 24
Farset river, 11,13, 14, 15, 16, 26, 27,
   33, 40, 58, 59, 61, 62, 64, 91, 97,
   102, 103, 119, 146, 147
Ferra, Mathew, 82
ferry service, 118, 119
Fisherwick, 169
Fitzgerald, Elizabeth née Nugent,
   countess of Kildare, 27
FitzGerald, Garrett, earl of Kildare, lord
   justice, 42, 43
Flanders, 107, 115
food, 107, 108
ford 12–15, 19, 24–5, 26, 31, 31, 34,
   37, 43, 45, 53, 56, 118
Forth river, 11
fortifications, 34, 40, 81, *see also*
   ramparts
Fountainville, 155
Four Corners, 143
Foyle river, 18, 119
France, pirates from, 17–18; trade with,
   107, 115, 156
Franciscan friary, Carrickfergus, 40, 46
freemen, 9, 67, 80, 82, 83, 110, 116,
   162
Friar's Bush, 39, 46
Friarstown, 46

Gaffikin, Thomas, 4, 15, 172–3
Galway, 89
Gardner, Robert, printer, 142
Garmoyle, Pool of, 18, 113
Garner, Mathew, potter, 139
garrison, 19, 45, 46, 47, 53, 74, 75, 79,
   100, 121, 145
gates 76–78, 104
Geashill, Co. Offaly, 82
geology, 3–7
Germany, trade with, 117
Getty, Edmund, 47
Giant's Ring, 11
Gilbert, J.T., xiv
Gillespie, Raymond, xii
Glas an Bradden river, 30
Glascock, R.E., xi

Glasgow, 106, 120, 121, 141
Glengormley, 24
Glynns, The, 42
Gordon Street, 76, 99, 107, 138, 148
Gormlaithe, 24
Grace, James, 29
grand jury, 110–11, 119
graveyard, 39, 46, 132
Great Bridge of Belfast, 109
Greencastle, 30, 33, 34, 37, 38, 39
Greene, Robert, land agent, 154
Gregg, Thomas, 2, 162
Grocers' estate, Co. Londonderry, 57,
   58
Grosvenor Road, 7
guilds, 111

Hamilton, James, earl of Clanbrassill,
   119
Hamilton, Sir James, 63, 118
Hampton, Christopher, archbishop of
   Armagh, 60
Hanover Quay, 149
Hanover Square, 118, 150
Hardy, Philip Dixon, 3
Harland and Wolff shipyard, 1
Harris, Walter, 157, 159
Harte, Carew, 68
Head, Richard, 75
Hennessy, William, xiv
Henry III, king, 31
Henry VII, king, 37
Henry VIII, king, 47
Henrystown, 26, 39
Hercules Street, 145–6
High Street, 11, 13, 14, 16, 35, 41, 60,
   61, 62, 71, 91, 94, 97, 100, 102,
   107, 115, 137, 145, 146, 147, 148,
   151, 169, 172, 173
Hill Street, 98, 138, 140
Holland, trade with, 115, 117, 141
Holywood hills, 5
Holywood, Co. Down, 18, 32, 34, 63,
   72, 115
houses, xiv, 1, 10, 60–1, 94–5, 97–9,
   103, 104–06, 137–8, 141, 145, 148,
   161, 169

industry, 1–2, 99, 105, 138–42, 156–8,
   172–3
inn, 72

James I, king, 47, 121
James II, king, 119–20, 121
John, king, lord of Ireland, 27, 32
Johnston, Robert, 112
Johnston, William, 100, 155
Joy, Francis, printer, 142
Joy, Henry, xiii

Karryn parish, *see* Knockcairn parish
Kildare, earls and countess of *see*
    Fitzgerald
Killemna, 39; chapel, 38
Killyleagh, Co. Down, 72, 135
Kilmakee townland, 39
Kilpatrick, 39; chapel, 38
King, William, bishop of Derry, 93,
    141, 152
Knock, 27, 32, 40
Knockagh, 37
Knockbreda, 24, 36, 132
Knockcairn parish, 39
Knock-Columcille, 27
Knox, Thomas, 112

L'Estrange, Thomas, xiii
Lagan river, 1, 5, 6, 7, 10, 11, 16, 24,
    25, 26, 30, 32, 33, 43, 46, 48, 54,
    59, 81, 97, 143, 146, 149
Lagan valley, 5–7, 8, 10, 11, 27, 32, 89,
    107, 117, 118, 157
Lambert, Lord, 56
Lane, Ralph, 48, 53
Larne, Co. Antrim, 18, 44
Lawson, Captain Robert, 8, 74
Le Ford, 25–6
le Squire, Henry, 74, 78
leases, xiv, 154, 168, 169
Leathes, Captain, sovereign, 139
Leathes, Robert, 109
Legg family, 112
Legolghtorp, 25
Legoniel, 5, 11, 15
Leslie, Henry, bishop of Down, 72
Limerick, 119, 143
linen hall, 2, 157–8, 170, 171
Lisburn Road, 6
Lisburn, Co. Antrim, 8, 66, 72, 74–5,
    89, 101, 108, 115, 117, 122, 128,
    157
Liverpool, 115
Logan, John, 25, 26
Lombard Street, 59

London, 115, 172
Londonderry plantation, 61
Long Bank, 148–9, 151
Long Bridge, 13, 14, 118, 119, 122
Long Walk, 147
lottery, 132
Lough Neagh, 160
Lowry, T.K., 30
Lowther, Christopher, 65
Lurgan, Co. Armagh, 59, 60, 89, 115,
    117, 155, 157

Macartney, George, 83, 100, 101, 104,
    109, 112, 113, 117, 118–19, 132–3,
    140, 151, 155
Macartney, Isaac, merchant, 93, 118,
    122, 149, 152, 158
MacCana, Fr. Edmund, 15, 17, 72
MacDonnell, sons of, 44
Maclanachan, John, cartographer, 39,
    128–51
MacQuillin, 36
Mac tSabhaoisigh, 43
Mac Uibilin, *see* MacQuillin
Mael Mura of Othain, 12
Magazine Street, Derry, 133
Magee, James, printer, 143
Magh Cobha castle, *see* Seafin castle
Maguire, W.A., xii
Makeon, castle, 42
Malachy, archbishop of Armagh, 28, 29,
    30
Malby, Nicholas, governor of
    Carrickfergus, 45
Mallusk parish, Co. Antrim, 30
Malone Road, 1, 6, 15
Malone sands, 6, 15
Malone, 37, 39, 55, 72, 75, 112
Manx settlers, 58
market, 54, 108, 110
market house, 41, 99, 100–01, 112,
    143, 171
marketplace, 62–5, 69, 102, 143
Marlborough, duke of, *see* Churchill
Martin, George, 66, 81
Mary Fortune, ship, 18
Mary, The, ship, 115
Massareene, earl of, *see* Skeffington
Matudán, 24
Mayddedowneard, *see* Blackstaff river
mayor, *see* sovereign
McArt's fort, 3, 4, 10, 24

McBride, John, 135
McIlwhan's hill, 5
McHugh's bar, 151
Meek, Francis, Captain, 82
members of parliament 67, 152–3
merchants, 8, 62, 66, 91, 97, 100, 107,
    108, 112–19, 142, 151, 152–3,
    158–9, 160, 171
merchants' tokens, 110, 115, 117, 130
Methodist College, 6
Michael Harrison's Lane, 145
Mile Water river, 11, 14
military barracks, 93
military hospital, 82, 121
Mill Gate, 77, 104–05, 106, 143
Mill Street, 113, 144, 145, 168, 173
Millfield, 11, 169
mills, 1, 143–4
Moira, Co. Down, 117
Molyneux, Thomas, 92, 128, 137,
    138–9
Monaghan, Co. Monaghan, 115
Monck, George, General, 81, 88
Moneymore, 108
Montgomery, Hugh, Viscount Ards, 74,
    81
Moylinney (Magh-line, Molynne), 42,
    44
Muff parish church, Co. Londonderry,
    57, 58
Mulholland, Roger, 169
Munroe, Robert, Major General, 69,
    78, 79, 80, 133

Narrow Water castle, 33
Neill, Patrick, printer, 141, 142
New England, 115, 157
New Forge, 8, 66, 74, 75, 155
Newry, Co. Down, 47, 61, 121, 128,
    159; canal, 160; customs house, 160
Newtownards, Co. Down, xiv, 5, 59,
    89, 102, 157, 160, 161
Nicholas IV, Pope, 26
Nine Years War, 54
North America, 2, 8, 115; migration to,
    159
North Circular Road, 35
North Gate, 104, 105 133, 143, 145
North Queen Street, 1
North Street, 27, 59, 61, 64, 76, 77, 83,
    91, 133, 161, 169, 171

O'Byrne, Cathal, xi
O Coloran, David, 25–6
O'Donnell, Aedh, 36
O'Donnell, Conn, 36
Ogle, Samuel, 152–3
Old Forge, 8
O'Neill, Aodh, 42
O'Neill, Aodh Buidhe, 36
O'Neill, Brian, 33
O'Neill, Brian, 36
O'Neill, Brian Fertagh, 27
O'Neill, Brian MacPhelim, 45, 46
O'Neill, Conn, 35, 42
O'Neill, Feidhlimidh, 35–6
O'Neill, Henry, 35, 42
O'Neill, Hugh, 43
O'Neill, Niall, 40, 42
O'Neill, Niall, son of Aodh, 53
O'Neill, Niall Óg, 43
O'Neill, Seán Mac Briain, 53
O'Neill, Shane, 44–5
O'Neills of Clandeboy, 27, 36–7, 38,
    39, 41, 42–3, 45, 48, 53
O'Neills of Tyrone, 36, 40, 42, 43, 44
Ormeau Avenue, 146
Ormeau Bridge, 7
Ormeau Road, 7
Ormond, marquis of, see Butler, James
Ostend, trade with, 115, 122–3
Owenvarra river, see Blackstaff river
Oxford Street, 7

Parliamentary Commissioners, 69, 82
Patrick, St, 27
Perrot, Sir John, lord deputy, 53
Peter of Bilbao, ship, 18
Peter's Hill, 2, 27, 168, 169, 173
Phillips, Thomas, cartographer, 14, 57,
    59, 65, 69–71, 76, 77–8, 91–106,
    129, 145
Pilson, James Adair, 17
piracy, 17–18, 19
Plantation Commissioners, 40–1, 55–6,
    58, 60–1, 69, 72
Plantation, The, 105, 168
Pococke, Archdeacon Richard, 39, 132,
    133, 148, 154
Poleglass, 35
poorhouse, xiv, 132, 101, 170
population, 71, 73, 89, 93, 128, 159
port, 97, 111, 158, 171
Post Office Entry, 148
pottery, 5, 35, 116, 140–41

Pottinger, Thomas, 120
Pottinger's Entry or Lane, 103, 147
Presbyterian Church, 72–3, 78–9, 93, 111, 133–5, 141, 146, 152, 157
print trade, 141–3
Purdy's Burn river, 10

Quakers, 133
Quay Lane, 148
quay, 66, 97, 149, 151, 152
Queen Street, 77
Queen's Bridge, 13, 14
Queen's Island, 1
Queen's Square, 151

Radcliffe, Thomas, earl of Sussex, lord deputy, 4–5, 44
Rainey, William, 147
ramparts, 75–8, 105, 143, 147, 167, 172
Rathbreasail, synod of, 28
raths, 9–10, 35
Raven, Thomas, cartographer, 11, 14, 72, 78
Rawdon, George, 117
rents, 73, 154, 169
Revenue Commissioners, 149, 151
Richard of Exeter, 30
Richardson, Moses, 147
roads, 5, 160
Rosemary Street, 59, 133, 134, 146, 147, 148
Roughan castle, Co. Tyrone, 56
Route, The 36, 44
Rowan, Andrew, 114–15, 117
Royal Avenue, 76, 146
Royle, Stephen, xii

Sacheverell, William, 115, 128, 139
Saltwater Bridge, see Boyne Bridge
Sandal, son of, 42
Sandy Row, 11, 16, 155
Scarrenenegragh river, 44
Schomberg, Friedrich Herman, duke of, 121, 122
Schoolhouse Lane, 148
schools 57, 82–3, 118, 120, 135, 155, 162
Scotland, 66, 73, 106, 113, 115, 117, 141
Scots, 44, 73, 74; merchants, 119, 122; settlers, 58, 73, 133; soldiers, 74, 78–9, 80

Seafin castle, Co. Down, 33, 34
Shaftsbury Square, 7
Shaneen Park, 10, 35
Shankill parish, 28–30, 32, 38, 39, 122; church, 11, 26, 27, 29, 56; rectory, 28; see also Belfast parish church
Shankill Road, 15, 27
Shaw's Bridge, 11, 118
shipbuilding, 1, 113
shipping, see trade
Shore Road, 7
Sidney, Sir Henry, lord deputy, 12, 45, 47
siege, 81
Skeffington, Clotworthy, earl of Massareene, 154
Skegoniel, 25
Skipper Lane, 99
Skipper Street, 62, 93, 95, 97, 98
Smith, David, merchant, 139–40
Smith, Mr, sovereign, 139
Smith, Patrick, merchant, 140
Smith, Sir Thomas, 45
Smithfield, 1, 2, 143, 173
Solemn League and Covenant (1643), 79
sovereign, 66, 79–80, 100, 110, 111, 120, 139, 141, 152
Spain, 152; trade with, 107, 115
Squire's hill, 4, 5, 15
St Anne's church, 26, 47, 168, 170
St Columb's cathedral, Derry, 57
St Columba's church, Knock, 40
St George's church, 14, 26
St Nicholas's church, Carrickfergus, xiv, 58
Stevenson, Noragh, xi
Stone Bridge, 142
Story, George, 121, 128
Strabane, Co. Tyrone, 155
Strand gate, 76, 77–8
Strand, 95, 99
Strangford Lough, 5
Stranmillis Road, 6, 46
Stranmillis, 8, 11, 16, 39, 75
Sugar House Entry, 113
Suir river, Co. Waterford, 119
Sussex, Lord Deputy, see Radcliffe, Thomas
Swayne, John, archbishop of Armagh, 36

Talbot Street, 169
Talbot, Richard, earl of Tyrconnell, 120
Taughmonagh, 24
Taylor, Jeremy, bishop of Down, 72
Telford's, ships' chandlers, 149
Test Act (1704), 152
Theaker, George, 59
Theaker, Thomas, 79
Thompson, Lewis, 115, 157
Tisdall, William, vicar, 153
Titanic, 1
topography, 3–8, 10–19, 24–5, 55, 91–4
town fields, 107
town hall, 68–9, 100
townlands, 38
trade, 2, 18–19, 48, 65, 89–91, 97, 108, 112–19, 121–3, 128–9, 156–60, 171
Traill, James, merchant, 135, 152
Trian Chongail, 36, 40, 42
Trim, Co. Meath, xv
Tuath Cinament, 37
Tuath le Fall, 37, 38
Tuathal Techtmar, 12
Tullyrusk chapel, 38, 39
Twiss, Richard, 170
Tyrconnell, earl of, *see* Talbot
Tyrone lordship, 33

Ua Domnaill, *see* O'Donnell
Ua Neill, *see* O'Neill
Udward, Nathaniel, 8
Ulaid, 12, 24
Umgall parish, Co. Antrim, 30
United Irishmen, 162

Venables, Robert, 81
Vesey, John, sovereign, 58, 66
vicarage, 73
Victoria Square, 11, 15, 146, 147
Victoria Street, 148
Virginia, 115, 157

Waring Street, 8, 13, 58–9, 64, 58, 60, 61, 62, 66, 69, 74, 83, 89, 91, 93–9, 107, 130, 136–43, 148, 151, 167, 168, 169, 170, 171, 173
Waring, Samuel, 138
Waring, Thomas, 83, 95, 99
Waring, Westenra, 151
Waring, William, 99, 151
Waringstown, Co. Down, 138
water bailiff, 111
water supply, 16, 108–09, 112, 155–6
Waterford city, 89, 115, 119
Wentworth, Thomas, earl of Strafford, lord deputy, 74, 114
Westone, 26
Whitehaven, England, 65, 107
Whitehouse, 15
William III, king, 17, 120, 121
William Street, 76
Wilson, Robert, 77
Wilson, Samuel, printer, 142
Wolf Hill, 4

Ymenaught, 25
York Street, 1, 173
Youghal, Co. Cork, 82
Young, Arthur, 171